No Beauty in the BEAST

Israel Without Her Mascara

BY MARK GLENN

Published by
THE BARNES REVIEW
in conjunction with
JTB PUBLISHING

FRONT COVER ILLUSTRATION: Detail of the back panel of the *Maesta* by Duccio depicting the Pharisees accusing Christ of an assortment of criminal transgressions. Above, illustration in full width. Pontius Pilate is in the center facing the wrangling mass of complainants. Christ is to the right, hands bound, surrounded by armed guards, immune to their worldly insults.

No Beauty in the Beast:
Israel Without Her Mascara

ISBN No. 978-0-9742303-1-3

Published by:

THE BARNES REVIEW
P.O. Box 15877, Washington, D.C. 20003
www.barnesreview.org

with

JTB PUBLICATIONS
P.O. BOX 27
CAREYWOOD, ID 83809
www.CrescentandCross.com
www.notmywords.com

©2005 by JTB Publications

*All rights reserved. Portions of this book may be reproduced
as brief quotations embodied in critical articles, essays or reviews.
Credit must be given to the author and publishers as well as full contact information.*

When reproducing any of the contents of this work cite:
Mark Glenn, P.O. Box 27, Careywood, ID 83809
www.notmywords.com

First printing: 2005
Second printing: 2007

Table of Contents

Introduction
Elegant and Eloquent 2

Part I —
No Beauty in the Beast
Words of Gratitude 4
Lost in Translation 7
In Their Own Words 17
Reasons 39

Part II —
Israel Without Her Mascara
The Rest of the Story 127
Grabbing a Wolf by the Ears 139
With Friends Like These 147
The New Sanhedrin 159
One Less Than Six Million 175
Birds of a Feather … Israel and America 190
Through the Eyes of a Muslim 202
History's Forgotten Braveheart 217
Those Who Hunger and Thirst for Justice 236
Ten Good Men 253
No Beauty in the Beast 267
Independence Day 281
Parting Thoughts 299
Bibliography 301

Introduction

Elegant and Eloquent—
Mark Glenn's Exposition of the Truth

Over the past several years the name "Mark Glenn" has become familiar worldwide via the Internet. Those who have accessed Internet news and information relating to the problems surrounding the state of Israel and its aggressive imperial aims in historic Palestine and beyond have had the opportunity to read Glenn's eloquent writings. And now, with the release of Glenn's book, *No Beauty in the Beast*, much of Glenn's writings, previously available only on the worldwide web, are now accessible for those who don't care for the glare of the computer screen.

Anyone who is familiar with the problem of Israel and honest enough to acknowledge that Israel is indeed just that—a problem—knows full well that there are three consistent components in Israel's mode of operation (and in America's continuing support for Israel): 1) lies, 2) bullying, and 3) double standards. In *No Beauty in the Beast*, Mark Glenn demonstrates, beyond any doubt, that Israel "without her mascara" is no beauty, but, instead, a beast.

That, of course, is an inflammatory thesis to those who have come to believe in the message of "the beauty of Israel" that is pounded into their eyes and ears and thus into their brains by the tired-and-worn pro-Israel propaganda emanating from the print and broadcast mass media in America. But for those who are open-minded and capable of digesting unpleasant realities, Glenn's book is a feast for truth-starved folks who hunger for honesty.

While Glenn's words are often hard-hitting and literally in-your-face, his writing style is nonetheless both elegant and eloquent and founded on the basis of his deeply-felt Christian beliefs. A native born American of Lebanese descent, this proud father of six children is a former school teacher, whose broad historic and cultural knowledge is quite apparent. Having taught American history and the history of Western civilization, as well as the Latin, Italian, French and Spanish languages, Glenn's writings reflect a remarkable bundle of learning that vibrantly and conclusively contradicts the recent claim by hard-line Zionist ideologue Richard Perle that critics of Israel and U.S. policy toward Israel are "illiterate."
In a day when Christianity is often treated by the controlled media as some form of fatal virus, Mark Glenn is an unapologetic Christian who spares no words in defending his faith—Christianity—and pulls no punches in daring to outline—in their own words—some of the vile, anti-Christian teachings of those who put

INTRODUCTION

Israel and the Zionist cause first and always.

Glenn is not afraid to point out that what he calls "The New Sanhedrin" is engaged in an open and vicious war against Christianity. And in a time when targeting the Muslim peoples for attack and defamation has become the favorite sport of the American media (even by some so-called American "nationalist" organizations), Glenn does not hesitate to say, candidly and forthrightly, that "concerned, conservative Christians should remember (or else come to realize) that is not the Koran, the Islamic religion, nor its adherents whom they need to fear."

"This fear they have adopted," writes Glenn, "is nothing more than a program of managed sentiments that those who control the flow of information have imposed upon Christians and for obvious reasons." Instead, Glenn writes, America's Christians should recognize that their real enemy is those who "literally decide who becomes president, where and against whom America goes to war, and what information people in America see, hear, and read."

One particularly valuable chapter in *No Beauty* is an eye-opening compilation of direct quotations from these sorry and sordid characters, along with a fascinating overview of some valuable (and sometimes forgotten) quotations from those brave few who have dared to publicly challenge the power of Israel and Zionism.

Another especially interesting chapter entitled "With Friends Like These" is a candid overview of Israel's crimes against not only the Christian and Muslim Palestinian Arabs, but against America and the rest of the world. This essay lays to rest, once and for all, the outrageously false theme that Israel is somehow "America's best friend."

This brief overview of *No Beauty in the Beast* is simply that: a brief overview. This classic is a compendium of historical truth devoted to traditional Christian ideals of justice and fair play, hitting the lies and bullying and double standards put forth by Israel and her American adherents—of which there are unfortunately too many—today.

—MICHAEL COLLINS PIPER

MICHAEL COLLINS PIPER is the author of *Final Judgment*, which nails down the Mossad connection to the assassination of President John F. Kennedy, who was working assiduously to prevent Israel from building nuclear weapons of mass destruction, *The High Priests of War*, the first-ever full-length published account of the rise of the hard-line pro-Israel neo-conservatives, *The New Jerusalem*, an up-to-date survey of Zionist power in America, and *The Judas Goats*, the shocking history of the infiltration and subversion of the American nationalist movement. An assembly of Piper's published essays is entitled, *Dirty Secrets: Crime, Conspiracy & Cover-Up During the 20th Century*. He is also a regular contributor to *American Free Press*, the national weekly newspaper based in Washington (see americanfreepress.net) and *The Barnes Review*, the bimonthly historical Revisionist magazine (see www.barnesreview.org).

Words of Gratitude

When a person opens his or her eyes and comes to grasp evil in its true essence, it can be a paralyzing and debilitating circumstance. In this situation it is very easy to lose all hope in mankind, and at sometime after that point, to succumb to the debilitating effects of depression and despair. What is used in pulling oneself out of this pit is the goodness of those few people who still possess this rare and much despised gem known as humanity, and it is these individuals who deserve to be acknowledged now.

To my beautiful wife Victoria, who is, whether she realizes this or not, co-author of this work. The nights she spent listening to me rant and rave, acting as a sounding board for what has become the central argument within this work, none of this would be possible were she to have considered her own selfish interests rather than the interests of others who are suffering under these present injustices.

To my children, whose tears and barely contained anger over what they saw happening to the peoples of the Middle East reminded me everyday that what I was doing was the right thing. Whether they realize it or not, they are in effect co-authors of this work as well, for many of their insights and observances have made their way into the words of this book. May God bless them with the destruction of this beast before it enters their lives and devours them as well.

To my friends around the world who I know only through the sterile confines of the internet, who have encouraged me and provided me with more inspiration to keep plowing forward than they could know. Truly without you, this work would not have been possible had I not came to know you, for it is in seeing that there are others out there who feel the same way as I do that has compelled me to add my own voice to this most important symphony.

To actor Mel Gibson, one of the few Christians for whom I still maintain some respect as a result of the film he made depicting in a dignified manner the humble carpenter from Palestine turned freedom fighter. I know that you spent many nights worrying about what could happen to you and your family as a result of making this film, and that you will spend many similar such nights in the future as well. May this film be "the shot heard 'round the world" and that in some way, it will remind Christians of who they are, and wherein lies their duty with regards to the present situation today.

And just so that there is no ambiguity....

To Hassan, for his wise words and brotherly concern; To Kim for her worrying and her willingness to give from her heart in our times of need; To Maisoon for her fearless voice and tireless temperament; Barbra for her insight and her outrage; To Dr. El Najjar, who has caught a lot of heat for publishing my works; To all those who gave me permission to use photos and excerpts, without which this work would have seriously suffered.

To Mom, Byron, Bill, Edwin, Arthur, Johanna, Sara Rae, Al, Michael, the folks at JTR, Nick, Paul, Jules, Nancy, Susan, Meike, Ed, et al.
To those writers and speakers who have kept the barely visible flame alive over the last century concerning the danger posed by the Jewish supremacist agenda. Were it not for you, the flame would have died under the deafening wall of obstructive noise that this agenda uses in silencing its critics and thus there would have remained no light by which mankind could see. In particular, I wish to thank Michael Collins Piper for risking literally life and limb in his effort at exposing the nature of this beast, as well as his colleagues at *American Free Press*, Don Wassal at *The Nationalist Times*, Theodore Pike, Michael Hoffman II, Dr. Gordon Ginn, Eustace Mullins, Douglas Reed (may he rest in peace) and all the others whose writings and wisdom have led me towards a more enlightened position as well as an understanding of wherein lie my own duties with regards to this desperate situation.

To the Zionists, whether you are Jew or Christian, for being the bloodthirsty animals that you are, and for finally showing your true spots and thus jump-starting my conscience back to life. I know that God is just, and that since you obviously would rather rule in Hell than to serve in Heaven, may your wishes be granted. I say this not as a curse but rather as a blessing, since I know that this is what you would prefer; spending an eternity in Hell with those who share your infected way of thinking rather than having to share Heaven with others whom you view as inferior.

To those Jews who, having been raised in the strangulating atmosphere of Zionist supremacist thinking, nevertheless managed to escape from what has no doubt been the real holocaust of the Jewish people. By rescuing your humanity from the clutches of the supremacists who wield terrible power over you, you have become and will remain for the duration of my stay here on earth heroes in my eyes. By speaking out against the injustices being wrought by those who have been the source of your own misery for the last 2,000 years, you have become like the patriots and prophets of old who risked life and limb in exposing the Synagogue of Satan before the rest of humanity. In particular, it is important that we remember names such as Israel Shahak, (may he rest in peace) Israel Shamir, Mordechai Vanunu, Henry Makow, and Professor Norman Finkelstein.

To those in the Middle East, and particularly the Muslims, who have inspired me by their courage and their steadfastness in the face of what has been unimaginable suffering. By your example I have come to understand wherein lies my duty as a Christian, and for the sake of my own soul as well as for the souls of those around me, may I never forget this duty, nor you.

And finally, I thank the children of Palestine, and in particular Amir Ayyad, who lost their lives to the beast and who still have yet to receive the remembrance and honor they deserve from a civilized world. Even if what remains of humanity has forgotten you, I never will, and I will continue reminding the world of who you were and what happened to you. I pray above all else that your sacrifices will not have been in vain, and that by such, the identity of this beast may be revealed and that by this he will be destroyed. May I be so fortunate as to see your beautiful, unscarred faces one day in Paradise, as well as the faces of those who mourned you for what to them felt like an eternity.

Lost in Translation

In addition to having taught several foreign languages over the course of many years, as well I have served as an interpreter on a few occasions when someone found him or herself in a pinch. Translating was something from which I derived a certain amount of satisfaction, not only because of what was my love for these various languages, but as well due to the fact that I was able to provide a service to others who found themselves disadvantaged by virtue of the obvious communication barrier.

Likewise, I found it to be a very fulfilling thing as well when I began this business of "translating" much of what I saw taking place in the world around me into the written word. Having individuals come to me and express their gratitude at things I have said has been a source of great reward for me, and something that hopefully I will be able to continue doing in the future.

However, despite the fact that I managed to hit a few small home runs in the course of my very modest writing career, it hasn't always been a complete success. Besides the fact that there are those who are decidedly against the position I have taken, there are those as well who simply have a hard time understanding what it is that I am trying to say. This is a situation that has become exponentially more pronounced the more that I have become acquainted with the mechanics of this situation in the Middle East, since, obviously, the more I understand it, the more there is to analyze and more to discuss.

In fairness to the rest of humanity who make an attempt at considering what it is that I have to say, there is good reason for them to walk away from these encounters scratching their heads in a bewildered manner. It certainly would not be the first time that I have heard it come from the mouths of others around me that I am oftentimes somewhat cryptic and possibly a little bit too allegorical in the pictures I attempt to paint. Perhaps it is that 'left-brained, right-brained' issue that many are always discussing, the battle between the practical and abstract aspects of the human mind. In any case, I cannot blame such individuals for not 'getting it,'...that is, understanding the point I am trying to make. Sometimes I leave myself confused.

Having said this then, the reader of this work will find a *plethora* of allegories, similes, comparisons, and what nots. I am of the opinion that they are not *too* vague or abstract, but then again, this is coming from the mouth of the one who is painting the picture and knows what it is that he has in mind. Still, the servant of humanity that I wish to be requires that I not construct an intellectual obstacle course too difficult to master, and therefore I owe it to the others who are affording me a few hours of their time all the assistance that I can without cheating them out of what I hope will be a profitable mental workout.

Therefore, for the benefit of the reader, I have decided to start things off on the right foot by giving a brief run-down of the argument that I am trying to make within the pages of this book so that he or she will be in possession of a road map of sorts in guiding them through what is a somewhat lengthy and complicated journey.

The title of the work itself, **No Beauty in the Beast**, should, given the times within which we find ourselves, cause several parts of the mind to fire-off recollections and recognitions. In this age of the apocalyptic paradigm that is daily fare on the various outlets of Western media and wherein the 'end times' and all that they portend are regularly discussed, then certainly this topic of *the Beast* has an undeniable relevance. One could make the argument (and especially given the amount of discussion *already* taking place by those in the apocalyptically-minded world of the Christian West) that there is no room for any additional commentary. It could be argued that the bank of debate is already bursting at the seems, and that my additional two cents is not only going to overload the discussion, but as well differs in no substantive way from the rest of the coins found within it. It is easy to see why there would be those who would argue this, particularly since it is a topic that seems to never take a break and therefore has become a religion in and of itself for many people.

NO BEAUTY IN THE BEAST 9

However, it is precisely *because* of the fact that it is the nucleus around which many Christians are living their lives today that I have decided to add my voice to this contest. Understanding that doing so only adds to what has by now become a cacophony of sorts, (the noise that is produced by all of these various instruments within this discussion) nevertheless, I am of the opinion that most of those who are playing are on the wrong page and furthermore are not the musicians that they think they are. For the most part, they are simply making noise in the same way that a child who is unlearned in any of the disciplines of playing a musical instrument cannot help but to replace the peace of silence with the anxiety of nerve-grating discord. It is not my intention to add to this discord, even though we must remember that dissonance is going to be an unavoidable by-product of my 'joining the band' as it were, and even if I *did* manage to play the piece perfectly.

I once heard an individual in his attempt at scoffing at the business of believing in prophetic visions say that were we to put 1,000 chimpanzees in a room, give each of them a typewriter and have them bang out a bunch of senselessness, that we could, after piecing together the various things that were produced, come up with a work of art. His assertion of course was that of typical rationalists who see an indivisible barrier between the natural world of human events and the divine world that created it. And in all fairness to the rationalists, this tendency that they maintain these days is completely understandable, given the times in which we find ourselves today. After all, a war against 1.5 billion people, with all the suffering and injustice that accompanies it has been launched and fueled in no small part by the efforts of those who have taken the business of biblical prophecy to a new mania. In light of these facts, it is easy therefore to see why there would be those who would avoid trying to associate themselves with any study of biblical prophecy as if it were some kind of vessel containing the plague.

I, however, take a different approach to this. To me it makes no sense to throw out the baby with the bath water, as the rationalists will often do in their dismissing of prophetic words. I think that there are great things to be learned and gained by considering these things, and I do not subscribe in any way to the idea that these events taking place and conforming as they have been to that which has been predicted centuries past are but a fluke. And although I will only do the safe thing in coming to broad conclusions about these things and of avoiding the minutiae that no one has the capability of discerning and decoding, nevertheless I have seen enough efficacy in the nature of these prophetic warnings for them to make a believer out of me.

Having said this, let me state then that it is my opinion that we are in the 'end times' that, centuries ago, were predicted to be forthcoming. I will ascribe neither a timetable nor hair-splitting particulars to these things in the same manner that many in this business do, a tendency that is a danger in and of itself for anyone trying to maintain any credibility. Nevertheless, there are generalities that can be safely adopted when decoding all of this, something that for obvious reasons is in the best interests of all parties concerned. I do not subscribe to the way of thinking that many rationalists have adopted, namely that prophecy is on the same level as palm reading and Tarot cards. Like all things, there are charlatans and there are bona fides, and to consign all of it to the realm of foolishness just because of the charlatans makes no sense, despite the fact that they possess such a formidable position in religious discussions today. For those who look at these things with an open mind however, there is no way to avoid noting that there have been people in the past who have made predictions that have been validated and vindicated with frightening accuracy, not the least of which have been those which foretold the arrival of the freedom fighter from Nazareth, Jesus Christ.

Therefore, what we find ourselves doing over the next few hours is discussing my understanding of the events that took place 2,000 years ago in the land known as Palestine, and in particular the social, political and religious struggle that took place between a peasant carpenter named Christ and the gangsters running the state of Israel who opposed him. We find ourselves discussing the roots of this contention that, as of this date I have not yet heard being discussed, as well as what kind of relevance this contention has had not only on the last 2,000 years, but also more importantly on today. We find ourselves discussing the warnings given in the prophetic vision that was experienced by a man named John on the island of Patmos, the vision of the Beast who would appear at the end of time for the purpose of destroying all that Christ the freedom fighter had envisioned.

In short, this is my attempt at bringing into practical, visible terms and images the cryptic and often misunderstood and even moreso misapplied picture which humanity is facing now concerning the event for which the world has been waiting now for 20 centuries. And whether this beast is personified as the "man of sin," as he is called by the Christians, "Dajjal," as he is imagined by the Muslims, or as the "Messiah" by the Jews, the image of the beast is the same. And although all three of the main faiths emanating forth from the Holy Land see the same picture, for two of them he represents an image of evil whereas for one of them he represents the long-awaited savior.

I have already experienced a certain amount of reticence on the part of fellow Christians concerning things I have written or said on this topic, individuals who are obviously made very uncomfortable by the manner in which I have depicted the two main persons within this issue, Christ and Antichrist. This is understandable, since man is by nature an animal very much susceptible to the laws that govern inertia, and whether the issue concerns mass and matter or whether it concerns philosophy makes little difference; a body at rest tends to stay at rest. And although I will say that this tendency is understandable, I will not go so far as to say that it is excusable. What I have seen on the part of people such as these are uncritical, knee-jerk reactions to ideas that are not that revolutionary concerning this man, Jesus of Nazareth, who was without question a revolutionary himself. What reactionary individuals such as these have done, unfortunately, is to lump my argument in with the many other arguments that are offered today by those who have a vested interest in defaming Christ and his legacy. Again, I will say that this reactionism is understandable, since a good portion of those in the Christian world have developed this 'siege mentality' when it comes to what have become the ever-increasing attacks on their faith and therefore are justifiably suspicious about anything new being introduced.

Being on the receiving end of the criticism though offers me a different vantage point, and as such I cannot help but consign all of this reactionary business to the category of unjustifiable guilt by association and which possesses absolutely no validity. This is even moreso the case since (and especially so in light of today's events) I hold this man and his deeds to be insurmountable in their excellence and perfection. Were it not for the fact that I view the opinions of such uncritical individuals with pity, I could be led towards being seriously offended by their accusations, particularly since one of the things I am trying to accomplish within the text of my argument is the elevation of this man before the eyes of the rest of mankind. I will take it one step further by saying that it is because of this uncritical foolishness that has been embraced by those in the Christian West, a foolishness rooted in the refusal to see Christ in this obvious light that we find ourselves in the mess that we have today.

So, in sum, what we are discussing here is the Apocalypse, albeit in a vastly different light than that which encompasses how it is discussed today. The argument being made here is that we are now living in the age of Antichrist, not necessarily as a man, but rather as the resurrected form of Pharisaical Judaism that was defeated 20 centuries past and which has now re-emerged as the ideology known as Zionism. The *abomination of desolation sitting in the holy place* is none other than Pharisaical Judaism's return to the land of Israel from whence it was chased 20 centuries before, while the *whore of Babylon* is a depiction of modern-day Christianity and its adherents who have apostatized by adopting the very same tenets of the Jewish supremacist agenda which Christ came to destroy, adherents who, by so doing have betrayed their rightful spouse and have thus become prostitutes for the Zionist agenda.

My reason for doing this, in addition to satisfying my own curiosity, is to shed what I hope is some kind of enlightenment upon others for their own benefit. Realizing that all of this appears to carry an air of pompousness attached to it, nevertheless, I must add what are my two cents to this, especially since nothing that anyone else is saying makes and sense. I am of the opinion that the larger portion of the Christian world, to which I proudly maintain my own membership, is *dead wrong* about most of what they envision concerning these times. When I view and then analyze what it is they have to say about all of this business, I am reminded of that scene in the movie *Indiana Jones and the Raiders of the Lost Ark*, wherein a rival group of treasure hunters are furiously digging away at what they believe is the location of this great find, but doing so in vain. As in the movie, this has taken place as a result of the fact that they only possess half of the information, and with that find themselves at present engaged in the business of utter foolishness.

It is my sincere hope that I am able to make this discussion profitable to all of us who find ourselves here considering this most important topic. It is my greater hope though that what I have envisioned within the puny confines of a limited human intellect will be able to find cogent, clear expression in what I have written, and that as a result, nothing has been lost in translation.

Mark Glenn
The Christian season of Lent, 2005

"... And I saw a beast coming out of the sea. He had ten horns and seven heads, and on each head a blasphemous name. The dragon gave the beast his power and his throne and his great authority. One of the heads seemed to have had a fatal wound, but the fatal wound had been healed. The whole world was astonished and followed after the beast. Men worshipped the beast saying, 'Who is like the beast? Who can make war against him?' The beast was given a mouth with which to utter proud words and blasphemies and to exercise his authority for forty-two months. He was given power to make war against the saints and to conquer them. All inhabitants of the world will worship the beast, all those whose names have not been written in the book of life."

—*Book of the Apocalypse:* Chapter 13

Above: *A detail from an Albrecht Durer engraving of the events of Revelation.*

In Their Own Words

"However, if you do not obey the Lord your God, all these curses will come upon you and overtake you: The Lord will cause you to be defeated before your enemies....The Lord will afflict you with madness, blindness and confusion of the mind.... The Lord will drive you and the king set over you into a nation unknown to you or your fathers....You will become a thing of horror and an object of scorn and ridicule to all the nations where the Lord will drive you...The Lord will bring a nation against you from far away, from the ends of the earth, like an eagle swooping down, a nation whose language you will not understand, a fierce looking nation without respect for the old nor pity for the young...You will be uprooted from your land, and then the Lord will scatter you among all nations, from one end of the earth to the other...Among those nations you will find no repose, nor any resting place for the sole of your foot...There the Lord will give you an anxious mind, eyes weary with longing and a despairing heart...You will live in dread both night and day, never sure of your life."
— *The warnings given by Moses to the future inhabitants of Israel of what kind of future they would face as a result of their disobedience,* **Book of Deuteronomy**

"Every time anyone says that Israel is our only friend in the Middle East, I can't help but think that before Israel, we had no enemies in the Middle East."
— *John Sheehan, S.J. (a Jesuit priest)*

"Again, I want to point out that it was this same group of Ashkenazi Jews, communist, socialist, Bolshevik Jews who migrated from Russia to Israel, gained control of the Zionist movement and have dominated the government of Israel since its beginning in 1948."
— *Jack Bernstein, author of the book* **'The Life of an American Jew Living in Racist Marxist Israel.'**

"And Jesus shall be a sign for the coming of the hour of Judgment. Therefore have no doubt about the hour. When Jesus came with clear signs, he said 'Now I have come to you with wisdom, therefore fear Allah and obey me,

for Allah, he is my Lord and your Lord so worship him, for this is the straight way.'"
— ***The Qur'an,*** *Islam's most holy book, Surah 43*

"So when you see standing in the Holy Place the abomination that causes desolation, spoken of through the prophet Daniel, let the reader understand...for then there will be great distress unequaled from the beginning of the world until now, and never to be equaled again."
— *Jesus of Nazareth*

"Whosoever disobeys the rabbis deserves death and will be punished in Hell by being boiled in hot excrement."
— ***The Babylonian Talmud,*** *Judaism's most holy book, Erubin 21b*

"Arab Palestinian Christians and Arab Palestinian Muslims lived side by side for the past 1400 years, and for anybody to say that the Arab Palestinian Christians have been persecuted recently by Muslims is absolutely another big lie, like the big lie that spoke of Weapons of Mass Destruction in Iraq."
— *Riah Abu El-Assal, Christian Bishop of Jerusalem*

"When Palestinian Moslems and Christians occupied Palestine, there was a religious aura. But since the Zionists took over and set up the state of Israel, it has become one of the most sinful nations in the world. Israeli laws suppress all religion, for instance, it is against the law to try and convert a Jew to another religion even if the Jew is an atheist. A Christian is permitted to preach the gospel in a church building, but for the clergy or anyone else to even tell anyone about the teachings of the Bible outside the church building will bring a 5-year prison sentence. This same kind of religious suppression applies to those of the Islamic faith who, in an act of kindness gives a gift of any kind to a Jew. A 5-year prison sentence can result."
— *Jack Bernstein, author of the book **'The Life of an American Jew Living in Racist Marxist Israel.'***

"Why should they, the Americans, have trusted us? We were a bunch of Russians, socialist Russians."
— *Isser Harel, former head of Mossad, speaking of the unlikely union between America and the Marxist state of Israel.*

IN THEIR OWN WORDS

"......The Israeli soldiers shoot with silencers. The bullets from the M-16 rifles tumble end over end through the children's slight bodies. Later, in the hospital, I will see the destruction: the stomachs ripped out, the gaping holes in limbs and torsos. Yesterday at this spot the Israelis shot eight young men, six of who were under the age of eighteen. One was twelve. This afternoon they killed an eleven-year-old boy, Ali Murad, and seriously wound four more, three of who are under eighteen."
"Children have been shot in other conflicts I have covered, but never before have I watched as soldiers enticed children like mice into a trap and murdered them for sport."
— Christopher Hedges, American Journalist on assignment in Gaza

---

"Knowing that the White House was totally protected by electronic countermeasures, the Mossad focused on the phone in Lewinsky's apartment. They began intercepting explicit phone calls between the president and Lewinsky. The recordings were couriered by diplomatic bag to Tel Aviv. On March 27, Clinton once more invited Lewinsky to the Oval office and revealed that he believed a foreign embassy was taping their conversations. In Tel Aviv, Mossad strategists pondered how to use the embarrassing taped conversations since they were the stuff of blackmail. Some saw the recordings as a potent weapon to be used if Israel found itself with its back against the wall in the Middle East and unable to count on Clinton's support."
— Gordon Thomas, author of **'Gideon's Spies: The Secret History of the Mossad.'**

"I want to tell you something very clear, don't worry about American pressure on Israel, we, the Jewish people control America, and the Americans know it."
— Israeli Prime Minister Ariel Sharon to cabinet member Shimon Peres, October 3rd, 2001, as reported on Kol Y'Israel radio.

"You'd have to be a recent immigrant from Outer Mongolia not to know of the role that people with Jewish names play in the coarsening of American culture. The sad fact is that through Jewish actors, playwrights, and producers, the Berlin stage of Weimar Germany linked Jews and deviant sexuality in all its sordid manifestations just as surely as Broadway does today. Much of the filth in American entertainment today parallels that of Germany between the wars."
— Rabbi Daniel Lapin, President of **Toward Tradition**

"They were seen by New Jersey residents on Sept. 11 making fun of the World Trade Center ruins and going to extreme lengths to photograph themselves in front of the wreckage."
– Excerpt of a police report concerning the arrest of 5 Israeli intelligence operatives after they were seen by witnesses filming the destruction of the Twin Towers in New York and cheering.

"When the van belonging to the cheering Israelis was stopped by the police, the driver of the van, Sivan Kurzberg, told the officers: 'We are Israelis. We are not your problem. Your problems are our problems. The Palestinians are your problem.'"
– ABC's program **20/20** covering the involvement of members of Israeli intelligence in the attacks of September 11.

"You stiff-necked people, you are just like your fathers! Was there ever a prophet they did not persecute? They even killed those who predicted the coming of the Righteous One. And now you have betrayed and murdered him – you have received the law that was put into effect by angels but yet you refuse to obey it."
– St. Stephen, 1st Christian martyr, killed by the Sanhedrin

"We Jews are in a state of panic, given the fact that dead Jews are precious and deserve a special burial. The fact that 5-10 Jews might be lost forever among some 125,000 gentiles is pretty horrifying, as I am sure you can see."
– Comments of an Israeli worker sent to Indonesia following the tsunami in late 2004 to prevent the bodies of dead Jews from being defiled by being buried in mass graves with non-Jews.

"Behold, the angels said; 'O Mary, Allah hath chosen thee and purified thee and has chosen thee above the women of all nations. O Mary, Allah giveth thee glad tidings of a word from him. His name will be Jesus, the son of Mary, held in honor in this world and in the hereafter, and of those nearest to Allah."
– **The Qur'an,** Islam's most holy book, Surah 3, Al Imran

"Miriam the hairdresser, mother of Jesus was a whore and the descendant of princes and governors who played the harlot with carpenters."
– **The Babylonian Talmud,** Judaism's most holy book, Sanhedrin 106a

"We are Judeo-Nazis, and why not? If your nice, civilized parents, rather than writing books about their love for humanity had instead come to Israel and killed six million Arabs, what would have happened? Sure, two or three nasty pages would have been written in the history books, and we would have been called all sorts of names, but we would be here today as a people of 25 million! What you don't seem to understand is that the dirty work of Zionism is not finished yet, far from it."
— Ariel Sharon, 1982

"If a gentile hits a Jew, the gentile must be killed."
The Babylonian Talmud, Judaism's most holy book, Sanhedrin 58b

---

"But if the enemy is disposed towards peace, do thou also be disposed towards peace, and trust in Allah, for he is the one that heareth and knoweth all things."
— **The Qur'an,** Islam's most holy book, Surah VIII

"Jesus the Nazarene, along with his disciples, practiced sorcery and black magic, led Jews astray into idolatry, and was sponsored by foreign, gentile powers."
The Babylonian Talmud, Judaism's most holy book, Sanhedrin 43a

---

"The anti-Semites will become our most loyal friends, the anti-Semite nations will become our allies."
— Theodore Herzl, founder of Zionism

"There is no need to exaggerate the part played in the creation of Bolshevism and the actual bringing about of the Russian Revolution by these international and for the most part atheistic Jews. It certainly was a very great one, and it probably outweighs all others. The majority of the leading figures were Jews, and moreover, the principle inspiration and driving power comes from the Jewish leaders."
— Winston Churchill, 1920

"Then I saw another beast coming out of the earth. He had two horns like a lamb, but he spoke like a dragon. He made the earth and its inhabitants worship the first beast whose fatal wound had been healed, and he performed great and miraculous signs. He deceived the inhabitants of the earth and ordered them to set up an image in honor of the beast who was wounded by the sword and yet lived."
— **Book of the Apocalypse**, Ch. 13

"The state of Israel must invent dangers, and to do this it must adopt the methods of provocation and revenge.... And above all, let us hope for a new war with the Arab countries so that we may finally get rid of our troubles and acquire our space."
— *From the diary of Moshe Sharett, Israeli's first Foreign Minister from 1948-1956, and Prime Minister from 1954-1956.*

"No rabbi can ever be punished with Hell."
— **The Babylonian Talmud,** *Judaism's most holy book, Hagigah 27a.*

"You snakes! You brood of vipers! How will you escape being condemned to Hell? Therefore I am sending you prophets and wise men and teachers. Some of them you will kill and crucify, others you will flog in your synagogues and pursue from town to town. And so upon you will come all the righteous blood that has been shed on earth from the blood of righteous Abel to the blood of Zecharia."
— *Jesus of Nazareth addressing the Sanhedrin*

"The fact that young Jews in Hollywood feel comfortable creating 'Jewy' characters isn't surprising. That's what happens when you Gentiles forget to keep scaring us. You let us join your country clubs, gave us your women and encouraged our most annoyingly self-righteous member to run for president. So now that we've assimilated to the point where we're completely the same as white people, we're trying to re-create a community by shoving our culture down your throats. The bizarre part is that the same masses who saw The Passion of the Christ are into it."
— *Jewish-American columnist Joel Kline writing for the LA Times*

"Israel controls the United States Senate. Around 80 percent are completely in support of Israel; anything Israel wants it gets. Jewish influence in the House of Representatives is even greater."
- *United States Senator William Fulbright*

...and He spake 'Lo, I am the slave of Allah. He hath given me the scripture and hath appointed me a prophet, and hath made me blessed wheresoever I may be, and has commanded me to prayer and to almsgiving, so long as I remain alive, and hath made me dutiful towards her who bore me, and hath not made me arrogant or unblest. Peace be upon me the day that I was born and the day that I die, and the day that I shall be raised alive.' Such was Jesus, son of Mary, this is the truth about which there is no doubt."
— **The Qur'an,** *Islam's most holy book, Surah XIX*

IN THEIR OWN WORDS

"Tell me, do the evil men of this world have a bad time? They hunt and catch whatever they feel like eating. They don't suffer from indigestion and are not punished by Heaven. I want Israel to join that club. Maybe the world will then at last begin to fear us instead of feeling sorry. Maybe they will start to tremble, to fear our madness instead of admiring our nobility. Let them tremble, let them call us a mad state. Let them understand that we are a savage country, dangerous to our surroundings, not normal, that we might go wild, that we might start World War Three just like that, or that we might one day go crazy and burn all the oil fields in the Middle East. Personally, I don't want to be any better than Harry Truman who snuffed out half a million Japanese with two fine bombs."
— Ariel Sharon, 1982

"It is interesting, but not surprising, to note that in all the words written and uttered about the Kennedy assassination, Israel's intelligence service agency, the Mossad, has never been mentioned. And yet a Mossad motive is obvious. On this question, as on almost all others, American reporters cannot bring themselves to cast Israel in an unfavorable light — despite the fact that Mossad complicity is as plausible as any of the other theories."
— US Representative Paul Findley, March 1992

"Since the Mossad had all the security arrangements in hand, it would not be a problem in bringing the killers as close as they wanted to President Bush and then staging his assassination. In the ensuing confusion, the Mossad people would kill the 'perpetrators,' scoring yet another victory for the Mossad. With the assassins dead, it would be difficult to discover where the 'security breach' had been, except that several countries involved in the conference, such as Syria, were regarded as countries that assisted terrorists."
— Ex-Israeli Intelligence officer Victor Ostrovsky, describing in his book **'The Other Side of Deception'** how the Mossad planned to assassinate President George Bush at the Madrid peace conference in October of 1991 for the purpose of blaming it on Arab extremists.

"Clearly there are laws on the books which have outlawed the inciting of riots or acts which endanger human life. Mel Gibson's movie will incite violence against Jews and put the lives of million of Jews in danger. Under Section 802 of the 2001 USA Patriot Act, any crime which endangers human life is defined as an act of domestic terrorism. Mel Gibson's incitement of anti-Semitism is a crime which endangers human life and under the Patriot Act his film The Passion is an act of domestic terrorism.

We hereby call upon Attorney General John Ashcroft, the Department of Justice, Homeland Security Secretary Tom Ridge and the Department of Homeland Security to arrest Mel Gibson as a terrorist, confiscate all prints of The Passion, confiscate all materials related to the film as terrorist paraphernalia and shut down every terrorist hate-site on the internet supporting the film."
– *Rabbi David Feldman, spokesperson for the group* **Jews Against Anti-Semitism**

"The books of the Christians must not be rescued from fire, but must be burned."
The Babylonian Talmud, Judaism's most holy book, Shabbat 116a

----

"Thou wilt find that the most hostile to mankind are to be found among those who are Jews and idolaters. And thou will find the most affectionate to mankind are those who say 'Lo, we are Christians.' That is because the Christians are not proud, and there are found among them priests and monks who are men of learning and who have renounced the world."
– **The Qur'an,** Islam's most holy book, Surah V

"Nearly all Arab Moslems and Arab Christians do have respect, even reverence towards the holiness of the land, but only a small minority of Jews have the same respect. 95% of the Jewish population in Israel are either atheists or secular humanists and are not impeded by the Ten Commandments or by any other restraints on sinful human behavior. When the Zionist/Bolshevik Jews won control of the Holy Land, every form of sin began seeping into it. Within a few short decades, the holy land became a modern-day Sodom and Gomorrah. Drug trade and abuse, illegal weapons sales, prostitution, gambling, labor racketeering, murder, extortion, blackmail, insurance fraud, loan-sharking and corruption of government officials and police became a part of daily life in Israel. Israel has a highly organized crime syndicate headquarters in Bat-Yam near Tel Aviv. Many members of the syndicate are ex-convicts and ex-commandos from the Israeli army, highly skilled in the use of weapons and explosives. This syndicate operates in the open because of corruption in the government. Some officials are paid off by the syndicate and some are actively associated with the criminal operations."
– *Jack Bernstein, author of the book* **'The Life of an American Jew Living in Racist Marxist Israel.'**

IN THEIR OWN WORDS   25

"It was with some astonishment that I discovered what an integral part of American Jewish life crime was. Our forefathers made names for themselves as gangsters, murderers, musclemen, hit men, acid throwers, arm breakers, bombers and all the other professions open to nice Jewish boys. Prostitution, vice, alcohol, gambling, racketeering, extortion, and all the other things that fill the newspaper today and that I gladly have been attributing as character flaws in other groups...those were our things. I was shocked at how deep our roots are in all the sinks of depravity and corruption. The Jews were the first ones to realize the link between organized crime and organized politics. They led the way in corrupting the police and city hall. They first realized the value of gang/syndicate cartels in business to reduce the killing of each other. They were monopolists of the highest order. We wrote the book, so to speak, on crime, but it's all forgotten."
— Marvin Kitman, Jewish critic and writer

"Thai police discovered a production studio operated by Australian Jewish gangsters who had been involved in the making of child rape pornography and ritual murder movies. Four Thai and ten Australian Jews were arrested after Thai police discovered they had been kidnapping Thai children between the ages of three and nine years old from the countryside in Thailand, and then filming them being tortured, raped, and murdered in ritualistic sacrificial scenes. The all-Jewish customers, including 2500 in Australia, 4500 in Israel, and an unknown number in the United States, paid as much as $1500.00 per one hour digital file downloaded off the internet of the ritual rape and murder of the little children. All of the scenes on the movies are too horrific to describe but most involved an altar shaped as a Star of David, and participants acting out ritualistic torture, rape and sacrificial murder scenes. Officials connected with the Israeli intelligence agency Mossad are paying Thai officials to cover the story up."
— News story covered by many media outlets, including the **Guardian of London,** describing the international ring of Israeli gangsters operating a child snuff porn business that was discovered in the summer of 2002.

"In giving to us the land of Israel, God had done teshuva, repentance, and with the magnanimity of his gift of giving us victories over the Arabs, we forgave him for all the evil he had done to us."
— Yossi Klein Halevi, author of **'Memoirs of a Jewish Extremist.'**

"In the name of God the Merciful and the Compassionate: Behold this promise to the people of Jerusalem of safe conduct for their persons, property, their churches, their healthy and their sick. Their churches shall neither be

used by us as dwellings nor destroyed, and no constraint shall be exercised among them in religion nor shall any harm be done to any of them. This document is placed under the surety of God and the protection of the Prophet Mohammed, the Caliphs and the believers, on condition that the inhabitants of Jerusalem pay the jizya (tax) that is due from them."
— **The Treaty of Jerusalem,** *signed between Caliph Omar and the Christians of Jerusalem in 636 AD promising them that they would suffer no religious persecution under Muslim rule.*

"They come in broad daylight and throw filthy materials like diapers and poisonous substances inside the spring's source. Last year as many as 12 children in the village were diagnosed with liver infections and many others developed stomach pains as a result of drinking contaminated water."
— *Ayid Kamal, mayor of the Palestinian town of Madama, commenting on the decades-old Israeli practice of poisoning the water sources of the Palestinians.*

"This country exists as the fulfillment of a promise made by God Himself. It would be ridiculous to ask it to account for its legitimacy."
— *Israeli Prime Minister Golda Meir*

"The big winner today, intended or not, is the state of Israel. There is no question that as a result of these attacks the Israeli leadership is feeling relief."
— *George Friedman, director of www.stratfor.com, a pro-Israeli intelligence think tank, commenting upon the attacks of September 11th.*

"Regarding what took place on September 11, well it's very good...Well, it's not good, but it will generate immediate sympathy for Israel."
— *Israeli Prime Minister Benjamin Netanyahu's response to the attacks on America as reported in The Jerusalem Post, September 12, 2001.*

"We must use terror, assassination, intimidation, land confiscation, and the cutting off of all social services to rid the Galilee of its Arab population."
— *Israeli Prime Minister David Ben-Gurion, May 1948*

"The anti-Semite has no morals and no conscience. We must fill our jails and our asylums with anti-Semitic lunatics and we must harass them to such an extent that none will wish to become fellow travelers."
— *Rabbi Leon Spitz, writing for* **'The American Hebrew,'** *1946*

IN THEIR OWN WORDS

"In most cases, "anti Semitism", old or new, is not an irrational hatred or sickness in the Gentile soul. It is a healthy defense mechanism of mainly Christian and Moslem nations, cultures, races and religions that are threatened by the gradual and insidious process of extinction under the Zionist agenda."
— Henry Makow PhD, anti-Zionist Jew and Internet writer

"I am a Jew, I am an Israeli, I am a Zionist, and I am both racially and intellectually superior to you, the non-Jew. For your lies, your pathetic stupidity, and your anti-Semitism, your people will suffer under the punishment of the world's future super-power, Israel!"

"You seem to forget Israel's nuclear capability. No country will risk getting hit with an atomic bomb, and therefore Israel's survival is assured. We will also, at a certain point in the coming decades, finally realize the need to exercise ruthlessness, and will blow our Arab neighbors to kingdom come. I am sure you will have the joy of witnessing the first example of the latter policy, when Israel takes action against Iran (and perhaps also Syria) in the coming months."

"Jews are superior to dirty-blooded non-Jews like you. While your ancestors were sleeping with the swine in the forests of Europe, my ancestors were building the city of Jerusalem. Israel will come to be the world's newest superpower. It is our destiny, written in the prophecies of god, written in our ambitions, written in our blood!"

"Beware, for your kind will come to fear us. The coming 30 years will make your eyes twitch my gentile!"

"I am a Jew, you are not. I have the privilege of having god by my side, as well as the world's supreme nation. Perhaps you do not yet see that the worst is awaiting your kind, in the face of the coming Islamo-Christian War, from which my kind will arise victorious."

"I am only 14 years old, but I have enough wisdom to see that you are nothing but a piece of gentile filth. No matter, perhaps god will find it suitable that a terrorist attack will end your misery. I shall personally pray for it to be so."
— Orri Joseph Avraham, an Israeli citizen

"Dishonoring Christian religious symbols is an old religious duty in Judaism. Spitting on the cross, and especially on the Crucifix, and spitting when a Jew passes a church, have been obligatory from around AD 200 for pious Jews. In the past, when the danger of anti-Semitic hostility was a real one, the pious Jews were commanded by their rabbis either to spit so that the reason for doing so would be unknown, or to spit onto their chests, not actually on the cross or openly before the church. The increasing strength of the Jewish state has caused these customs to become more open again but there should be no mistake: The spitting on the cross for converts from Christianity to Judaism, organized in Kibbutz Sa'ad and financed by the Israeli government is considered an act of traditional Jewish piety. This barbarous attitude of contempt and hate for Christian religious symbols has grown in Israel. In the 1950's Israel issued a series of stamps representing pictures of Israeli cities. In the picture of Nazareth, there was a church and on its top a cross -almost invisible, perhaps the size of a millimeter. Nevertheless, the religious parties made a scandal and the stamps were quickly withdrawn and replaced by an almost identical series from which the microscopic cross was withdrawn."
— *Professor Israel Shahak, former Israeli citizen and holocaust survivor*

"I think the government should put bombs in Palestinian hospitals, but unfortunately the government doesn't do it, so it is up to the people to do those things."
— *Noam Federman, member of the Israeli terrorist organization* **Kach,** *of which the JDL (Jewish Defense League) is an offshoot.*

"Here lies the saint, Doctor Baruch Kapal Goldstein, blessed be the memory of this righteous and holy man, may the Lord revenge his blood, who devoted his soul for the Jewish people, the Jewish religion and the Jewish land. His hands are clean and his heart is clear. He was killed as a martyr of God on the 14th of Adar, Purim, in the year 5754. "
— *The inscription as it reads on the grave of the mass-murderer Baruch Goldstein, an American physician and an Israeli settler of Hebron who indiscriminately murdered 29 Palestinian worshippers kneeling in prayer in a mosque in 1994.*

"I have learned that the state of Israel cannot be ruled in our generation without deceit and adventurism."
— *Moshe Sharett, Israel's first Foreign Minister and later a Prime Minister*

"I am going to church to give thanks to my friends and to God, Jesus Christ for the support of the last 18 years, but before I do, I want to tell you something very important. I suffered here 18 years because I am a Christian, because I was baptized into Christianity. If I was Jewish, I wouldn't have all this suffering here in isolation for 18 years...only because I was a Christian."
— Mordechai Vanunu, a Morroccan-born Jew later turned Christian who was imprisoned 18 years in an Israeli jail for having revealed the truth about Israel's nuclear weapons program.

"I've never seen a President — I don't care who he is — stand up to the Jews. They always get what they want. If the American people understood what a grip these people have got on our government, they would rise up in arms."
— Admiral Thomas Moorer, Chairman of the Joint Chiefs of Staff from 1970 to 1974

"I'm trying to be realistic. Preserving my people is more important than any universal moral concepts."
— Israeli writer Benny Morris

"American security services overnight stopped a car bomb on the George Washington Bridge. The van, packed with explosives, was stopped on an approach ramp to the bridge. Authorities suspect that the terrorists intended to blow up the main crossing between New Jersey and New York."
— A story appearing in **The Jerusalem Post** concerning the arrest of a team of Israeli intelligence operatives posing as Palestinians on September 12, 2001

"Our goal is to break the West's confidence in the existing Egyptian regime. This terrorism should cause arrests, demonstrations, and expressions of revenge. The Israeli origin should be totally hidden while attention should be shifted to any other possible factor. The purpose is to prevent economic and military aid from the West to Egypt."
— Col. Benjamin Givli, the head of Israel's military intelligence who outlined the purpose behind the wave of Israeli-orchestrated terrorist acts taking place in Egypt during 1954 in what came to be known as the Lavon Affair.

"Let us never tolerate outrageous conspiracy theories concerning the attacks of September the 11th."
— President Bush, speaking to the United Nations.

"Never in her history has Israel had the luxury of having 500,000 foreigners fight her wars for her, until now."
— Abba Eban, Foreign Minister to Israel, in reference to the 1st Gulf War.

"The Marxist Zionists who rule Israel and the Marxist Zionists in America have been trying to trick the U.S. into a Middle East war on the side of Israel, and if more Americans are not made aware of the truth about Marxist/Zionist Israel, you can be sure that, sooner or later, those atheists who claim to be God's chosen people will trick the U.S. into a Middle East war against the Arabs who in the past have always been America's best friends."
— Jack Bernstein, author of the book **'The Life of an American Jew Living in Racist Marxist Israel.'**

"The Mossad (Israeli Intelligence) was busy at the time preparing for Operation Brush Fire, aimed at getting the United States involved militarily in the Middle East in general and in the Gulf region in particular. By January 1989 the Mossad machine was busy portraying Saddam as a tyrant and a danger to the world. The Mossad activated every asset it had, from volunteer agents in Amnesty International to fully bought members of the US Congress...The media was supplied with "inside information" from "reliable sources" on how the crazed leader of Iraq killed people with his bare hands and used missiles to target Iranian cities. The Mossad wanted the Americans to do the work of destroying that gigantic army in the Iraqi desert so that Israel would not have to face it one day on its own border."
— Ex-Israeli Intelligence officer Victor Ostrovsky, describing in his book **'The Other Side of Deception'** how the Mossad maneuvered the American government and military into fighting Iraq in the first Gulf War.

"The 2nd war in Iraq was conceived by 25 neo-conservative intellectuals, most of them Jewish, who are pushing President Bush to change the course of history."
— Ari Shavit, writer for the Israeli newspaper **Haaretz**

"Fight in the cause of Allah those who fight you. But do not transgress limits, for Allah loveth not transgressors. And fight them on until there is no more tumult or oppression and there prevail justice and faith in Allah.

IN THEIR OWN WORDS

But if they cease, let there be no more hostilities except against those who practice oppression."
— ***The Qur'an,*** *Islam's most holy book, Surah II*

"During the nights, the Jewish squatters used to bring drugs for the soldiers on my roof. The soldiers would inject themselves, and afterwards would sit on the floor breathing heavily for hours. On one occasion a soldier fell from the roof. He was having difficulty breathing and raving on the ground as if he were dying. I called the IDF headquarters and asked for a military ambulance to take this soldier. When the unit officer came to check the story, the soldier claimed that he was having an 'epilepsy attack'. In another event I saw a soldier beating his colleague seriously and trying to take away his weapon after he took drugs. The soldiers claimed that their colleague was ready to shoot into the Arab homes nearby. Dr. Tayseer Zahdeh from Hebron claims that he saw the Israeli soldiers taking heroin injections in front of his private room, where he and his family hid themselves from them. He took the used syringes and used them to support his story, but the military commander said that these syringes were used by Dr. Tayseer himself. The commander forgot that the IDF syringes have a special color which is not allowed to be used by Palestinians."
-excerpt from **'IDF Soldiers and Jewish Squatters: Shit, Drugs and Abuse... The Daily Life of Kawther Salaam.'**

"President Bush announced that we are here not for WMD but for freedom of the Iraqis. That's the biggest crock we have ever heard over here. Every soldier and marine here knows that the people don't want us here. They see us as exactly for what we are, foreign occupiers of their country who have killed tens of thousands of civilians including thousands of women and children in so-called 'collateral damage.' We all saw the video on NBC of the mosque shootings of wounded and I can tell you it is a lot worse than that. We often killed the helpless, the wounded and many civilians. My own squad did. I did. And I will do whatever I am ordered to do, but it doesn't stop me from not liking it. I didn't join the service to kill women and children! We do a lot worse than what you saw on the video.

In Fallujah when we come to an apartment building, we shout for the people to come out. Most times because of the lack of translators we couldn't even say to come out in Arabic, and these people don't know what an English "come out" sounds like anymore than you reading this would know it if I said it in Arabic. A lot of people are too afraid to come out. But after we would warn them, we would go in. You know how? We would riddle the *building and every window with high-caliber, armor-piercing machine gun fire, then often we would throw in a grenade for good measure. If any civilians were in there they ended up either dead or wounded. I can tell you that over the duration of a week I myself saw at least a hundred bodies in the burned out and attacked apartments, and I only saw a little sliver of Fallujah. And what did we do with the wounded? I'll tell you. We did nothing. We just moved on to the next building. We were fighters, not medics, but there were no medics behind us. I believe the thinking is that it is better for the wounded enemy to die so they can't fight us anymore. It is true that we have to kill civilians if we are to survive because we can't know who the enemy is, but how in the world can our leaders put us in this situation? If it takes the killing tens of thousands of civilians for us to be here, for God's sake we shouldn't be here! And if we have to kill innocent civilians and destroy tens of thousands of people's homes, then how can we say we are fighting to bring them freedom? Tell that to the grieving mother and father I saw who at their feet lay their little girl with her head half shot off."*

"None of us can figure out why we are really here. The people here on the streets have a name for us, they call us the Jews! At first I never understood this, but when I found out how Israeli agents in the American government like Perle and Wolfowitz were behind the war, all of it began to fall into place. It was never a war for America, it is one where thousands of Americans are being killed or maimed for life for the benefit of Israel, not America. We want to get back to our families, not because we are afraid, but because we realize that this war is the craziest war America has ever fought, an unnecessary war that has only caused more human suffering, both for us Americans here doing our duty and for the innocent here who suffer and hate us with all their heart. And as for terrorists, we are making 10 new ones for every one we kill."
— Letter from an American serviceman in Iraq

"The 16 year old girl stayed for three days with the bodies of her family who were killed in their home. When the soldiers entered she was in her home with her father, mother, 12 year-old brother and two sisters. She watched the soldiers enter and shoot her mother and father directly, without saying anything. They beat her two sisters, then shot them in the head. After this her brother was enraged and ran at the soldiers while shouting at them, so they shot him dead."
— Dahr Jamail, an American reporter for **Inter Press Service** covering the war in Iraq.

IN THEIR OWN WORDS 33

"Five of us were trapped together in our house in Falluja when the siege began. On 9 November American marines came to our house. My father went to the door to meet them. We were not fighters, and so we thought we had nothing to fear. I ran into the kitchen to put on my veil, since men were going to enter our house and it would be wrong for them to see me with my hair uncovered. This saved my life, for as my father and neighbor approached the door, the Americans opened fire on them. They died instantly. My 13-year-old brother and I hid in the kitchen behind the fridge. The soldiers came into the house and caught my older sister. They beat her and then shot her, but they did not see me. Soon they left, but not before they had destroyed our furniture and stolen the money from my father's pocket."
— *Hudda Fawzi Salam Issawi, an Iraqi girl from the Julan district of Falluja testifying as to what happened to her family by the Americans.*

"Some messengers were endowed with gifts above others. To some of them Allah spoke, to others he raised to high degrees of honor. To Jesus, son of Mary were given clear signs, and who was strengthened by the Holy Spirit."
— **The Qur'an**, *Islam's most holy book, Surah II*

"All gentile children are animals."
The Babylonian Talmud, *Judaism's most holy book, Yebamoth 98a*

"Why would Iraq attack America or use nuclear weapons against us? I'll tell you what I think the real threat is and has been since 1990 — it's the threat against Israel. And this is the threat that dare not speak its name, because the Europeans don't care deeply about that threat, and the American government doesn't want to lean too hard on it rhetorically, because it is not a popular sell."
— *Philip Zelikow, member of the President's Foreign Intelligence Advisory Board (PFIAB), which reports directly to the president.*

"I was not involved in the September 11 attacks in the United States nor did I have knowledge of the attacks. There exists a government within a government within the United States. The United States should try to trace the perpetrators of these attacks within itself; to the people who want to make the present century a time of conflict between Islam and Christianity. That secret government must be asked as to who carried out the attacks. The American system is totally in control of the Jews, whose first priority is Israel, not the United States."
— *Osama Bin Laden, September 2001*

"Israel must be like a mad dog, too dangerous to bother."
— *Israeli defense minister Moshe Dayan*

"Our armed forces are not the thirteenth strongest in the world, but rather the second or third. We have the capability to take the world down with us, and I can assure you that this will happen before Israel goes under."
— *Remarks of Martin Van Creveld, a professor of military history at Israel's Hebrew University.*

"We do not know which irresponsible Israeli Prime Minister will take office and decide to use nuclear weapons in the struggle against neighboring Arab countries. The weapons that Israel is holding can destroy the region and kill millions."
— *ex-Israeli nuclear technician Mordechai Vanunu*

"......And it may be that this astounding race may at the present time be in the actual process of producing another system of morals and philosophy as malevolent as Christianity was benevolent, and which, if not arrested, would shatter irretrievable all that Christianity has rendered possible. It would almost seem as if the gospel of Christ and the gospel of Antichrist were destined to originate among the same people, and that this mystic and mysterious race had been chosen for the supreme manifestations of both the divine and the diabolical."
— *Winston Churchill, 1920*

"Be on your guard against the yeast of the Pharisees."
— *Jesus of Nazareth*

"Ultimately, the Americans fell for the Mossad ploy head over heels, dragging the British and the Germans somewhat reluctantly in with them."
— *Ex-Israeli Intelligence officer Victor Ostrovsky, describing in his book* **'The Other Side of Deception'** *how the Mossad tricked the American government into bombing Libya for the benefit of Israel.*

"A sly rabbi debates with God and through trickery defeats Him. God is forced to admit that the rabbi won the debate."
— **The Babylonian Talmud,** *Judaism's most holy book, Baba Mezia, 59b.*

"Woe to you, teachers of the law and Pharisees, you hypocrites! You are like whitewashed tombs, which look beautiful on the outside but which on the inside are full of dead men's bones and everything unclean. In the same

way, you appear to people on the outside as righteous, but on the inside you are full of hypocrisy and wickedness."
— Jesus of Nazareth addressing the Sanhedrin

"If a Jew is tempted to do evil, he should go to a city where he is not known and do the evil there."
— **The Babylonian Talmud,** Judaism's most holy book, Moed Kattan, 17a

---

"There is no doubt that many sexual atrocities were committed by the attacking Jews. Many young Arab girls were raped and later slaughtered. Old women were also molested."
— General Richard Catling, British Army Assistant Inspector after interrogating several female survivors at the Deir Yassin massacre.

"The Jews I find are very, very selfish. They care not how many get murdered or mistreated as long as they themselves get special treatment. When they have power, physical, financial or political, neither Hitler nor Stalin have anything on them for cruelty or mistreatment of the underdog."
— US President Harry S Truman

"When a Jew murders a gentile there will be no death penalty. What a Jew steals from a gentile he may keep."
— **The Babylonian Talmud,** Judaism's most holy book, Sanhedrin 57a

---

"What are we accomplishing?" they asked. "Here is this man performing many miraculous signs. If we allow him to go on like this, everyone will believe in him, and then the Romans will come and take away our place and our nation." Then one of them named Caiphas who was High Priest that year spoke and said "You know nothing at all. Do you not realize it is better that one man die than that the whole nation perish?"
— **Book of John**

"And the unbelieving Jews plotted and planned to murder Jesus, but Allah is the best of plotters."
— **The Qur'an,** Islam's most holy book, Surah III

"Jewish blood and a goy's (gentile's) blood are not the same."
— Israeli Rabbi Yitzhak Ginsburg

"Nothing of any good could come from the world. According to the rabbis, the Goyim (non-Jews) could fix your car and send satellites into space, but they couldn't understand truth or the meaning of life. Only Jews had a link with God."
– Yossi Klein Halevi, author of **'Memoirs of a Jewish Extremist.'**

"A Jewish man is obligated to say the prayer every day, "Thank you God, for not making me a gentile, a woman or a slave."
– **The Babylonian Talmud,** *Judaism's most holy book, Menahoth, 43b-44a*

"The best of the gentiles – kill them; the best of snakes – smash its skull; the best of women – is filled with witchcraft."
– **The Babylonian Talmud,** *Judaism's most holy book, Kiddushin 66c*

"One million Arabs are not worth one Jewish fingernail."
– *Rabbi Yaacov Perrin, Feb. 27, 1994*

"My view of history was that billions of people who lived and suffered and died were no more than extras in a Jewish drama, and that human experience was really Jewish experience. I came to believe that the anti-Semites were right, except in the reverse; that the Jews did secretly control the world, but benevolently. How else to explain the Holocaust if not as evil trying to destroy the source of all good? I was ready to concede that there were decent people who weren't Jews, but decent peoples? Only the Jews."
– Yossi Klein Halevi, author of **'Memoirs of a Jewish Extremist.'**

"Woe to you, teachers of the law and Pharisees, you hypocrites. You give a tenth of your spices, but you have neglected the more important matters of the law: justice, mercy, and faithfulness."
– Jesus of Nazareth

"The thesis that the danger of genocide was hanging over us in June 1967 and that Israel was fighting for its physical existence was only a bluff, a deliberate lie which we developed after the war to justify our actions."
– Israeli General Matityahu Peled

"The Jews and 'the world' could never co-exist; at best we would endure each other from a distance. Some of our religious laws seemed to be meant

IN THEIR OWN WORDS

not to bring us closer to God, but rather to separate us from the Goyim (non-Jews)."
— Yossi Klein Halevi, author of **'Memoirs of a Jewish Extremist.'**

"By rejecting Christ, the Pharisees placed the Jewish people in perpetual opposition to the best interests of humanity, to the ultimate and inevitable path of human spiritual evolution."
— Henry Makow PhD, anti-Zionist Jew and Internet writer

"The reason that there are so many Jews in the porn business is because Jewish families tend to be more liberal than Christian ones, and they aren't obsessed by the fear of the devil or of going to hell."
— Ron Jeremy, Jewish porn star who proudly admits to having acted in or directed over 1,500 porn videos, explaining why there is such a disproportionate number of Jews involved in the pornography industry.

"About one-third of the Israeli parliament belongs to the one of Israel's communist, socialist, or other Marxist-oriented parties. That fact alone should put to rest the lie about Israel being the only barrier against communism in the Middle East. In fact, it is the Arab countries that form the barrier that has stopped the spread of communism in the Middle East. Israel is one tentacle of the New York/Moscow/Tel Aviv/ triangle which is behind the communist movement."
— Jack Bernstein, author of the book **'The Life of an American Jew Living in Racist Marxist Israel.'**

"The Israeli soldiers took the two Palestinians, Firas Al-Bakri age 21 and Samih Rahal age 24 to a deserted hotel in the Southern part of Jerusalem, then they tortured them. They beat their victims, burned out their cigarettes on the victims' bodies, then one soldier held one victim, forced him to open his mouth and to close his eyes. Then the other soldiers urinated in his mouth and forced him to swallow it. The soldiers threw the victims ID's into a hole full of urine and feces and then ordered them to crawl on their abdomens and to pick up their IDs with their mouths. The soldiers were spitting at the victims all the time, they beat them with the butts of their rifles, all the while cursing Arabs, Muslims and Palestinians. The Israeli soldiers put an end to their sadistic scene as they ordered their victims, under threat of shooting, to jump from the first floor of the Hotel. This caused the victims injuries and several broken bones. The Israeli soldier Mikael Merolofski asked journalists during a meeting in Jerusalem, 'Why are you are making such a big deal and bothering us about this? We didn't

do anything, we just forced two Palestinians to drink urine, one of us beat a Palestinian, and the second beat the other one. Our commander recommended us to get revenge on the Palestinians and before they sent us to serve in the West Bank they showed us a film about the killing of two Israeli soldiers and how they were thrown from the first floor in Ramallah.'
– *excerpt of a news report concerning Israeli brutality against Palestinians authored by Palestinian journalist Kawther Salaam.*

"By way of deception thou shalt do war."
– *Motto of the Mossad, Israeli's foremost intelligence agency.*

Reasons

"Charity begins at home..."

It has been said an incalculable number of times, and certainly, a good number of those who have said it have done so without much thought as to what kind of wisdom it is supposed to contain.

One could easily make the argument today that those troubled times have at last arrived that were predicted would come, perverse times in which the world would be filled with individuals *"ignorant and unstable, distorting the truth to their own destruction"*. It is without question an age of wanton violence, represented not only in what is being done to men's bodies, but as well in what is being done to men's hearts and minds.

Today, it should be obvious to all that there is an undeniable agenda at work whose interests lie in debasing humanity to the level of beasts, and as such, the precepts of truth and wisdom acting as the natural impediments to this debasement must be eradicated if such an agenda is to succeed. And so it is in this age therefore that one finds these ignorant and unstable individuals proliferating—not in numbers of one's or two's, but in the tens and hundreds of millions—distorting the truth into something perverse, knowingly or not. And as bad as this may sound, the prospect of living amongst such base, and to a certain degree, dangerous individuals, it gets much worse.

Unfortunately, individuals such as these never are and never will be content with leading only themselves down the road to destruction, but instead insist upon taking everyone else with them as well. This is easy to see, and particularly so in the West, when considering the manner in which today many (and especially those who proudly decorate their exteriors with the garb of feigned religious principles or patriotism) distort what is the beauty and majesty of truth in their attempt at justifying the unjustifiable. One such attempt that I have witnessed more times than I care to remember over the last two years has been the abuse of the statement that initiated this discussion concerning charity.

This theme (in one of its varying forms) is what I have experienced from individuals during the course of my many in-depth discussions concerning events as they pertain to the Middle East. I say "in one of its varying forms" because as of yet I have not actually heard those particular words, but certainly the theme has been undeniably present. And now, two years later, it is a sentiment for which I have developed a certain amount of distaste, not only because I have been the recipient of its "wisdom" on too many occasions, but rather because I know what it is that these individuals are *really* trying to say.

Human nature and the behavior that it creates can be a curious thing to watch, particularly when people take things that are in their basic essence good and then turn them into something perverse, or at best, abused to absurdity. Like many old sayings, the one concerning charity has been used with such frequency that many have forgotten what it means, while others, hoping to capitalize on its efficacy, use it in the interests of aggrandizing themselves or their argument way past what is rightfully due. Either way, like many things that used to command a certain amount of respect in a more noble age, today it is used cheaply and usually for ignoble purposes.

Once it has been decoded, in whatever context it maybe used, the theme that it is supposed to carry is one of loyalty, and loyalty in a very discriminating sense. It speaks of the righteousness of coming to the aid of those in the immediate vicinity as opposed to assisting those in the more remote. Coming to terms with the origins of this tendency should be no mystery, for in truth it is just another aspect of human nature that is as innate to mankind's being as cold weather is to January. This nature, being what it is, is such that people are imbued with natural affections which lead them to consider what is best for those who are closest to them as opposed to those who are out of sight and thus out of mind.

However, despite the altruistic spirit that this saying may appear to possess, what should be considered is that the real essence of this theme is rooted in self-preservation, albeit of a more subtle type, and it is probably safe to say as well that one of the reasons for this saying having been encoded within our sociological wiring is tied to the simple issue of rewards. As unpleasant as it may sound, the truth of the matter is that man is a self-centered animal who prioritizes all things in relation to how they affect him personally. As such, oftentimes then we find that the only difference between those things that are brazenly self-centered and those that take on the *appearance* of being altruistic contrast each other only by degrees.

This being the case, even the concept of "charity beginning at home" does not escape the rigors and regimen of human nature, particularly in that all people understand the fact that the closer the recipient of such charity is, the better the chance there may be of the giver being rewarded with some type of fringe benefit. Walking alongside this statement concerning charity can be found its near identical sister that speaks of the insoluble ties that are bound by blood, and again, it is safe to say that the interest that is at work here is the instinct of self-preservation, albeit not as easily apparent. And although there may be those who may wince at hearing these expressions (due to the fact that they appear to justify a certain amount of callousness with regards to others) what must be remembered here is that we are talking about human nature, which is a tough program to alter, and a condition that rarely responds to negotiation.

Therefore, the reader of this work, in glancing over what no doubt appears to be an incendiary cover and title, as well as scanning over the material that is covered within it will no doubt ask at some point where the reason may lie in my not following that more near-sighted line of thinking that seems to be the norm in today's world. As an American Christian whose country is at war with those in the predominantly Muslim Middle East, why, they will ask, have I not adopted that more 'familiar' charity as opposed to concentrating on the events that are taking place in the lives of those whom I have never met? In addition to this, such individuals will ask what it is that I hope to gain by speaking on this topic and in this fashion.

For those who know me by my writings, and who know me well, there should be no ambiguity as to where my position lies concerning this topic, as I have been anything but vague or unspecific. I have painted the picture (at least as I see it) in stark terms — black vs white, good vs evil, and rarely do I run into someone who, after reading something I have written, is asking for clarification. Instead, my correspondence varies between those who love what I have to say and those who hate it, and within that group of "haters" there are those who are not as bold in their opposition and who attack what I am doing by stealth, using the tactic of intellectual distancing and the protected position that it affords by asking the question we discussed previously, which is "why?"

Of course, the question "why" for the most part is merely the primer, and this is what I meant in the first part of this discussion when I said that I have come to understand what it is that these individuals are *really* trying to say. For most of them, what is at issue is that they simply do not *like* what I have had to say, and are really not interested in what my reasons are for saying it. Rather though than to expose the truth of who they are and what they are really about, they attempt to cloak the fact that they have come to the discussion having already made up their minds about this topic with no interest in reviewing it in any manner, a concealment that they attempt to accomplish by "intellectualizing" their approach with a series of questions. "Why" is simply a smokescreen that many of them use to disguise the fact that they are on a seek-and-destroy mission, (whether they know it or not) individuals who are disposed towards the "shoot first and ask questions later" approach that has come to typify the American mindset. This seek-and-destroy mission is the attempt to silence a message that conflicts with something that these individuals may prize and as such is oftentimes camouflaged within the context of an interrogation of sorts which I have experienced now dozens (if not hundreds) of times in the last 2 years and which is a variation of that *"charity begins at home"* theme that introduced this discussion:

"Where is your concern for those at home? Where is your consideration for your own blood, being that you are (whether you like it or not) an American? Where are your tears for those who lost their lives on September 11? Where is your loyalty for those men and women in the service who have lost their lives in fighting for our "freedom" in Afghanistan and Iraq?"

And of course, the predictable accusation-framed-as-a-question from those whose agenda lies in seeing to it that the well-being of the state of Israel is maintained above all other issues, *"Where are your tears for the innocent Jews who are being killed by suicide bombers? Where are your tears for the victims of the Holocaust, whose survivors today are only doing what any group of persecuted people would do were they faced with similar circumstances?"*

On a superficial level of course all of these questions appear to have hit the bulls eye, and for those who (in what is the most generous of terms) employ a level of thinking that is shallow, it would appear that they have made a good point. What we must remember though is that, intellectually speaking, this is the age of professional wrestling and other types of gladiatorial games that easily amuse an unthinking mob. Therefore, we should not let these questions take on the intellectual equivalent of mortal blows within the context of this debate, for in truth they are only fancy maneuvers with no real substance behind them.

In the first case, let us be frank by saying that these "questions" are not questions at all, but are instead charges and accusations. By implication what is being stated here is that I am neither a patriot nor a lover of freedom, that I know no loyalty to those around me, and worse still, that I am one of those detestable "mentally deranged bigots" who has nursed a certain amount of unwarranted animosity for the Jews, a sentiment which today is the only remaining unpardonable sin. The individuals who engage in this type of interrogation vary between the clever and the not-so-clever; the clever being those who know that there is nothing to gain for their position in an honest, substantive discussion of the facts surrounding this issue, and the not-so-clever being individuals who know that they do not have enough information or gray matter necessary to manage such a debate without looking like a fool.

In either case, what should be remembered is that this technique at debate and discourse is nothing new, as the individuals who engage in this type of interrogation (whether they realize it or not) are merely mimicking that which they have seen take place everyday in America on her radio and television talk shows as of late. It is the process (even if done within the confines of what appears to be an air of civility) of shouting down the person and his message, and by so doing, making an example of him or her so as to discourage others from aligning themselves with that position. The difference between those who ask (in the more muffled tones) the previous questions and those who eventually lose all sense of composure and become like rabid dogs is only a matter of degrees. The point is that they are not individuals interested in any kind of intellectual discourse, but rather are interested in silencing a message which happens to complicate or thwart some idea or agenda that they have constructed for themselves for whatever reason.

For the *most* part, these people are not, in the strictest sense, ideologues. The truth is that they simply do not know what they are about, at least not in America. In the larger sense, their support for America's present involvement in the Middle East did not come into being as a result of careful consideration and research of the facts. They are individuals who have, after being given the option of choosing chocolate or vanilla, chosen one as a result of their distaste for the other, while being unaware that there were other options open to them as well. In the most unflattering sense, they really are like the proverbial spectators at the coliseum who are being deliberately kept in a state of distraction and confusion for the benefit of a ruling elite who are busying themselves with bigger projects of which the others remain unaware. They are the "common clay" who have friends or loved ones in the American military who are fighting in the Middle East, or who see in this war an opportunity for America to regain the prestige she lost during the Vietnam era. Absent these factors, they may be individuals who have "religious" reasons for taking the side that they have chosen, fundamentalist Christians who believe what has been told to them by a Jewish-owned media that the Muslims pose the most serious threat to their religion and way of life that has ever existed. And of course, there are those of the more maniacal variety present within this group as well, who have constructed this elaborate series of events that culminate in the return of Christ, and who have demonstrated what is a willingness on their part in facilitating whatever situation is necessary in order to hasten this Second Coming, no matter how horrible such situations may be to the innocent peoples living in those affected areas.

Despite the fact that they may not be ideologues, nevertheless, this 'mob' must be handled somewhat delicately, since these individuals still pose a formidable danger by virtue of the instability that has permeated their thought processes. They have demonstrated aptly in recent years their willingness and their ability to participate in just about anything, including violence in order to protect this agenda and see it thrive. More important than this is the fact that this loss of all sensibility is not an accident, but is rather the result of their being manipulated by other "interested" parties who (at least as of the moment of this writing) prefer to remain unseen and unconsidered. Those making up the mob are not necessarily evil people, just foolish, but nevertheless with this in mind what must be remembered is that in any honest discussion of these facts such individuals do not deserve the benefit of the doubt when it comes to understanding their position, and particularly not when considering the fact that they are not in any real sense interested in finding out the truth.

Of course, we said "for the most part" in describing those who make up the bulk of what is considered the cheering section of America's involvement in the Middle East conflict. There is however another component to this section as well, made up of a few individuals who are not being led by the nose unwittingly and who understand this situation in its clarity, and these are the individuals who must be watched with the utmost concern, for it is they who possess a danger that surpasses that of the mob. The truth of the matter is that there would be no mob at the coliseum were it not for *these* individuals, and it is in dealing with them that we must remain, as a rather perceptive man once said, *"as wise as serpents"*.

Pearls before swine

The situation involving what is and has been taking place in the Middle East is not as complicated as some would like to make it out to be, and an individual does not need an advanced degree in order to understand its mechanics. The truth is that it is a story which, were it told accurately, possesses a simplicity in its explanation that could be grasped by mere kindergartners. However, those who enjoy what is an uncontested monopoly over the various information mediums in this country have tried to paint the situation in confusing and contradictory images, at least when such a picture works in their favor.

Understanding that due to the decades of mind-numbing programming that he or she has received, the average Westerner suffers not only from what is a very short attention span but as well from a seriously reduced capacity for critical thought, what those who enjoy this monopoly over the media have done is to make *certain* themes within the discussion of the Middle East situation easy to understand, and others more difficult. Obviously, those themes that have been made easy to understand are those that have been wrapped in duplicity, themes that, when reduced to their irreducible minimum, encompass an argument that is based upon what is a very simplistic, chauvinistic and supremacist position. In an age where the thoughts and policies of the people are confined to easily remembered and easily regurgitated slogans, the chant heard 'round the animal farm from all the various outlets of intellectual discourse is more often one that supports unquestioningly the Jewish agenda in some manner.

Although few realize this to be the case, (with an even fewer number who are willing to admit it) it is an age wherein the Jewish supremacist agenda reigns, wherein all other issues, at least in the Western world, are subverted in the interest of furthering this agenda. In such a situation, all information, at least that which we would call 'mainstream' or 'official,' must pass through a filter of sorts that colors it in such a way so as to conform it's essence to the precepts of this agenda as well as in assisting in its efforts. This may not be readily apparent to the individual who is just coming to this discussion for the first time, since those who manage the news in the West have made the business of lying a new art form in a category all by itself. The bad news for such individuals coming to this discussion is that they are about to be confronted with a version of reality that is so controverted to that which they have imagined that it borders on the unbelievable. The good news though is that the disparity between the truth and that which the Jewish supremacist agenda spews out on a daily basis is so wide that the individual who is beginning this journey into opening his or her eyes doesn't have to dig very deep in order to find that for which he is looking, a situation that becomes more pronounced everyday.

There is this thing that occurs and which finds its way into the mechanics of all gangster agendas during their ascent to power, that being a sloppiness of sorts that creeps its way into the process of maintaining that subterranean existence that they must endure when living amongst civilized people. All healthy societies simply will not tolerate gangsters living in their midst, as much as they would not tolerate a vicious animal living among them and terrorizing their every waking moment. Those who are friendly to gangster agendas know this, and this is the reason why they are said to be a part of the "underworld," since they cannot allow the citizen body at large to know that they are parasites who are infecting the political system with their activities. In time however, as this gangster agenda grows and becomes more confident in itself, it no longer maintains with the same efficiency and energy this subterranean existence that it did previously, and once it has become assured of its power, it boldly comes crawling out from the sewer from whence it existed and begins mingling with the masses in a manner that reveals how completely unconcerned it is with what might take place down the road.

This is precisely the case today with regards to the Jewish supremacist agenda, wherein those who are the operatives within this conspiracy have become so confident in their success that they no longer go to the painstaking lengths that they used to in insulating themselves from the light of day. Besides the daily instances of outright murder that are taking place in Palestine, we find as well a mountain of available information concerning the hundreds of Israeli spies who were arrested and deported back to Israel in the days just following September 11th, the involvement of Israeli intelligence in the goading of America into attacking Iraq and the Abu Ghraib prison scandal, not to mention all the talk concerning the Zionist agents working in high positions of influence within the Bush White House. And although obviously the bulk of this supremacist agenda deals with the Middle East situation and how it effects this thing known as the state of Israel, what we must remember above all else is that this agenda is concerned with far more than simply this.

The Zionist agenda, although obviously very interested in the politics of this little terrorist country in what used to be called the Holy Land, is an octopus whose tentacles are spread across the entire globe and plugged into all issues. There is not an avenue or alleyway of human existence, at least not in the West, in which it has not in some way attempted to ensconce itself for the purposes of monitoring what takes place, much in the way that Big Brother of George Orwell's *1984* could be found watching and listening at all times and in all places. This agenda is interested in what people think, how they make and spend their money, how they raise their children, what they do in their spare time, what god they profess to worship and in what manner they do it. During the course of the last century, it has wormed its way into every facet of human life in the West, including the influential avenues of finance, information systems, academia, entertainment, and lest we forget, government, and enjoys within these various spheres a 'back-door' into each that allows it an incredible amount of power over the lives of those who find themselves within this agenda's radar. Thus we find that this agenda, in addition to being interested in harnessing the labors and sentiments of those living on its newly acquired plantation, the industrialized West, is capable as well of 'popping-in' from time to time and taking a peek at what is going on sociologically within these societies so as to better serve its own interests.

In light of these facts, the mystery is better solved then as to why so many things of such monumental importance take place in the West, the origins of which are said by those who manage the flavor and flow of information to be clouded in obscurity. Economic cycles, periods of boom and bust that always seem to work in the favor of a few recurring individuals no longer appear to be mere accidents. Wars that begin in some part of the world where there is to be found some valuable commodity or why suddenly there is all this contrived hysteria concerning some 'hold-out' who refuses to bow before the Jewish supremacist agenda begin to make more sense. The manner in which the moral trends of the West suddenly take a dive for the worst, from issues involving when human life begins to what constitutes marriage ceases to be a mystery when one comes to understand better the mechanics of this thing known as the Jewish supremacist agenda. It becomes clearer why it is that young people suddenly begin dressing and acting like the court jesters of the Jewish supremacist agenda; those pop and film stars who introduce on what has seemingly become a weekly basis new trends that should shock the sensibilities of normal people anywhere. All of these things, as well as others too numerous to mention here suddenly begin to fit as individual pieces of a puzzle that is fascinating and at the same time terrifying to behold.

As we said, and unfortunately so, the intricate machinery of this agenda is too large and too encompassing to cover within the span of this discussion. Besides the fact that such a discussion is beyond the scope of this work as well we are hampered by the fact that those studying it must do so, not as a team of scientists with the resources of a modern industrial state behind them, but rather as treasure hunters and sleuths who must finance this mission out of their own blood, sweat, and tears. They are individuals who must put the pieces of this puzzle together with nothing more at their disposal than their own wits, and who must do so while wading through what are oceans of disinformation that are effortlessly spewed forth by the other side. And if this weren't bad enough, what makes it worse is the fact that they must do so as outlaws of sorts, since the success of the supremacist agenda that such sleuths are attempting to uncover hinges on the maintenance of the same secrecy and duplicity found in all criminal conspiracies. Thus, those who are working to expose this 'elephant in the room' that no one appears to be able to see must do so in the midst of being hounded, ridiculed, chased, threatened, as well as being exposed to all the other methods of corruption that this agenda is capable of wielding against their mission, which, needless to say is quite formidable.

Conversely, what must be remembered is that those who are working for the interests of this supremacist agenda *do* have all the resources of the modern industrial world at their fingertips, and who, with the utmost of ease, can shut down this treasure hunt that has been undertaken by those few who today dare to try. Character assassination, property and wages being seized, trumped-up charges, libel suits, imprisonment, houses and cars fire-bombed and even an assassin's bullet are all common methods that the other side has used and is using with accelerated frequency as of late against those who attempt to bring the reality of this situation to the attention of their fellow man.

What we must remember as well is that this is not some new development that has just recently emerged within the sphere of human events, but is rather the product of *2,000 years* of planning, trial and error, and fueled no less by a fanaticism that is unparalleled in mankind's history. Therefore, in covering this theme of this supremacist agenda, what we are forced to do in this discussion is to remain within the boundaries of broad ideas and conclusions, hoping of course that by so doing we will be giving future investigators and analysts a leg-up when they come to the business of studying this thing more intensely.

Returning then to our discussion concerning those who are to be found within the cheering section of the Zionist agenda in the Middle East, we should not make the mistake of thinking that *these* individuals, operatives within the Zionist lobby who are trying to shout down any substantive discussion of the topic concerning the supremacist agenda are doing so because they are ignorant of the facts surrounding it. For the most part, (unlike their counterparts sitting in the stands at the coliseum) they *are* ideologues and individuals who are "interested," meaning that they stand to profit or lose something of great value depending on what circumstances take place with regards to this situation. As opposed to those who make up the mob, by contrast the "true believers" have invested much more in this situation and therefore have to be taken much more seriously. What's more is the fact that they are motivated by a fanaticism that surpasses anything yet seen in human history and have the resources of a nation-state behind them, including all the mechanisms of law and media, as well as possessing the ability to "silence" their opposition permanently, both in the figurative and literal sense. And lest we make the mistake of assuming that we here in America are protected from such violations by a government steeped in the Western tradition of respect for human rights and the rule of law, perhaps such optimism should be tempered, and particularly after considering the fact that in the days and weeks following the attacks of September 11th, *our own government* deported hundreds of Mossad officers back to Israel, many of whom were caught in circumstances as incriminating as filming the jetliners crashing into the towers while cheering. Added to this, we have the recent revelation that Lyndon Johnson, President of the United States during the Six Day War in 1967, ordered his fact-finding team to rule that the attack of the USS Liberty by Israel was a mistake, an act of murder and treachery that left 35 Americans dead and almost 200 wounded. And finally, lest we forget, there is the recent UPI story detailing the manner in which Israel has publicly announced her intention to being a program of assassination against her "enemies" found abroad, irrespective of whatever countries to which such persons may be citizens or where they may be found. The United States government, which is now engaged in the business of exporting war pre-emptively in the interests of protecting its citizens, in perfect contradiction to what has been her stated justification for the war in Iraq has had nothing to say about this ominous new development other than that this was a "policy decision" within Israel over which the United States government is powerless in doing anything.

What all of this means is that there are few opportunities that exist today in the mainstream for a substantive, honest discussion of what are these undeniably momentous and unprecedented events. I myself, in what by comparison has been a very limited scope, have encountered too many individuals whose ability for rational thought has been replaced by fits of madness — individuals who have taken the most undeniable, unarguable pieces of truth and have turned them into pretzel knots — to entertain much hope in there being any productive discussion on these matters. In truth though what we should remember is that there is nothing about this condition that is unique, since it has become just one aspect of the madness that has gripped the formerly Christian West over the course of the last century. The various symptoms of this cultural decay, the list of which grows every passing day, all mimic each other in the duality of their natures, manifested in their reverence for deceit as well as in their abhorrence for the truth.

In many ways, the process of debating the topic of this ugly agenda mimics the debates that have taken place in the past surrounding other institutions of inhumanity and totalitarianism such as slavery and the slaughter of the unborn. The defenders of such institutions know full well that their argument cannot withstand the light of day, and therefore are devoted, at all costs, to preventing the truth from being revealed concerning the mechanics of these processes. Such individuals steer the debate away from any discussion of pertinent facts — namely that what is taking place is the process by which living human beings are dehumanized, brutalized and then systematically destroyed — and instead, cloud the issue with ethereal, hypothetical, abstract discussions of vague topics involving supposed laws and rights which in reality do not exist. Individuals such as these do not need someone to patiently sit down and discuss the mechanics of this issue, since for the most part they know full well by virtue of natural law and common sense what is taking place.

Likewise, those whose interests lie in defending what is and has been taking place in the Middle East for Israel's benefit, individuals who bow at the feet of the Zionist agenda know *full well* what issues are at stake here. They understand the concept of invading a land and of murdering and displacing its people. They understand what is meant by a military occupation and the process of dehumanization that goes along with it. If we are to take their constant tirades seriously, they, *better than anyone else* understand what is meant by terms such as "genocide," "holocaust," and "racial supremacism". They understand full well that the Zionist ideology that they have elevated as their golden calf is an expansionist, aggressive and pitiless sibling within the Marxist family whose founders have, in instances too numerous to count, boldly asserted that their agenda lies *far beyond* simply possessing a sliver of land 12 miles wide along the eastern shores of the Mediterranean Sea.

Therefore, it is for these reasons and many others that will be discussed later that individuals such as these do not deserve to be the recipients of "fair treatment" in any productive discussion concerning what is and has been taking place with respect to these events. Getting into the ring with individuals such as these is like showing up for a boxing match with your regulation gloves when your opponent has shown up with a gun. In the war of ideas, it is suicidal to afford them this benefit of the doubt, as much as it would be for an individual to allow his mortal enemy to be armed at his own expense. They are like the proverbial rabid dog whose condition is of such a dangerous nature that no one dares to find himself within its vicinity less they be bitten and infected.

Rather, what is necessary when dealing with a beast such as this is that it be left alone or else that it be dispatched from some distant position, but we can dismiss the idea of trying to wrestle with this thing, since doing so would be an act of sheer madness. In like manner therefore must we deal with those whose thinking has been infected with the rabid ideology of militant, supremacist Zionism, either leave them alone or "deal with them," intellectually and politically speaking, from a distance. As I stated, individuals such as these are not on a treasure hunt for the truth, but rather are there to prevent anyone else from finding that treasure, since the very existence of such threatens the agenda for which they have been in a state of salivating expectation for the last 20 centuries. The process of trying to reason with them is tantamount to sitting down with an abortionist and attempting calmly to explain that what is taking place in this process is murder, or as maddening an experience as sitting down with someone who traffics in human slaves and trying to reason with them as to how grotesque and inhumane their business is. They already know this too well, and such a discussion is, in its simplest sense, casting pearls before swine.

And, finally, (as well as risking the charge of sounding too harsh) what should be remembered is that individuals who engage in this type of interrogation are not as harmless as the environment of discussion and debate may make them appear to be. Not only are they dishonest, but in addition they contain within their affections a secret admiration for totalitarianism, whether they are willing to admit it or not. It is the "win at all cost" program that drives their behavior and which dictates their tactics. Such individuals have demonstrated over the course of the last century that they owe no allegiance to anything but the agenda which they serve, an agenda that has supplanted all accepted norms of morality found in any society at any time. In better understood terms what we must remember is that they are individuals who derive a certain amount of power from the Zionist agenda, and whether this power is real and measurable or whether it is simply that which manifests itself in some type of blind, unhealthy zeal for an ideology that mankind periodically embraces beyond reason, the results are the same. All institutions throughout history that have graduated to the level of totalitarianism had as part of their gestation process a developed hatred for the truth and the willingness to suppress it at all costs, no matter how dirty such a process of concealment had to get. Therefore, the student of history would be wise to consider the fact that these types of tactics employed by the advocates of the Jewish supremacist agenda — the use of innuendo, suggestion, subtle words and images, veiled threats — all done in the interest of clouding the truth and of thus undermining an opponent's confidence and stability are and have been the traditionally used methods of neutralization that are common fare in all totalitarian systems.

Nevertheless, for the benefit of making my point, I'll play along.

Why *am* I concerned with the injustices that are being wrought against those in the Middle East, the supposed "perpetrators" of the crime that led to America involving itself in this war? Where *is* my loyalty to my country? Where is my loyalty to the friends and family members who are risking their lives fighting for my "freedom?" Where is my concern over the future of my children, when they stand the risk of becoming victims of some "terrorist attack" at sometime in the future? Where is my love of justice that I am supposed to possess as a Christian? Where is my patriotism which leads me to want my country to be safe? Where is my concern for the future of my Christian faith which is said (by those aligned with the Zionist agenda who mold public opinion) to be threatened as never before and by such a fanatical enemy? And, last but not least, where is the kinship I am supposed to feel towards my "elder brethren," the Jews, whose religion and heritage were the harbingers of the faith which I practice today? Do I not live in a "Judeo-Christian" country, a "Judeo-Christian" civilization, and possess "Judeo-Christian" values?

As I said, it is only the shallow-minded who succumb to such kindergarten-level arguments, who cannot master anything more complex than putting two and two together, but for the benefit of the unconvinced I will explain myself nevertheless.

The simple answer is that the reason that I have turned my attention towards the events taking place thousands of miles away is because I understand now *better than ever* what is encompassed in the expression "charity begins at home". It is because of the fact that I have come to embrace the idea that "blood is thicker than water" that my thoughts now reside with the goings on in areas such as Palestine, Afghanistan and Iraq. It is due to the fact that I love my children and my country more than myself, as well as the fact that I possess a great reverence for the precepts of justice and that I desire a safe future that I am standing here before you now speaking these words. And, last but not least, it is due to the fact that I possess, if not a kinship or idolatry, than certainly what can be called simple respect for those who are, in whatever context, Jewish, that same respect that is owed to any individual by virtue of his or her membership in the human race.

In short, all the childish charges that my detractors may level at me for the positions that I have taken are blown away like paper tigers in a windstorm when reviewed in light of the bigger picture, as well as when an individual takes his eyes off of his immediate surroundings and glances towards the horizon.

Supremacism by any other name

Before going into this explanation though, let us take a brief detour into something that needs to be covered if there is to be any progress made in this discussion. What must be stated before going any further is that there is a massive distinction between this "respect" that is owed the Jews by virtue of their membership in the human race and the "respect" that is demanded from those who are the worshippers of Zionism and its blood-thirsty bastard child known as the state of Israel. These days, given the amount of propaganda that is mercilessly beamed at those living in the West, it cannot be assumed that the reader understands this concept in its proper context, and this demands therefore that a certain amount of discussion takes place on this issue. Having perfected the Orwellian process of managing the affections of the masses for their own benefit, the doctors of disinformation and psychological warfare have endeavored mightily to blur this distinction, and in judging from the conversations that are to be had with the average Westerner, they obviously have made good ground. Therefore then, let us begin this discussion with the understanding that the "respect" that is demanded by the Zionists is not respect at all, but rather idolatry, albeit somewhat haphazardly masked. In its most unvarnished form it is supremacism, pure and simple, and not really that different from the flavor of supremacism made famous by the Nazis and which the West makes the pitiful attempt at pretending to despise.

A brief examination of the personages and sentiments involved with this apocalyptic ideology, the Jewish supremacist agenda responsible for the invasion and conquest of Palestine yesterday and the rest of the Middle East tomorrow reveals nothing that even remotely resembles any precepts devoted to humanitarianism or good intentions. Zionism is, was, and always will be a racist, exclusivist, ethno-centric sibling within the Marxist family, and possesses just as much a propensity for shedding innocent blood as has been famously possessed by her other sisters, Bolshevism, Leninism, communism, et al. This is by far one of the most peculiar things to note in the "friendship" that the West, and in particular America, has maintained with the Zionist state, considering the fact that there was this thing known as the 'Cold War' whose identity was inextricably wound within the mission of containing militant socialism. And yet, what we find is this contradiction that is impossible to explain rationally; the incalculable amount of resources, both in money and man hours that were expended over the course of several generations in countering the dialectic socialism of Russia, compared to the amount of money and man hours spent in propping up the dialectic socialism of Zionism. It was a situation that even the Zionists themselves had a hard time explaining, as evidenced by one of the remarks made by one-time director of Mossad, Isser Harel, in his description of the unlikelihood of a union between America and Israel, given the fact that the Zionists were Russian socialists themselves.

And if an individual can lose sight of the truth when weaving his way through the maze of political theory and debate, the area from which there can be no loss of focus is when all of this is viewed in human terms that should be easily understood by all, and especially after considering the events that have taken place over the course of the last century. If there were ever a time period within which mankind could point to incomparable instances of human suffering on a mass scale that were the product of policies that were enacted by a few evil individuals, then certainly the 20th century should have left an indelible mark upon the collective memory of the West and remained for some time. What's worse is that in many respects, many *do* make the pretenses of understanding the seriousness of these events, but again, only in particular instances, not general. Those in the West will obediently drone on and on about the evils of the Holocaust against European Jewry, but yet when a program of executing *the very same kind* of bloody supremacist agenda is implemented against the Arabs, there isn't even a blink of recognition that a repeat performance is taking place. Even only a cursory study of the architects of this disaster reads like a who's who in the genealogical tree of Murder Incorporated, a crime family of vampires and sociopaths who entertain not an ounce of concern for human life, and particularly not if such interferes with the agenda that they worship with unrivaled fanaticism. Never before, with the obvious exception of what took place in Bolshevik Russia by those who (both in the literal and figurative sense) were the cousins of today's Zionists has humanity been witness to such a legion of beasts, individuals bereft of all moral restraint and respect for the laws governing right and wrong. These individuals have been and remain to this day just as despicable and as worthy of all the derision that the civilized world can muster for them as were the same Nazis whose deeds and history are constantly paraded before mankind as the paragon of inhumanity.

This supremacism, forming the lifeblood of their ideology, is easily recognized in the manner by which they categorize all issues into one of two camps, a process of discrimination that differs greatly from that which is to be found among the rest of the world's peoples. While the majority of the world's peoples may categorize things into one of two camps of *objective* right and wrong, those working for the benefit of the Jewish supremacist agenda — in what has now become the perfected process of purification and distillation — weigh and categorize all things against the question of whether something is *good or bad for the Jews*. This spirit of tribal solidarity that is impossible to avoid noting surpasses that which is to be found in other cultures and in what could be considered healthy and acceptable levels. This supremacism that has supplanted the moral values which are supposed to be the building blocks of all civilized societies has progressed to such an extent that there is no violation nor any breaching of any moral boundary that cannot be justified in the interests of benefiting the tribe. As far as the interests of the agenda are concerned, if a million people have to die, a million people have to die, and as you will see later, *if six million have to die, than so be it*. It has become the ultimate golden calf representing the notion that the end justifies the means, an apocalyptic picture of a people who remain frozen in the classical stance of the revolutionary pose, an army of supermen marching forward with their fists in the air, shouting towards the heavens in absolute defiance and who pay no mind to the laws of men nor the laws of God.

Instead of settling for the kind of egalitarian "respect" that demands fairness and impartial treatment for all people, what these individuals demand is the elevation of their cause to such a position of superior status that all the rules of right and wrong do not touch or effect them in any way. The "respect" that they demand is superstar status, accompanied with the assurance that no matter what things they may do, irrespective of how nefarious, inhumane or infamous they may be, that these acts will be praised or at the very least excused and forgotten. This "respect" that they extort from the West is nothing short of the deification of their people and of the Zionist ideology that fuels their agenda and which acts as a lubricant for the machinery used in constructing it. In the marketplace of people and ideas, there is no room for principles or platitudes that revolve around the theme *"all are created equal"* as far as they are concerned. Rather, their agenda mimics that which was described in George Orwell's book *Animal Farm*, which in its essence was *"all are created equal, but some are more equal than others"*.

And thus, in such a way, these individuals have, just as was promised, *deceived the inhabitants of the earth* and have *set up an image in honor of the beast* and who now demand that all worship this beast, and those who do not are, as is seen on a daily basis, "handled" in their own particular way.

Therefore, when we talk about the "respect" that is owed a group of people by virtue of their being members of the human race, we should not include within it a special category that designates some as a "chosen people" over others, nor any other form of supremacism that today has come to typify the manner in which many view the Jews and how they should be treated. We should not maintain a sliding scale, or better yet, a *graduated system* of benefits for those who may or may not be a member of a particular racial or religious group. Despite what demands these individuals may make upon the rest of humanity, the truth is that people are people and deserve to be judged and handled according to their merits and faults, and nothing more. Despite the picture they insist on imposing upon the rest of the world, there is no such thing as the modern day equivalent of the god-men who used to occupy important positions among the various religions of the Greeks, Romans and Vikings. And the fact that they, "God's chosen people" have suffered does not change anything as well, especially since (in contradiction to the image that is depicted today by what is the Jewish monopoly over information and its dissemination) they are not the only people who have suffered, nor have they even suffered the worst. The argument which they put forth today and which functions as one of the vertebrae within the backbone of the Jewish supremacist agenda that posits the notion that such individuals possess the moral right to murder people en masse and in all other ways be given an exemption over the rules governing objective right and wrong is farcical beyond rational thought, despite the fact that it is so widely embraced today. The fact that large numbers of those in the West have so blindly ingested this type of thinking and have made it an integral part of their civilization is an indicator as to how far the degeneration of their cultural health has progressed.

For those who would try to deny away the existence of such a tendency, (this partiality in quantifying the suffering of some based upon their membership in a particular group) we need only look at the reaction that takes place on the part of those in the Zionist community (Jew or Gentile) when the argument that they themselves use in justifying their hellish behavior is employed by someone else.

What they reveal by such a reaction is the fact that in their agenda there exist no *general* principles, only *particular* ones, and, as we discussed earlier, the peculiarities of these principles change by virtue of *who* happens to be the affected entity. And thus, expanding on the theme we discussed earlier, within this supremacist agenda all instances of suffering are equal, *but some types of suffering are more equal than others.*

Therefore, in these Orwellian times in which we find ourselves, a particular action has no objective, organic qualities of its own. What these individuals dedicated to the Zionist agenda reveal is that there are two standards that are used in determining the character of a particular action, and the sole criteria used in designating the value assigned to that character is based on how it may or may not assist the Jewish supremacist agenda. Violence against innocent Arabs is dignified and justified with what is by now the effortless manipulation of words; a magic act that the Zionists have perfected to an art form. Noble language such as "pre-emptive military operations" are used to describe in the most sterile manner the murder of Palestinian school children, while Arabs who use justifiable violence against hostile invaders of their homeland are called "insurgents" and "terrorists". The suffering of the Jews under Hitler, (an occurrence made possible only through the assistance of Zionist organizations at the time) is used in justifying the invasion of a land and of murdering those within it, but yet the suffering that is the result of ugly Jewish supremacism does not warrant anything from its victims other than their quiet submission to what has been a century now of murder, rape, and dehumanization. In what has been the same traditional spirit of hypocrisy that has been the calling card of Jewish supremacism for 20 centuries now and counting, the world watches as those who employ the logic of Cain go about the business of devouring their victims and who *demand* that such brutality be applauded or at the very least excused.

And thus it is that we find that in the Zionized Christian West there is only one acceptable discussion concerning victimhood and only one acceptable arena of debate concerning those who hunger and thirst for justice, and for easily discernible reasons when one considers the parameters surrounding the Jewish supremacist agenda. One needs only to look at history in determining why it is that intellectual cowards and hypocrites such as these are so maniacal in making sure that the discussion of victimhood involves only them, since they would be left with quite a hefty price to pay if accounts were ever to be settled with those whom they have brutalized in the past.

Besides what is and has been done to the Arabs, there are the Africans who suffered for centuries under a slave-trading system monopolized by Jewish supremacist interests, an abomination that, although being eradicated in name, still continues to this day through a deliberate program of dehumanization, the welfare system, and a ghetto life of violence, drug addiction and despair. Standing in line next to them are the Christians of Russia, Ukraine and all the other Slavic and Eastern European nations who suffered—not the loss of a mere six million, but rather more than *sixty* million at the hands of Jewish Bolsheviks—and who have (if we are to apply the same standards that are used in excusing what is done by the Zionists) *ten times* the right to sidestep the rules of right and wrong in exacting some form of justice, as well as in "pre-empting" any future suffering at the hands of those who were their violators.

But yet, in perfect ideological contradiction, there is to be found only one group who possesses such a dispensation, and it is those Jews and their Gentile lackeys who have become worshippers of the beast known as Zionist supremacism.

There is an important and often overlooked item attached to this as well in that there certainly does not exist any such dispensation for those Jews who have been ideologically opposed to the supremacism that has infected the thinking of their cousins. Receiving the benefits of membership in the tribe has certain requisites, not the least of which is the adoption of this corrupting business of self-worship as a code and as a creed, and for those Jews who do not adopt such and who decide instead to become partners with the rest of humanity, the benefits of such an insurance policy do not apply. In proving this, one need only look at the invective that is defecated out upon those few individuals who, to their own credit, have escaped from the same spiritual and intellectual holocaust that has reduced the rest of their people to the imprisoning, destructive and virulent ethos of greed, haughtiness and egotism and who have against all these obstacles carved out a peaceful, productive existence for themselves without utilizing the power of the tribe. They are branded as traitors, are the constant recipients of death threats, and in all ways are shunned by the group and labeled with such nonsensicals as "self-hating Jews," a charge that truly defies comprehension. Thus the Israel Shahaks, Israel Shamirs, Norman Finkelsteins, Mordechai Vanunus, Henry Makows, Alfred Lilienthals and Benjamin Freedmans of the world must endure a lifetime of looking over their shoulders everywhere they go for fear of what the tribe may have in store for them. Verily, such individuals, the true heroes of the Holocaust, deserve to be remembered and honored as such for their bravery, and the fact that they must endure this type of character crucifixion goes a long way towards revealing what is the hypocrisy that flows through the veins of today's Jewish supremacists.

The tip of the iceberg

Those who attempt the futile argument that no such supremacist agenda exists (whether they be Jew or Gentile) are trying to argue away the existence of something as apparent and as irrefutable as are the four seasons. It is the proverbial 'elephant within the room' noted by one Jewish-American writer in the period leading up to the invasion of Iraq which no one is willing to acknowledge but yet which is apparent and impossible to avoid noting. For those on the sidelines who are susceptible to such arguments, you should realize now that you are doing so at your own peril, as well as at the peril of those whom you love. Not merely the existence, but the *prevalence* of this supremacism is so abundant in the political and social air breathed by the West that all should be suffering the intellectual and spiritual equivalent of choking fits as a result of its effects. For those who insist upon remaining within the protective confines of their delusion however, let just a few items, taken from a mountain of similar facts be considered.

*It is no accident that the decline of Western Civilization has taken place simultaneously with the ascent of the Jewish supremacist agenda. Those who have acted as the agents of this agenda can be found in instance after instance during the course of the last century assisting in the introduction of all the various plagues that have all but decimated the West, from communism to the moral relativism that has supplanted the order of these various societies. It is no accident that individuals such as these are to be found directly involved in the financing and hands-on machinations of the various communist revolutions in Europe which have left the heart of Christendom, Europe, a rotted out shell of what it once was, as well as in bringing to fruition two world wars that left the Christian world decimated and destabilized for generations.

*It is not incidental that the West now finds itself fighting a war against the Muslims and that the entity that benefits the most from it is Israel. It is no accident that many of George Bush's advisors have been throughout their careers paid agents for the Israeli government, nor is it an accident that Bush has staffed his cabinet with individuals who are of the same stripe of Jewish supremacist thinking and who elevate the well-being of this little terrorist state of Israel over the well-being of their own nation and people. This little project has been on the drawing table for quite a long time, and an honest examination of what was done to the careers of previous presidents reveals what was a concerted effort on the part of the Jewish supremacist agenda in placing "their man" in the White House for the furtherance of wiping out Zionism's enemies. Under Reagan it was Libya and Lebanon, under Bush the Elder it was Gulf War I, and under Clinton a failed attempt at Gulf War II.

*It is not by chance that all the main institutions of power in the West; media, academia, law, and finance are and have been dominated by those loyal to the Zionist agenda for the last century. By controlling all the organs of the political body, all bodily functions, including life and death, are harnessed in such a way so as to serve the interests of the host. Thus, all policies as well as all debate and discussion are carved out of a schedule which puts the interests of the Jewish supremacist agenda at the very top.

*It is not by coincidence that the intellectual process found in the average Westerner is such that the bulk of his affections and sentiments are arranged so as to be in near perfect conformity with the Zionist agenda. In bombarding those in the West with a minute by minute assault on their thinking processes through media programming designed to reduce their intellects to that of functioning idiots, what has been created is a civilization of people who cannot reason for themselves outside of the parameters that have been set for them by their overlords working for the Jewish supremacist agenda.

*It is not an accident that spies working for the furtherance of the Israeli agenda are routinely caught in the act of sabotage and afterwards released without any fanfare. Despite one man's conviction, Jonathon Pollard, nothing has been done with respect to the spying that has been successfully realized against not only America, but as well against the entire Western world. In addition, the West has stood by and done nothing with respect to bringing to justice those working for the Jewish supremacist agenda who have been responsible for acts of terror and war against the countries of the West, just a few instances of which include the Lavon affair, the bombing of the King David Hotel, and the attack on the USS Liberty, in addition to the various assassinations of Westerners, both civilians as well as powerful members of Western governments.

*It is not by chance that every vice known to be such—pornography, abortion, sodomy, et al—is now celebrated and has been elevated to the level of virtuousness to the obvious detriment of a healthy society resulting from over-powering effect of the Jewish supremacist agenda upon the institutions of the West. In such a way, the Western nations are peopled with immoral, unprincipled individuals who now for the most part do not possess any conscience when it comes to killing innocent people, and short of that, robbing them of their wealth and reducing their vitally necessary infrastructures to rubble. The reason for this deliberate program of breaking down the morals of the West appears to have been done with the intent of creating an entire civilization of beasts willing to go out and slaughter for the benefit of the Jewish supremacist agenda not only the entire Muslim world, but as well anyone else who gets in the way.

*It is no accident that in most countries of the West, special laws now exist (as they did in the first country that was the manifestation of the Jewish supremacist agenda, the Soviet Union) which forbid the criticism of Jews or Zionism. These laws did not just 'pop-up' in the intellects of the average Western lawmakers as something that appeared to be a good idea. As we discussed before, the adherents of the Jewish supremacist mindset enjoy a love affair with totalitarianist thinking, and these laws are but one example of the proof of this tendency. For those deluded individuals who do not think that such laws exist, what can be said? Obviously they are members of the flat-earth society and suffer by virtue of an ignorance that has been born of the complacency that affects virtually all persons and institutions in the West under the overpowering influence of the Zionist agenda.

*It is not by some unexplainable circumstance that all the pillars that used to act as the bearing members of Western Civilization are groaning under the weight of its decay. It must be remembered that in watching as the descendants of Abel built a civilization that is unparalleled in its success, that the Jewish supremacist agenda has been grinding its teeth slowly and continuously over the course of the last 2000 years. When the new ideology of Christianity was born in 1st century Palestine and thus threatened and rivaled the agenda that those in the leadership positions of Pharisaical Judaism had constructed, a program for its extermination was implemented immediately. The fact that this extermination did not succeed, and that an entire civilization was built up around it has been like salt in the wound of the Jewish supremacist agenda for the last 20 centuries. Just as Cain slew his brother Abel out of envy, so too do the apostles of this supremacist agenda hate the brother whom their father favored, the Christian West, and have therefore embarked upon this course of removing it from the world in the interests of taking its place. It is for this reason that Christianity, its precepts, institutions and legal system in the West have been hounded and assaulted in the manner that has taken place.

All one needs to do is to trace the history of the present situation backwards just a bit, study what institutions and which persons were responsible for bringing all of this to fruition, and the mystery for this catastrophe ceases to be such. And for those who will, in what is the most pitiable excuse of intellectualism, attempt to maintain a reticence in accepting the reality of these notions, all that would be necessary to do in exposing the double-standard that they maintain would be to switch the characters around a bit. If what were being discussed in such conspiratorial themes was the "Islamic supremacist agenda," we would not find such scoffing taking place among individuals such as these, a drama which in truth is but a ridiculous attempt at hiding the fact that they are "compromised" parties and therefore enjoy what is in the best of terms a conflict of interest.

In either case, what we should not make the mistake of doing is to ascribe all the aspects of this tragedy to chance, especially since the one who first attempted to protect mankind against these people and their agenda 2,000 years ago ruled out the possibility that this tragedy could be the product of mere coincidence. He predicted that a day would come wherein the weeds of destruction would be found proliferating within the garden of humanity, weeds that did not *accidentally* find their way into this garden, but were rather the result of deliberate human action, a circumstance that he noted by saying *"an enemy hath done this"*.

And now, as a result of this policy of acquiescing to the demands of the Jewish supremacist agenda and of having received the mark of this beast, not only are hundreds of thousands, dare we say *hundreds of millions* dead, but in addition, millions more are scheduled to suffer and die, all because a handful of people have elevated the interests of a few over the well-being of the world at large by virtue of the blood in their veins. All this because certain individuals, discontent with the arrangements that have been put in motion by the creator of the universe and by the weight of history have decided that such arrangements must take a back seat to their own agenda. And thus, such individuals, whether they be Jew or Gentile, ignorant and unstable, distort the truth to the destruction of not only themselves, but to the rest of the world as well. And this, in the final analysis, is but one aspect of the leaven of supremacism, pure and simple.

Homeland security

Rather than spend too much time at this point addressing these thorny issues, let us go back to the question that we began addressing earlier as to "why" we are having this discussion today over this issue. To put it in the simplest of terms, the reason we are having this conversation today is because of *storms*.

I have become a storm watcher since September 11, not in the same sense as those who go about the countryside chasing tornadoes for fun, but rather in the sense that I am a person who possesses a certain amount of responsibility for a large number of people, and that means watching the political weather. This means that in order to take care of "homeland defense," in order to live by the motto that "blood is thicker than water," I must pay attention to what is brewing on the horizon and how it may or may not affect those at home where charity begins. And despite the fact that my family may be enjoying itself with a day at the beach, with its blazing sun and brilliant sky, I still must scan the horizon for dark threatening clouds, and when I can see that a significant system is headed our way, that means I have a decision to make and a job to do, as unpopular as it may make me with those in my charge who are busying themselves with a good time.

Since September 11, I have come to understand the nature of this storm known as the Middle East conflict in a better way. I certainly am no expert, as obviously there are others whose knowledge of these circumstances makes what I have come to know merely a grain of sand on a beach full of information. And having said this, I understand that I may have made (and will continue to make) mistakes regarding some of the conclusions to which I have arrived. And lest the reader assume that I am some pedantic, brainy individual who is doing this simply for the thrill of impressing others, let me make something clear as well. I am no intellectual giant at all. I am probably one of the least competent individuals to discuss these themes, considering what kind of minds are out there, nor do I consider myself to be that gifted of a writer. If some extraordinary ability can be attributed to me, it is merely that I am willing to say what other more competent individuals should be saying but won't. And despite what appearance is created by my willingness to take to the podium as it were and speak my mind about a given topic in such a public manner, the truth of the matter is that I am not as smart as such a willingness suggests. The truth of the matter is that I consider myself to be gifted with what is at best a slightly above average intellect, but that is all. I am no genius, and I am certainly no saint, and I say this with no feigned or effected sense of modesty. The things I have written or said, the analyses I have produced and the conclusions to which I have arrived are not as earth shaking or novel as some may think. An individual does not need to have a degree in meteorology to see that an approaching storm, with it violent display of lightning and thunder is a force with which to be reckoned. It is simply common sense, for lack of better phraseology, and nothing more. The fact that I may be the first (or at least one of a very few number) of those willing to say it does not denote anything stupendous about my own abilities as much it is an indictment upon the rest of humanity as pertains it unwillingness to note what is the obvious.

Having said this then, I hope that it is more easily understood what I mean about "charity beginning at home". Not only my country, but my civilization is at war with 1.5 billion people and I need to find out why, particularly when this storm is producing winds that carry the whispers of a mandatory military draft that would include not only the young men in my family, but the young women as well. But this is by no means all of it, since there are several aspects of storms that have to be considered as well, and which we will soon discuss.

What became apparent early on (and by that I mean as early as 30 years ago when I was a boy) was that there was a particular group of people posing as meteorologists and who described the storm in such a way as to best benefit themselves. What I am describing here of course is a media controlled by those devoted to the Jewish supremacist agenda who have depicted the Arabs and Muslims as violent, blood-thirsty, irrational people driven by an unquenchable fanaticism, juxtaposed to the image of the poor, beleaguered, fair-minded and ethical inhabitants of Israel who are just "trying to get along" with their neighbors so that they can merely survive. This was apparent to me even before I understood the more intricate mechanics of what was taking place in the Middle East, but something which obviously I have come to understand better since September 11.

And now, 3 years later, I can stand here and say with what is not a small amount of confidence that those who have been bringing us this information, the "weather men" who mold our opinions and thus our public policies, having been lying through their teeth about everything. I suspected this in the days following September 11, I just didn't know to what extent nor what the total reasons for it were. At the risk of appearing too cynical, or heaven forbid, *extreme*, let me nevertheless state that it is my position now (after having studied the methods and mechanics of this thing rather intensely) that the disciples of this supremacist agenda known as Zionism are of such a nature that they couldn't tell the truth about *anything* even if there were a fortune to be made in it. Their attachment to lying and disinformation as instruments of not just warfare but *mere survival* are almost *organically* ingrained within their natures, coupled with the sociopathy of having no conscience about what results from their agenda or what it does to the rest of humanity. It is no accident that the motto of Israel's intelligence agency, the Mossad, just happens to be a celebration of duplicity and violence. *"By way of deception, thou shalt do war"* did not just "pop-up" in someone's mind when the founding fathers of the Jewish supremacist state sat around thinking up clever slogans to adopt. Zionism, being a sibling within the Marxist family tree, carries within it the genetic programming of all Marxist ideologies, one of whose common traits is the reliance upon lying and done for the purpose of keeping their enemies unorganized and in a state of instability.

It is in light of these facts therefore that today I stand before you as an American Christian and say unequivocally that not only have we been had, but been had in an apocalyptic way. Everything we have come to know about our "lone ally in the Middle East" by way of the mouthpieces (who are nothing more than paid liars and intelligence assets) is and has been a farce of unsurpassed significance. We in the formerly Christian West have wedded ourselves not only to the worst enemies we have ever had, but to the worst we could *ever* have had. It is like the lamb agreeing to form an alliance with the wolf, or, more prophetically, with the lion, as there is an organic, unchangeable nature of the two characters that absolutely forbids any co-operation existing between the two of them. The philosophical paradigm that was the building block of the Christian West, the *anti-supremacist* ideology known as Christianity, is and was supposed to be of such a character and hue as to be inimical in every way to Zionism and the supremacism that embodies its essence. The two ideologies, Christianity and Zionism, are (if they are acting in accordance with their real natures) as compatible as water and fire, and the fact that today they have become so comfortable with each other is an indicator that something has gone terribly wrong in the nature of at least one of them, and we can dismiss the idea that it is to be found within the nature of the latter.

Perhaps I am way out of line in doing this, acting as a Johnny-come-lately in having this discussion, and particularly when so much injustice has been wrought against so many innocent lives. Perhaps others could bring this message in a more efficacious way, and particularly those who have witnessed it firsthand and thus can speak with more authority on the matter. Perhaps what I have to say is way too late, being as it is that the storm is now upon us, and the roar of the thunder and wind is such that nothing can be heard above its fury. As I said, I am no genius and am certainly no saint, I am merely a father who fears for the future of his children, and it is for this reason therefore that I have added my voice to those who are shouting against the storm.

On thin ice

Lest those reading what I have to say accuse me of being naive in thinking that shouting against this storm will actually serve to dissipate its destructiveness or chase it out to sea where it can do no harm, let me say that I do not entertain much practical hope for this taking place. In my opinion it is way too late to extricate ourselves from this situation and still come out of it in one piece. The watchmen on the towers who were supposed to warn us of an impending invasion were bought off long ago, and while we slept soundly, those who were charged with protecting us (our government, media, intelligentsia and religious leaders) unlocked the gates and allowed the enemy to position himself in such a way that no one is getting out alive. We are, literally, prisoners within our own country and within our own civilization. Our lifeblood has been used as collateral in paying the mortgage of Israel's agenda. Our children and grandchildren have been enlisted in the service of fighting all the future wars for Israel's benefit. The only difference between Bolshevik Russia, (the first attempt at imposing the Jewish supremacist agenda and the terror that is the stamp of its ingenuity upon the world) and the situation as it exists today is just a matter of cosmetics. Citizens in the formerly Christian West, numbering in the tens of millions are murdered each year in the aborturies, the secret police monitor all dissent and discussion, elections are rigged in favor of perpetuating the system as it exists for the benefit of the supremacist agenda, and a sham judicial process is in operation which has no basis in any substantive pursuit of the facts or truth. As the inheritors of what used to be the great legacy of Western Civilization, our situation is such that this enemy will allow us to live and live with a dusting of the freedoms we used to enjoy provided of course that we supply him with all the money and manpower he needs in realizing his agenda, and his agenda is not by any means modest in its scope. He intends to wipe out 1.5 billion people in the Middle East, seize control of the oil therein, and after he is through with that mission, he intends to wipe us, what remains of the Christian West, out as well. The only question is whether or not he intends to wipe us out literally, or whether he merely intends to destroy our culture and our civilization, if indeed this has not been accomplished already. In either case, it is a price that few would be willing to pay if they were but aware of it. And it is way too late to do anything substantive about it, as we literally have a gun to our head, and that gun is represented by the 200 nuclear weapons that the Zionists have threatened to unleash upon anyone who thwarts their agenda. Short of that (the use of the "Samson Option") what must be considered is the manner in which the economies and monetary infrastructures of the world's superpowers are monopolized by those working for the Zionist agenda and managed to such an extent that these individuals could bring everything crashing down with just a few carefully placed comments and a few keystrokes of the computer.

Those who would scoff at these notions suffer by virtue of the fact that they are poorly informed as to what comprises the complicated machinery of Western economies and infrastructures, and who do not realize how precariously balanced all of it really is. One need look back no further than the blackout that occurred in the Eastern section of the US a year or so ago that was the result of one computer glitch in some remote part of Ohio. The more complicated the machinery, the more susceptible it is to breakdown, and whether such a breakdown is the result of poor maintenance or sabotage matters not.

Those who *are* better informed concerning the precariousness of modern day Western life but who still scoff at any talk of future troubles as a result of the illicit love affair between Zionism and the formerly Christian West simply suffer by virtue of naiveté when it comes to understanding human nature, and in particular as it involves the aspects of greed and power. Such naïve sentiments, which are prevalent throughout almost all aspects of Western societies, are the product of the post-industrial era wherein such individuals view things from a purely materialistic perspective. In their very limited understanding, wars are caused simply from lack of basic necessities; food, land, water, shelter, etc, and therefore, given the fact that the capabilities of the post-industrial world are of such a character that anything can be produced in short time and with little effort, all issues involving greed and want can be neutralized as well. In the West (and more so in America) it is assumed that there is no problem that can't be solved by throwing a little bit of money and ingenuity into it. Disease has been conquered, as well as impoverishment, hunger, turmoil, etc, so why should this be any different?

The mistake that such individuals make is in forgetting that people can be motivated by other things besides the immediate hierarchy of their physical needs. There are some people who can have all the food, water, land, shelter and everything else necessary to sustain a comfortable life, and who *still* will go to war to achieve more. What individuals such as these fail to consider is the fact that history, and particularly recent history, is replete with examples of individuals who didn't just want their fair share of the pie, *but rather the whole thing*, and sometimes for no other reason than that they didn't want someone else to have any. What these Pollyannic individuals have failed to note is how powerful a motivator ideologies can be, and particularly those ideologies that are religious or tribal in their nature.

In truth though, what must be stated is that such individuals (who scoff at the notion that great danger is to be found in the Jewish supremacist agenda) are not really being honest in their position. They understand this issue well, the topic of ideologies and the manner in which their adherents can be motivated into committing the worst, but such individuals are *selective* as to when and against whom they will apply this understanding. And once again, just like the infectious disease that is the leaven of the Jewish supremacist agenda, the program that is in operation here is mere hypocrisy, for a quick examination reveals that individuals such as these will *only* scoff at such a notion if the group of people in question happens to be the Jews.

In such a process as they manage it, any discussion of a conspiracy rooted in "Jewish interests" cannot conform to the scientific method of fact-finding and deduction, as if there were an *organic impossibility* that such dangerous individuals could exist. When it is reduced to its irreducible minimum, the program under which such individuals have deluded themselves is that it is impossible that evil in any form may emanate from the Jewish quarter, and, conversely, that the only evil that can exist is that which works against the Jewish agenda. Like Pavlov's dogs, the sentiments of such individuals can be turned on like a light switch in defending the agenda of their masters, sentiments completely disconnected with any true intellectual processes and which vary between loyalty for the hand that feeds them and fear of the hand that can grab them by the throat. And thus it is in this manner therefore that we must view the intellectual parrying that takes place by today's skeptics as but a magic act, and particularly so when the other side of the coin is discussed.

Ask them however, about the threat posed by extremist ideologies attached to fundamentalist *Christians or Muslims*, and the whole tone they maintained with regards to the other side of the coin changes dramatically. Now they will acquire a very serious look in their eyes and nod gravely, noting that such entities pose a clear and present danger to the civilized world. Such individuals know well what is meant by the words "Islamic extremism" "Al Qaeda" and "suicide bomber," as well as "Christian Militia," "Aryan Nations" or "white supremacist" and yet who smirk when someone goes about the business of describing things such as the Irgun, Stern Gang or Talmudism, despite the fact that a mountain of documentation exists surrounding them.

Therefore, we should not put much weight in the arguments offered by these individuals who use the vehicle of ridicule during the debate covering the Jewish supremacist agenda known as Zionism and the danger that it poses for the whole of humanity. They are persons who are either ignorant of the facts or who are, as we said earlier, "interested".

Those who do accept that a danger exists but who downplay the depth of its seriousness, in my opinion, do so as a result of their failure to consider things in their proper scope, for in truth their argument is based upon superficial criteria. "How" they argue, "can an ideology such as Zionism, represented by a nation such as Israel of only six million people, pose any kind of substantive threat to a civilization such as that in the West, with over 1 billion people and the lion's share of the world's technology and wealth?" Of course on a kindergarten level this would be a good argument. It is like asking the question, "What can this little spider do to this gorilla?" If the spider happens to be of a deadly venomous variety though, and if the gorilla is sick and already dying as a result of having been bitten hundreds of times, then obviously that changes things considerably.

The difference lies in the dynamics of this situation, as well as in the pyramidal structure of power as it exists in the West. Never before has so much power been concentrated into the hands of such a few number of people, who literally can decide what countries live or die on a minute by minute basis. Never before has all the world's wealth been subject to the decisions of such a small clique of individuals, who can, as we said earlier, completely alter the economic, sociological, and legislative landscape of entire nations as if with the wave of a magic wand. And if this situation weren't bad enough, what makes it worse is the fact that the mental condition of this clique is such that makes the whole situation a ticking time bomb. It's true, on it's face, that such a threat from such a statistically small number of people makes no sense, except when considering what possibilities exist when this small number of people have the ear of the President of the United States, the most powerful man in the world. And, if these people can literally make the president dance on strings like a puppet, (as has obviously been the case with every American president since Lyndon Johnson) then it becomes apparent how such machinery can be made to operate. We are talking about an unprecedented concentration of the world's power in the hands of a few individuals who are, by any standards that can be used to measure, criminally insane. They possess 90% of the world's wealth, control the political machinery of the world's most powerful nations, control the informational infrastructure of these nations, and are imbued with the mindset that they have a right to possess all of this by virtue of:

A: Their superiority, and by
B. The inferiority of the rest of the world's inhabitants.

This situation does not paint a pretty picture, even to the most shallow-minded of thinkers.

Of course, by now the scoffers are having fits that swing between the extremes of laughter and rage, demanding to be shown the proof of such a cabal, and, of course, as if on cue, the typical bludgeoning that takes place in Pavlovian fashion of the anti-Semitic charge. The proof of this condition should be just as apparent as lightning and thunder are indicators of any storm, and anyone with eyes to see and half an ounce of sense should be able to connect the dots. The tragedy and the truth is that they *can* see it, but have chosen rather to convince themselves and others around them of the impossible notion that the "elephant in the room" is not really there.

What we need, literally, is a miracle, a miracle unprecedented in its magnitude, and from a creator whom we have treated rather shabbily in the last few decades. In my opinion, we will need to catch him on a good day if he is to honor such a request. Either way, we are in for a spanking that will leave us sore for quite a while.

David and Goliath

And so, the reader will ask the obvious question again, "why then are we having this discussion, if indeed there is not much hope for it doing any good?" And surely it will come as something of a surprise when I say frankly that for me it is for selfish reasons that I have involved myself in this business, a coin with two sides which you will soon see.

In the first case, the business of stirring up this brood of vipers (the disciples of the Jewish supremacist agenda and all the debasement that they peddle as an ethos) while indeed being a dangerous thing can be quite rewarding in its own small way. Seeing them scurry around like cockroaches when exposed to the light of day, watching them soil themselves in panic over the fact that truth, their mortal enemy, has touched them and their agenda in such a direct and undeniable way has elements of satisfaction in it that are their own reward. Watching as they turn purple over being exposed, of listening to them stutter and stammer when faced with the awfulness of who they are, what they have done and what they are about can be rich and delightful, even if it is transitory and brief.
in addition, witnessing the manner in which they will take the most undeniable and unalterable pieces of truth and turn them into pretzel knots, while indeed being a maddening experience, also has practical benefits attached to it as well. If nothing else, it serves to strengthen our own constitutions, functioning as a way of reminding us from

time to time that we are not crazy for thinking the things we do. For me, being involved in this business reaffirms my belief that there is this thing called the eternal struggle between good and evil and as well helps clarify for me what are the characteristics that define each of them, something that is especially important in a world where today the two are deliberately confused.

There are maneuvers that must be used in whatever form of warfare is being employed and which have existed from the beginning of time, and one from among these is the tactic of smoking out the enemy in the interest of learning his whereabouts and his agenda. In addition, by forcing him to engage in this fight, what inevitably results is the exposure of his techniques and of his weaponry, as well as the liabilities that each possess. And so, the business of kicking up this nest of vipers, of aggravating their progress, (even if only momentarily) and of bringing to light what is the reality of their agenda, this is a battle that must take place in the interests of any long-term strategy.

And make no mistake about it, *making war against this agenda is dangerous business, and not one to be taken lightly.* The history of the last century is littered with examples of people who "got in the way" of this agenda and paid the ultimate price for it, and one need look no further than what has been done to the Palestinians during the last century for validation of this theme. The footsoldiers of this agenda are as pitiless as were their Bolshevik cousins who didn't blink an eye at murdering over 60 million people when such a slaughter served their interests. They truly are the worshippers of Cain, the first murderer, and who have elevated him, if not formally, than symbolically as the founding father of their agenda.

What we in the West do have though in our favor is the fact that their power, like all complicated machinery, is quite vulnerable to certain breakdowns, and one of the most, if not *the most* vital aspect necessary for the smooth functioning of this complicated machinery lies in maintaining the delusion that has been imposed by their propaganda infrastructure upon the masses. As we discussed previously, such an agenda is very much akin to the manner in which other entities operating within the world of organized crime have had to maintain a sub-terranean existence for a period of time, and who, after the accumulation of a certain amount of wealth and power, surface in a public way but with what appears to be an air of respectability attached to them. Maintaining this delusion of respectability requires that these individuals mask what are the real mechanics of their business—murder, corruption and in all other ways anti-social activities—and replace them with "charitable" (there's that word again) institutions designed to fool the masses. Cross them, however, and the real nature of the beast is revealed, as periodically takes place. Today's gangsters operating within the Jewish supremacist agenda are no different than the gangsters of the last century who, by virtue of their expensive cars and clothes, enjoyed a certain amount of celebrity status within a city, and who fawned before an adoring crowd of people too stupid and weak to recognize that there was a parasite and a predator living among them. Bump into one of them accidentally though, and cause him to spill something on his expensive suit and then the world will be witness to just how undeserving he is of the celebrity status that he enjoys.

In like manner, the gangsters of the Jewish supremacist agenda can always be counted on to do what is expected of them in this regard, in that for all the "respectability" they make the pretenses of possessing—the speaking engagements, the television and radio appearances, the humanitarian causes, meetings with the President and whatnots which they use to hide the true nature of their images and of their agenda—all of this masquerade melts like a snowflake in a microwave when someone happens to "spill the truth" on them and soil the expensive veneer within which they have suited themselves. At that point, the teeth and the claws come out, a viciousness manifesting itself in the name calling, character assassinations, threats, and in more than a few cases, actual terrorism manifested in the various fire bombings and shootings that have come to typify how they do business.

If there can be said to be one thing about which we can possess some remaining hope as pertains this desperate situation, it is in the fallen nature of man, and in particular his instinct of self-preservation, that instinct that causes individuals to turn on even their best friends if their own interests are threatened in a serious manner. Therefore, by aggravating this beast to such a point that he does something foolish, something drastic, with luck this will result in this dangerous spell being broken, and thus will end this illicit, dangerous love affair with Jewish supremacism to which the Christian West has been party now for the last century. What must be considered though is that in today's terms, when we talk about something rash, what we are talking about (both in the figurative and literal sense) is Armageddon, since it is a fact that these individuals now possess the ability to wipe out entire nations at their fancy, as well as the willingness to do so if such suits their agenda. For those who would scoff at such a notion, perhaps they should read *The Samson Option* by the Jewish-American writer Seymour Hersh, as well as considering the many veiled threats that have been uttered by Israel's power elite over the course of the last two decades.

Casualties

The second reason for us having this discussion in the midst of what appears to be a hopeless situation, and which has as much an effect over me as the first, is the fact that as much as we may detest this beast called Zionism and the evil that is its essence, at the same time, there is an equal amount of compassion that is due to those who have been the victims of it.

The lines are indeed long, seemingly endless, of those who have perished within the jaws of this beast known as the Jewish supremacist agenda during the last century. We are talking about literally billions of people by now, when we count the bloodshed that took place as a result of the spread of communism, both world wars, as well as the slaughter of the unborn in the various countries making up the Christian West that have fallen so heavily under the influence of Jewish supremacist interests. Besides those who manifest the physically dead, there are the billion or so left today who make up the intellectually and spiritually dead in what was the formerly Christian West. When coming to terms with this situation one needs merely glance at what has become of these people, with their addictions to pornography, sodomy, promiscuous behavior, violence, materialism and in all other respects their undeniable attachment to triviality and self-centeredness. These are the "hidden" or "obscure" victims of the Jewish supremacist agenda, but who will one day, as historians look back over this time period, be included in the list of Zionism's formal victims.

As far as those who are on the formal list today, the numbers are staggering as well, with an abundance of tragedy and injustice encompassing their tale of woe.

The first of those on this list are the Jews themselves; not the dyed-in-the-wool Zionists, the *true believers* in the gangsterism that is the Jewish supremacist agenda, but rather the little people who have had to suffer by virtue of their oftentimes-involuntary association with them. Within this group can be found two sub-groups, one of them made up by those who have dropped their association with the supremacist agenda that pits them against the rest of the world's peoples and who have successfully assimilated into the cultures within which they dwell, and the other made up by those who make the *pretense* of not being supremacists but who nevertheless run to the defense of the tribe whenever it is criticized from the outside, irrespective of the conditions of that criticism.

It is true that the Jews are a group of people who have suffered, a point of fact that is constantly employed as a bludgeon in silencing the critics of Zionism by those whose interests lie in the supremacist agenda. What is never discussed though, the question that is never asked in coming to terms with this situation is *why* when it comes to determining the source of this suffering as well as discussing *who* has been responsible for authoring it. When pressed to account for this, those whose interests lie in perpetuating this situation, (their religious leaders or those closely associated with them) will use two avenues to explain it, one for the Gentiles, and one for the Jews themselves, and rarely have they allowed cross-pollination of the two explanations, until recently.

The reason put forth for consumption among the Gentiles by operatives within the supremacist agenda is that the "persecution" they have suffered has been a result of their forefathers' involvement in the crucifixion of Christ. For 2,000 years now, the vengeful, fanatical Christians have made these innocent, humanitarian, peace-loving peoples pay for what took place, culminating in the murder of 6 million innocent souls in WWII. Among the Jews themselves, the reason has always been attributed to an issue of envy, wherein the Gentile world knows innately the superiority of the Jewish people, (concomitant with their own inferiority of course) and that this is what has motivated them to treat "God's chosen people" with such, oh, how shall we say..."*irreverence*".

We have to give them credit for what has been a brilliant operation, this business of whispering into the ears of both entities the psychological triggers that have and continue to result in the perpetual clash between the two peoples. It is nothing more than an application of Hegel's dialectic theory, of thesis and anti-thesis being merged in the interest of creating a desired outcome. In contradistinction to what has taken place before though, now what can be found is that the two ideas are being preached side by side, (at least in the fundamentalist Christian camp) and which have been, by such ignorant and unstable individuals, swallowed wholeheartedly to their own destruction. As a result, the outcome is beginning now to take on a discernable shape and outline, and which is responsible for facilitating the murder and mayhem that is manifested in the Jewish supremacist agenda. But what we must remember is that there are other aspects to this dialectic besides the physical destruction of Israel's enemies in the Middle East.

The Christian world has to a large extent today, and without knowing what kind of dangers they have accepted by so doing, swallowed the cyanide capsule that has been prepared for them by the Jewish supremacist agenda, a program of intellectual, cultural and spiritual suicide which manifests itself in the notion that they *did* persecute the Jews for no justifiable reason, that all this took place simply out of pure malice and that they themselves are inferior to the Jews who are, just as the scripture reads, the apple of God's eye.

What is never mentioned however, are the very *real* reasons for this tragedy which can be traced — not to the crucifixion or other issues of envy — but rather to the part played by the supremacist gangsters who have always pitted the little people within their community against the Gentile world for their own benefit, beginning with what took place in 1st century Palestine.

The First Dominoes

In the first instance, what must be remembered is that the theme of enmity that was set as the tone for future relations between the two peoples was not the result of the Christians "making the Jews pay" for the crucifixion of Christ. In borrowing an often-overused comparison, such a statement is the equivalent of putting the cart before the horse, an accomplishment made all the more easy today by virtue of the fact that the Christian world has forgotten its roots and its own history. In their early days, and by that we mean for the first 300 years, the Christians were never in the position, political or otherwise, to effect any kind of pogrom against their kindhearted and kindred Jewish neighbors. Lest we forget, (and which is never mentioned in the discussion involving the history of this turbulent relationship and which serves as the lynch pin in understanding these present circumstances) is the fact that the Christians had to hide themselves *from the Jews* out of the very real fear of being imprisoned, tortured or killed. It was the Jews, under the direction of the Sanhedrin, who were bent upon the extermination of this rival sect and its adherents, and who utilized the same methods of bribery, corruption, false witness, threats, flogging and murder that they utilize today in seeing their agenda realized. It was the fanatical Jewish supremacists who 'swore an oath not to eat or drink' until the deed of wiping out the liberating message of Christianity had been accomplished, thugs and 1st century Bolsheviks who possessed no sense of humanity or decency that they accuse the Christian world of not possessing today. It was those who held sway among the Jews who were bent upon the destruction of a group of family members, refugees who had decided to abandon the supremacist agenda that was the ethos of 1st century Palestine, this intoxicating elixir that was the harbinger of Zionism and which was the source of empowerment for those who entertained big plans for themselves down the road.

On the other hand, it was the Christians who had to endure imprisonment, beatings, being hunted by the authorities and finally death, a fact that is *never* discussed when analyzing the roots of what has historically been a turbulent history between the two peoples. When discussing "man's inhumanity to man" and the history of Jewish suffering, (including within it of course the unavoidable discussion of the holocaust) *never* is there any mention made of what was done to the Christians by the Jews themselves. Therefore, when coming to terms with what were the first dominoes to fall that led to the present circumstances, these dramatic facts must be remembered, and particularly whenever Jewish interests go about the business of depicting themselves as a helpless minority that has been unjustly persecuted for centuries on end. And lest we forget, this unpleasant situation for the Christians endured for quite a while, including of course the infamous persecutions that took place under the Roman emperor Nero, who had converted to Pharisaical Judaism and was heavily under the influence of his religious advisors. It was this, and not the 'blood libel' that set the tone for future clashes between the two groups.

And if all of this weren't enough, what must be remembered is the fact that this little history was but the first of many similarly shaped dominoes that would fall and which would be responsible for planting the seeds of future animosity between the Jewish people and the rest of the world.

Predators and prey

One of the first Christians, Paul, once wrote that 'there is nothing new under the sun' in describing the cyclical, repetitive and eternal nature of human behavior. And just as the Jews of 1st century Palestine put in motion events that had explosive implications for themselves and for those who would be following in their footsteps down the road, so too throughout their entire history have they continued doing likewise. For those wishing to understand why there is this thing known as the Middle East conflict, and more importantly why there is this thing known as 'Islamic extremism' that has in recent years become the new buzz word, what should be considered is that there is nothing new to be found here. The sources of this turmoil have as a common thread running through them the very same theme that has led to friction between the Jews and the peoples around whom they have lived for the last 2,000 years, although one would find no such discussion of these items taking place today nor in the manner that it should. And the theme upon which all of this is based is the simplistic one of survival, of prey trying to save itself from the predator.
Imagine being a Christian, or any other non-Jewish person throughout the history of the last 2,000 years for that matter, and learning about what kind of religious precepts that "God's chosen people," your Jewish neighbors who are living amongst you entertain. Imagine finding out that Pharisaical Judaism entertains and fosters among its adherents the notion that all non-Jews, *the Goyim*, are animals with no rights and who have been created for the purpose of serving those who fancy themselves as being a "light

among nations. Imagine learning of the Talmudic teachings that speak of the manner in which the inferior non-Jew only *appears* to be human so as to be better equipped to serve the needs and desires of the master race. Imagine learning that there are special religious dispensations for your Jewish neighbors that permit them to steal, lie, cheat, molest and rape your children and your wives, as well as murdering you and your fellow citizens, and that not only are these abominations permitted, but that such acts are considered a *mitzvah*, or a religious duty.

Now imagine that upon learning these things, you see the manner in which these sentiments are implemented on a daily basis; that the local Jewish merchants have become cozy with whatever governing body exists at the time, and that laws and policies are being enacted that place them atop the rest of the non-Jewish subjects in a particular political community. Imagine that slowly but surely you find yourself dispossessed of your property, that you are working slave hours for slave wages, and that you are doing all of this as a service for your fellow Jewish neighbors who truly believe in all that business about their being "destined to inherit the earth". Human nature has a breaking point, and such has it been throughout history that peoples reach that breaking point, and thus arrive the "waves of persecutions" about which we are reminded on a seemingly regular basis. In the words of Henry Makow, anti-Zionist Jew and popular internet writer,

"In most cases, "anti Semitism", old or new, is not an irrational hatred or sickness in the Gentile soul. It is a healthy defense mechanism of mainly Christian and Moslem nations, cultures, races and religions that are threatened by the gradual and insidious process of extinction under the Zionist agenda."

And in a nutshell, we now have delineated the source of the conflict in the Middle East, in addition to all the particulars involving anti-Jewish circumstances throughout history that are too numerous to discuss here. The invasion of Palestine, the subjugation and oppression of the non-Jewish people therein, and the ambitiousness that is the religiously inspired/racial supremacist ethos of the Zionist agenda are the reasons for all this turmoil, pure and simple. Despite what dribble today's members of the ADL, JDL, AIPAC and all the other tentacles of the Jewish supremacist agenda will spew, "anti-

Semitism" is not a product of envy or jealousy, nor does it "spring up" out of nowhere for no discernible reason. Just as it has been throughout history with other peoples, today, the Arabs, both Muslim and Christian, know full well what the Jewish supremacist agenda known as Zionism entails, which is no less than the theft of all their land and natural resources, as well as the enslavement and murder of those living there, and all for the benefit of those who view themselves as being a "light among nations". And despite the effusions of denial that take place (wedded to the apoplexy that grips the mouthpieces of the Jewish supremacist agenda whenever anyone begins discussing the tenets of Pharisaical Judaism and the anti-Gentile, racist sentiments spanning some *2,000 pages* of its most holy book, the Talmud) nevertheless these items are literally in black and white and have been revealed by many who were fortunate and brave enough to rescue themselves from the imprisoning mentality of this agenda and who have made it their noble mission to warn the rest of humanity concerning its precepts.

Encores

If it can be said that there is nothing new under the sun, likewise we need to take stock of the wisdom contained in the old saying concerning "birds of a feather". Being that Zionism is a Marxist ideology, we should not be surprised then to see it nursing an admiration for totalitarianism, and thus we find it modeling much of its operational methods upon what was successfully achieved in that other famous implementation of the Jewish supremacist agenda in Soviet Russia.

Besides the wanton spilling of innocent blood, what we find as well is Zionism's penchant for Orwellian language in spelling out its demands as well as in justifying its deeds. And just as the Bolshevik cousins to today's Zionists employed code words for various themes, whose meanings varied greatly from the way in which they were conventionally understood by the rest of the world, so too does such a situation exist today within the paradigm of the Jewish supremacist agenda. Thus we find that any and all opposition to their designs is equated with 'terrorism,' and that the word 'peace' is what takes place when with their demands are met. The fact that the horrors that took place under the Bolshevik revolution were authored principally by those whom British Prime Minster Winston Churchill referred to as *"international and for the most part atheistic Jews"* is an important component as well in understanding why there is such enmity for these people found today among those living in the Middle East.

From the very beginning of this nightmare, the inhabitants of the Middle East have understood full well who was responsible for the deaths of millions of people during that time period known as the Bolshevik Revolution and its aftermath, and who therefore have entertained no desire in having as neighbors their like-minded cousins who carried with them the same diseased way of thinking. And anyone who foolishly wishes to deny the realities of this situation, what such school children need to do is but *read* the words of those who have been the pilots of this bloody voyage and find out the truth for themselves, although practically speaking, few probably would go to such lengths as investigating it with an open mind.

Therefore, when we include in the list of the victims of the Jewish supremacist agenda the Jews themselves, what is meant is that there are those who have had to suffer from the ambitiousness of their leaders now for 2,000 years. In truth the enslavement that the Jews suffered under the Pharaohs has been comparatively less than the enslavement that they have suffered under the Pharisees, and which is the *real* tale of woe and persecution that is yet to be told. The manner in which those who have been the Godfathers of this gangsterism—those embracing this criminal mentality of Jewish supremacist sentiments who have heaped derision and persecution upon those under them are the real villains, not the Gentile peoples who have risen up against such designs in the interests of their own defense.

Suicidal tendencies

If there *is* one area though in which the 'little people' can be blamed for the saga of their own suffering, then it resides in the foolishness that they have historically employed in allowing such predators to assume the roles of leadership among them, paired of course with their willingness in following vampires such as these down the road to ruin. This tendency appears to be a constant within their collective personality, beginning at least as far back as the flight from Egypt and up through the crucifixion.

What history has shown with regards to the 'little people' within the community calling itself Jewish is a schizophrenia of sorts when it comes to deciding wherein lie their best interests. Left to their own devices and sentiments, these individuals-with no more an ambition to rule the world than anyone else-have shown that they were willing to follow good leaders such as Moses and Jesus, men who had their best interests at heart and who wanted nothing more than to see their people freed from bondage. Unfortunately, and despite the fact that leaders such as these were willing to go to such lengths as walking through the desert or walking on water, the loyalty that the little people had for their own best interests proved to be short-lived, as history has aptly demonstrated. Like a child who chooses bad friends whose interests lie only in bringing trouble into his or her life, so too have the Jews historically done in allowing the leaders among them to drag them into schemes that have produced literally thousands of years of misery.

There is nothing original about this condition, as it is but a common theme found among peoples whose identity and individualism have been swallowed up by what are the demands of the tribe. The inevitable weakness of character and the inability to consider what are their own best interests in the face of the pressures brought to bear by the tribe can be a powerful force with which to reckon, and unfortunately, a force that all too often has proved to be insurmountable, as far as the Jews and their history have been concerned. Therefore, what we see is instance after instance wherein, within the proverbial blinking of an eye, when someone else holding some kind of sway over their thinking came forward and induced them into something antithetical to their own interests, they have turned like a bunch of mindless sheep against those whom a moment before were their kings. Whether it was betraying Moses or Jesus or the prophets whom they killed regularly, or whether it has been in adopting the Talmudic mindset which cannot but pit them against the peoples living in their midst, the story has been the same; swallow the lies and promises uttered by the gangsters among them to their own misery and destruction, never learning and never growing, a vicious cycle that can only lead to their own eventual destruction at the hands of the gentile peoples against whom they have been pitted for the benefit of their leaders.

And this tendency, more than all others, is and has been the *real* holocaust of the Jewish people, namely the inability to think for themselves and to consider their own best interests in contradistinction to what their leaders have crafted for them. The stereotype that they have suffered throughout history, the image of them as a race of immoral, self-centered and merciless Shylocks — while originating in the activities of the more profligate among them — nevertheless has been given assistance in the quiet compliance that the rest of the group has afforded to them throughout time. Throughout their troubled history and in every instance in which one from among their leadership was caught red-handed in some nefarious business that roused the anger of the Gentile population around them, what *should* have been done by the righteous members of the Jewish community, by those who fancy themselves as being a "light among nations," by a community who practiced what they preached and lived out the depiction that they have crafted for themselves as "God's chosen people" would have been to join the rest of humanity in condemning such business in the interests of objective right and wrong. Instead, what they have done, in perfect conformity with the program that has been installed in their intellectual hard drives was to run to the defense of those who were in truth planting the seeds of future misery for them and for their own children. In choosing to insulate the criminals from among them and in refusing to condemn what have historically been acts of wickedness committed by their own, what they did was to deny that there was any god higher than that which benefited the tribe. Over the course of thousands of years, what has taken place has been the institutionalizing of this criminal mindset and causing it to perpetuate itself in such a way that any behavior, *even the murder of millions,* is acceptable if the tribe somehow comes out on top of all of it. And thus, by so doing, what they in effect have done was to co-operate in fleshing out a picture of a monolithic conspiracy of Jewish interests in the minds of the various Gentile populations who existed in their midst, and with it all the predictable reactions and counter-pressures. The image that would finally take shape before the eyes of the rest of the non-Jewish people is one wherein the Jews could be counted on to excuse any evil that was committed by one of their own, and particularly if such evil happened to touch a Gentile in an unfortunate way.

And so, such it is today, as Israel goes about the business of implementing a program of extermination for the world's 1.5 billion Muslims and of stealing their land and oil, and few there are to be found from among the tribe who are willing to speak out against such criminal behavior. In such a way, there exists a nation of Manchurian Candidates spread throughout the globe, or as ex-Israeli intelligence officer Victor Ostrovsky named them, a world-wide network of *sayanim* who contain within their thinking a program that is initiated whenever they are exposed to certain trigger words and which compels them into executing a particular action for the benefit of their handlers who remain behind the scenes. It is no different than what took place in America during the 20th century with the Italians, who would protect and insulate the criminals living among them, and by so doing, fashion a prejudice among the rest of the community that all Italians were Mafiosi.

And thus we have the real reasons for the persecution of the Jews throughout history. Had the Jews not allowed themselves to be pitted against the rest of the non-Jewish world by virtue of the elitist, supremacist agenda that has been the vehicle for empowering the more profligate from among them, they would have assimilated and enjoyed what would have been a period of peace and cultural advancement. Had they abandoned the notion that they were a race apart, had they abandoned the idea that they were "God's chosen people" who were "destined to inherit the earth" and who would "make footstools of all their enemies," there would have been no pogroms and no holocausts. Had they listened to the liberating message preached by the Palestinian carpenter that contained within it the keys that would unshackle them from the enslavement of supremacist thinking that inevitably leads to conflict with other peoples, there would have been no Diaspora nor any captivity in foreign lands. Had they flushed down the memory hole the junk science formulated around the supremacist heresy going by the name of Pharisaism, Sanhedrinism, or its later politicized and popularized name, Zionism, there would have been no perpetual war between them and the rest of the world's peoples, as has clearly been the case. When examined in this light it is no mystery then why there is such hatred to be found for Christ within the pages of Judaism's "holiest book" the Talmud, and particularly after considering the manner in which Christ's liberating message threatened the agenda being constructed by the supremacists within the Sanhedrin. To call him a thorn in their side is an understatement. Rather, he was like a Robin Hood, a William Wallace or a George Washington, a revolutionary who threatened to undo everything upon which their power was precariously balanced.

Instead, by allowing this "master race" theory to take root in their behavior, and by empowering the gangsters within their own communities to implement such anti-social practices among the rest of the peoples around whom they have lived, what they have done is to assist in planting the seeds of their own misery and in paving the road to their own ruin, as is obviously the case today with regards to the Middle East situation. Their leaders, due to the empowerment that has been surrendered to them by those at the bottom have just picked a fight with 1.5 billion people, and even though the Americans may be deluded as to what this is all really about, the rest of the world's billions have not. Therefore when this blood bath reaches its unavoidable ferment, heaping suffering upon the rest of the world's inhabitants, such victims will, *as they have always done throughout history,* come looking for who is responsible, and thus will be ushered in a new wave of persecutions for "God's chosen people".

In closing upon this aspect of the discussion, let us say that it is in this light therefore that we can better understand what significance is contained in the curse that the Jews of Christ's time heaped upon themselves when they spoke out in one voice *"His blood be upon us and upon our children"*. In choosing what was and is the enslaving mindset of supremacist thinking rather than embracing the liberation found in the message of the Messiah who had been promised to them, what they chose in effect was the mark of Cain, humanity's first beast, a mark which has put them at enmity with the rest of the world's peoples. The willingness on the part of their leaders to subject the 'lesser' human beings around the globe to the crimes of lying, stealing, and murder that has been the product of their having adorned the precepts of envy and greed, just as Cain did to his own brother Abel, this can be said to be the real cause of their history of suffering, not the cryptic, mysterious, and enigmatic phantom of "anti-Semitism".

All things being equal

Lest the reader assume that I have succumbed to what is now the very prevalent disposition of wailing over the suffering of the Jews to the detriment of discussing the suffering endured by others, we shall move on to more pressing topics. In considering the plight of those who are the *real* victims of the Jewish supremacist agenda, obviously, such a discussion cannot take place absent the most obvious example of the tragedy that has destroyed the lives of those living in the Middle East.

There have been many things leveled at me by those critical of my position, not the least of which has been that I am an Islamophile way beyond any boundaries of justifiable reason. The application of this charge comes as no surprise when it originates from within the ranks of those making up the discipleship of the Jewish supremacist agenda, since right now the Muslim world is the only real impediment to the realization of its 2,000 year-old dream of world hegemony. When it originates from within the ranks of those in the Christian world however, it is — when considered logically — completely out of place. But then again, what must be considered is that when today's pundits and false prophets extol the virtues of the "Judeo-Christian" culture, they are saying a lot more than they or anyone else realizes.

This is, without a doubt, the hardest part of the writing that I have had to do for this work, not the least of which is due to the fact that as a Christian, I have had to arrive at some very uncomfortable conclusions about my fellow travelers. No doubt, the alienation that has crept between me and them as a result of what I have written over the course of the last 2 years will be widened as a result of what I am about to say now, but nevertheless, it is something that must be stated, for the benefit of all and in the interests of justice.

No apologies will be made for my assertion that the Muslims deserve much more credit than what is being given to them. The fact that many of my co-religionists have reacted to the empathy that I possess for what these peoples are enduring as well as my admiration for their forbearance goes a long way towards delineating in my mind what are some of the terminal symptoms afflicting what passes for Christianity today.

The systematic process of brutalizing and then demonizing the Muslim people by the thuggery of the Jewish supremacist agenda is so despicable as to almost surpass conventional imagination. It is so haughty and bold in its application that one has difficulty believing that its existence is not something out of some science fiction novel. In its least complicated form, what the Zionists have done is to subject these people to the horrors of a program of displacement, terrorism and genocide similar to the ones about which they constantly lament and then attempt to justify this by making it look as if the victims deserved it. What is worse is the fact that this program of unimaginable suffering, injustice and bloodshed is paired with its uncritical acceptance on the part of those in the formerly Christian West. For me, that to which it is all simply boiled down is a coin with two sides: On the one side is this thing called justice, and on the other side is this thing called gratitude.

Like it or not, the fact of the matter is that the *only* entity that is resisting this beast of Jewish supremacism is the Muslim world. While the Christians have *"laid down with the lion," "turned the other cheek"* and *"rendered unto Caesar"* and have in all other ways accepted the destruction of their cultures and all the order necessary for preserving them, the Muslims have not, and in large part due to the fact that they have seen what has happened to the West through its own abdication. Like it or not, the fact that must be recognized is that the suffering that these people are and have been enduring is real and in the near future will be unprecedented in its scope. The heart-breaking stories of the brutality endured by the Palestinians, of watching daily as their children have been deliberately shot while playing in their yards or while going to school, as well as what has been done to the people of Iraq over the course of the last decade is a situation over which the Christians of the West should be suffering sleepless nights in their contemplation. Like it or not, the reality is that the Muslim world has up to the date of this writing successfully repelled that to which the Christian world has already surrendered itself without so much as a whimper; the vices of abortion, pornography, sodomy, the degradation of marriage and women, and in all other cases the moral chaos that has flowed forth from the Jewish supremacist agenda. As day by day the Christian world becomes exponentially more ghoulish in its embrace of the culture of death that has been injected into its sociological bloodstream by the Kevorkian mindset of the Jewish supremacist agenda, by contrast the Muslims for the most part enjoy healthy, well-ordered societies. Like it or not, there is this thing called justice to which those in the Muslim world are entitled their fair share, the same justice requiring the world (and in particular the Christian world) to come to their aid in the midst of this assault under which they are laboring. And lest those in the Christian world attempt the foolish and elitist argument that no such justice is deserving for these people by virtue of their attachment to the religion of Islam, perhaps then they should consider the fact that millions of Christians are there who are suffering in these regions as well.

And, finally, like it or not, empirically it must be recognized that the Christian West owes a great debt to those in the Muslim world for one undeniable reason:

Were it not for the sacrifices made by those who are the adherents of the Islamic faith in resisting this beast, the world would be much further along in the hellish grip of the Zionist agenda, and particularly the Christian world, which is and always has been the real target of Pharisaical Judaism's program of extermination.

It doesn't take a mathematician or a military strategist to see the logic in this reasoning. For all the rot that has encompassed the Christian West—the fact that virtually every country within it has taken seriously ill as a result of having drunk from the well that has been poisoned by the Jewish supremacist agenda—such a condition would be much worse were it not for the fact that this agenda has had to divide its resources and energies between the West and the Middle East. Conversely, what this means is that once the Middle East "problem" has been "taken care of," thus freeing the Zionist agenda to concentrate its efforts on the West, the process of decay and destruction for Pharisaical Judaism's eternal enemy will be moving along at an accelerated rate.

Therefore, as a Christian and as a father of many children, I cannot help from entertaining what is a large measure of gratitude for what these people in the Muslim world have done. Were it not for the fact that they believe so strongly in right and wrong and are willing to fight for the rights of the omnipotent being who created them—were it not for the fact that they cannot be bought nor bullied—my children, whose innocence and lives are being eyed on a daily basis by the beast of the Jewish supremacist agenda would be much closer to the jaws of death than they are now. Were it not for the fact that the Muslim world has tied up the resources and energy of the Zionist agenda in such a formidable manner, we in the Christian West would be much further along in the process of losing our freedoms and our culture.

Therefore, I cannot in good conscience view their struggle in any other light than in the context of admiration and gratitude. The fact that the rest of those in Christian world refuse to do so and instead either align themselves with the Jewish supremacist agenda that wants the Muslims destroyed or else approach the whole subject in a spirit of nauseating ambivalence tells me that those in the Christian world have come to hold in quiet contempt a good portion of that which the peasant carpenter from the Palestinian town of Nazareth had to say.

Within the midst of this discussion that puts those in the Muslim world in a more favorable light, the epileptic fits that will be displayed by the modern day Pharisees who have elevated this supremacist agenda to the level of a god can be dismissed outright without the slightest consideration. It should be obvious to all by now wherein lies their intellectual honesty, and therefore how little of this discussion deserves to be occupied with their sentiments. All the screaming sessions that they orchestrate over the dangers of "Islamic extremism," when analyzed thoroughly, betray the fact that these sentiments are rooted in a self-serving agenda that cares little about the West or anyone else for that matter. What must be remembered is that in such a program, it is "Islamic extremism" today, "Christian extremism" tomorrow, "Hindu extremism" next week, "Buddhist extremism" next month, so on and so on, until they have subdued the entire planet. Remember that being totalitarianist in their thinking means that conventionally understood concepts have different meanings for them, and therefore when we hear the word "extremism" what we should understand is that what they really mean is *"opposition to their agenda"*.

But more important than this, what must be remembered above all else is that the real blame for this thing known as "Islamic extremism" falls squarely in the lap of those attempting to shove the Zionist agenda down the throat of the rest of the world's peoples and cultures.

Were it not for the extremism that is the Jewish supremacist agenda and the manner in which it has been forcibly applied to those around the world, and more importantly to those in the Middle East, there would be no such thing as "Islamic extremism".

It is the extremism of the Talmudic thinking that is the backbone of this supremacist agenda, an extremism steeped in self-absorbed narcissism and which views all non-Jews as animals fit to be enslaved and then slaughtered that has resulted in the Muslim world reacting in so violent a manner as it has.

Besides its track record in Bolshevik Russia and Eastern Europe, it is due to the history of what the Jews have done to the Arab peoples over the course of the last century that has created the situation as it exists today within the Muslim world. It is due to the fact that women and children have been shot, bombed, burned, raped, run out of their lands and forced to live like animals for 50 years by the thugs of the Jewish supremacist agenda that today has resulted in Palestinians strapping themselves up with bombs and blowing themselves up. It is the fact that nearly one million children in Iraq have been systematically and forcibly shoved into death's estate by being starved of food and medicine, not to mention the terrible disfigurements that have resulted as a result of the radiation poisoning they suffered after the first Gulf War that today is fueling and feeding what the Zionist agenda disparagingly calls "extremism". It is the fact that this same supremacist agenda which has been responsible for the murder of hundreds of millions, as well as for the nearly complete destruction of Western Civilization that today the Muslim world has become a place of seething hatred and violence.

Besides considering these facts, what we need to remember is that the "moral outrage" that those who bow at the golden calf of the Jewish supremacist agenda pretend to possess over the "extremism" possessed by those in the Muslim world is not genuine in and of itself, a fact that is easily proven when looking at it as it is viewed from the other direction. No such "moral outrage" exists on the part of Jewish extremists when discussing the manner in which the Jews of Europe subjected the Arab peoples of Palestine to what was inarguably a campaign of terrorism and wanton brutality. No one would dare to categorize the extremism that was committed by Zionist groups such as the Irgun, Palmach, Haganah and Stern Gang during the early days of the invasion of Palestine in the same negative light in which they categorize what the Muslims are doing today.

By contrast, the business of murdering over 250,000 people and of destroying over 400 Palestinian towns is remembered nostalgically, in perfect conformity with the Talmudic mindset that justifies genocide against non-Jews. Both Gulf Wars, set to coincide with the Jewish feast of Purim, *the feast of vengeance,* receive special remembrances when the acts of brutality that encompassed these events are recounted. And thus, the same spirit of hypocrisy that is and always has been the calling card of the Jewish supremacist agenda and which raised the ire of Christ is employed when determining which acts of violence are celebrated and which acts are condemned. What the Muslims are doing today is no different than what those in the Christian West or any other place would be doing if the same atrocities were committed against them, provided of course that their intellects and spirits had not been corrupted by the leaven of the Jewish supremacist agenda that robs its victims of the ability to reason properly.

And it is within this light therefore, of all things being equal, that the world should look at the efforts of those within the Muslim world and acknowledge that in the larger sense, they are justified in what they are doing, not only in the interests of their own self-defense, but as well for the benefit of the rest of the world, and especially for those in the West. They deserve the same dignity and the same level of respect for their "human rights" about which those in the Christian West are constantly running their mouths for the most trivial of reasons. A rose by any other name is still a rose, and when we are talking about bravery, faithfulness to the precepts of right and wrong and the willingness to sacrifice life and limb in the defense of innocent women and children, then it certainly is an injustice of the highest order when those who are fighting this fight are branded as terrorists, religious fanatics, and bloodthirsty savages. The fact that a good portion of the Christian world has done so in lock-step with its mortal enemy, Zionism, indicates what is a not-too-promising future for the followers of Palestine's first freedom fighter from the town of Nazareth.

Those in the West who have swallowed the bait concerning those in the Islamic world that has been provided for them by the Zionist agenda would be wise to remember that there has been no substantive war between Islam and the West for centuries, and anyone who has studied the history of this situation knows that Islam has been in a protracted period of withdrawal since that time. Within this time period, and more importantly, during the course of the last century, all that they have really desired is to be left alone and to have the stability of their societies left unmolested by the Jewish supremacist agenda. More nobly, what they want is freedom, *real freedom,* to manage their own affairs and to be liberated from the corrupt leaders who are and have been since the fall of the Ottoman Empire in the paid service of the Zionist-American cabal, traitors who have acted in Israel's interests by robbing these people of the wealth, their human rights and of their aspirations.

And after considering these items, perhaps those in the West should take their thinking one step farther and thus afford some credibility to the theory that one of the reasons that the extremists working in the service of the Jewish supremacist agenda have pitted this war between the Christians and the Muslims is out of their own fear that as a result of increased contact between the Muslim world and the West, that there would result increasing numbers of conversions to Christianity. Since Christianity (in its uncorrupted state, of course) forms a natural barrier, antidote and antiseptic to the ambitiousness and brutality of the Jewish supremacist agenda, and as such remains its *real* target of extermination, it is easy to see then why such conversions from Christianity to Islam obviously cannot be permitted to take place. This becomes all the more easy to understand when considering the way in which today the Muslims refuse to concede anything to the Jewish supremacist agenda, for if such people—possessed of such solid characters and constitutions were ever to embrace the religion of Christianity and take that message to the ends of the earth that are at this moment solidly in the hands of Jewish extremists—the Antichrist's game would be up for sure.

While we can dismiss the position held by Jewish supremacists in terms of how the Muslim world is viewed, we cannot afford to give the same exemption when it comes to those in the Christian world, as they do not possess any such immunity from their obligation of viewing this picture realistically. Besides the fact that they have been commanded to be as "wise as serpents," in addition they have been commanded to hunger and thirst for justice, and particularly for those who have been beaten by robbers and left by the roadside to die.

Therefore when those in the Christian world choose one of the two prevalent views concerning the *abomination of desolation* that is the Jewish supremacist agenda in the Middle East—the one which supports it and the other which does not care—what they are doing is to flagrantly disregard the very commands that were issued to them the week in which their Master was killed by the thugs of the Sanhedrin. Despite whatever noble pretenses they may use in justifying their position, the truth of the matter is that it is but sheer stupidity laced with the complacency that follows in the wake of a comfortable lifestyle that is to blame for their disinterest in what is going on in the Middle East. Their disgusting display of hypocrisy in refusing to speak up against the injustices that are being wrought against those in the Middle East, all done out of the pretended desire to remain *'religiously pure'* and *'spiritually loyal'* is an indicator as to how much of their thinking has been infected with the same 'leaven of the Pharisees' about which their Master warned them 20 centuries past.

For those with eyes to see, the obscene spectacle that is today the complacency of the Christian world towards the events in the Middle East is so dramatic and outrageous in its scope as to almost be surreal, and were it not for the fact that wise men predicted that such a situation would take place centuries ago, one would be quite pressed into accepting that all of it today were genuine. All the events about which they were warned for 2,000 years are culminating before their very eyes, and yet they mill about unconcernedly like stupid cattle in the field, exactly as they are depicted as being within the pages of Judaism's Babylonian Talmud. Their societies have been torn asunder, the load-bearing beams supporting the weight of their civilization have been devoured by the termites of the Jewish supremacist agenda, and few of them bother to ask anything pertinent with regards to what is happening, nor what substantive things can be done in reversing it. Not even the fact that in the *very land* in which their Master lived and died, the land where their faith was born and where the war for independence from Pharisaical Judaism took place, the fact that it is being drowned in innocent blood seems to matter to them. The locations that marked all the important events of his life are day by day being molested and demolished by the descendants of the same Sanhedrin who put him to death, an abomination that should be intolerable to today's Christians, and still they are not troubled. Those calling themselves followers of the peasant carpenter from Nazareth today sit by and watch as the Muslims endure this slow death, *this abortion on a massive scale* and stupidly amuse themselves with all the triviality that encompasses their Western lifestyles tainted with the leaven of Jewish supremacism. And thus it is that both by their active participation in these events and by their complacency they have become one of the heads of the beast, although few recognize this to be the case.

For Lack of Knowledge

It is obvious to anyone who has carried on a discussion of this type with today's Christians in the West that there are many of them who use the "perfume" of religious reasons to hide the ugly odor of their disinterest with what is taking place in the Middle East. The attitude that one constantly encounters is that wherein an individual justifies his or her ambivalence towards the tragedy by saying in essence that *"this war between the Jews and the Muslims is a war between two peoples who are not Christian, therefore I am not going to involve myself in it"*. The folly contained in this position is obvious in and of itself, simply by virtue of the fact that individuals such as these are very near-sighted in their vision. They *think* that they won't involve themselves, yet they are involved already, and up to their eyeballs. Their country is at war, their taxes are being used to pay for it, someone they know is fighting in the American military, and quite soon, their children stand a good chance of being drafted.

But besides the folly (which can be laughed away due to the stupidity that is contained therein) what cannot be disregarded is the fact that Christians such as these are not moved by the plight of those who are suffering, and suffering immeasurably so. The scope of the anguish and the injustice being wrought against the peoples of Iraq, Palestine, and Afghanistan is so horrible that it almost defeats the imagination. The callous disregard that those in the West maintain towards this suffering and injustice would be more tolerable were it not for the fact that so many of these individuals never miss an opportunity in aggrandizing themselves in some way by talking about Jesus and how much they "love the Lord" etc, etc.

As we said before, this malevolent neglect that such individuals are entertaining goes both ways, as those in the Christian West will soon tragically learn. It is not difficult to see *why* they were commanded to be as wise as serpents, particularly when considered in light of the manner in which many people throughout history have been destroyed *'for lack of knowledge.'*

The members of the Christian West, after considering the manner in which they have gluttonously swallowed the propaganda that has been put before their intellects by the Jewish supremacist agenda have spit out conclusions that indicate what is not a small degree of stupidity and moral laziness operating within their thinking processes. In complete contradiction to the precepts of enlightenment and respect for the truth (for which they boast the pretenses of possessing on a daily basis) such individuals have betrayed the fact that they have ceded over to the Jewish supremacist agenda their right to think logically and rationally, even when they find that their very lives are at stake. Engage in any discussion today with the average Christian and he will vomit out verbatim all the notions that have been concocted by the Zionist agenda concerning the Muslim world and what comprises its existence. The words "jihad," "holy war" and "infidel" are used by superiority-minded Christians as if they were in complete command of all the information encompassing what is the religion and culture of the adherents of Islam, but who make monumental fools of themselves in the process for their lack of knowledge.
Were they as informed and as superior as they presuppose themselves as being, they would have ventured into this exploration after 11 September with two indispensable weapons at the ready: The first of these weapons that should have been brandished yet which remained securely holstered and untouched was skepticism, particularly since the very entity that was providing all this information concerning the religion of Islam and its adherents was Christianity's own mortal enemy, the Jewish supremacist agenda which stood to gain the most from pitting the Christian and Muslim worlds against each other. The second weapon that they should have employed and which should have followed on the heels of the first was a sprinkling of research mixed with a dash of common sense.

Tragically, none of this was done, and now those in the Christian world find themselves in the suicidal position of fighting 1.5 billion people for the benefit of their own eternal nemesis. "Family values" Christians simply allowed liars such as Rush Limbaugh, Sean Hannity, Bill O'Reilly et all do their thinking for them, even when the conflict of interest surrounding these individuals was so great as to preclude the possibility of an honest discussion of the facts. And in the event that one jumps to the defense of his or her own particular sect of Christianity as being an exception to what has now become the rule, doing such in the interest of devaluing what is now a well-earned and much-deserved unpleasant generalization, what should be remembered is that this suicidal tendency cuts across all religious lines, be they Catholic, Protestant, non-Denominational, etc. By contrast, the numbers of Christians who can be found having *not* drunk the poison of lies offered to them by the Jewish supremacist agenda is so small as to almost be undetectable.

Had they bothered to read, had they bothered to question that which was being put before their consideration by the Zionist agenda, they would have found a mountain of lies so large that it would have joined the Great Wall of China in its distinction as being the only man-made structure visible from outer space. Before buying into the notion that the Muslim world poses an organic threat to a civilization based upon the *genuine* precepts of Christianity, what should have been considered is the manner in which he who founded this civilization, Jesus Christ, is revered and honored by the religion of Islam — the fact that he is considered the *Messiah* and that his return is awaited anxiously by those in the Muslim world in the end times for the purpose of defeating the Antichrist — the fact that his mother Mary is considered the highest, most noble and holy woman ever to have graced the human race or walked the earth — the fact that Christians, *true Christians,* are considered to be the greatest friends to the Muslims, since *"they are not proud, and have priests and monks among them"*.

Yet, rather than giving credit where it is due, the *"enlightened"* Christian West, in what will one day be given a special section in the annals of human folly, thoughtlessly drank the maddening wine from the chalice of the Jewish supremacist agenda, and in a state of intellectual inebriation, agreed to send her sons and daughters to the sands of the Middle East to fight the last remaining enemies to the Antichrist agenda of Zionism, and to the detriment of their own civilization.

And all of this, as unbelievable as it may be in the present, is all the more incredible when it is viewed from the perspective of the past, for the Christian world has always had in its possession a model from which it could derive the necessary wisdom in preventing the disaster that has taken place today. And if there are those in the Christian world who can claim ignorance and blame their state of half-wittedness on having no command of history nor having an understanding of its weighty implications, then certainly no excuse can be made by such individuals that they weren't warned, for clearly there have been dire words of caution that have been screaming out to them for the last 2,000 years by the very one whom they make the pretenses of calling their Master.

Lest we forget

"*You snakes! You brood of vipers! How will you escape being condemned to Hell? Therefore I am sending you prophets and wise men and teachers. Some of them you will kill and crucify, others you will flog in your synagogues and pursue from town to town. And so upon you will come all the righteous blood that has been shed on earth from the blood of righteous Abel to the blood of Zecharia*".

"*You belong to your father, the devil, and you want to carry out your father's lusts. He was a murderer from the beginning, not holding to the truth. When he lies, he speaks his native language, because he is a liar and the father of lies, and the reason that you do not hear what I have to say is because you are not of God*".

"*So when you see standing in the Holy Place the abomination that causes desolation, spoken of through the prophet Daniel, let the reader understand...for then there will be great distress unequaled from the beginning of the world until now, and never to be equaled again*".

"*The day will come when your enemies will build an embankment against you and encircle you in on every side. They will dash you to the ground, you and the children within your walls. They will not leave one stone upon another, because you did not recognize the time of God's coming*".

"Be on your guard against the yeast of the Pharisees".

"Watch out for false prophets, who come to you in sheep's clothing, but who inwardly are ferocious wolves. By their fruit you will recognize them".

"Do not suppose that I have come to bring peace to the earth. I did not come to bring peace, but the sword".

"Behold, I send you out as sheep among wolves, be ye therefore as meek as doves, but as wise as serpents".

"For I tell you that unless your justice exceeds that of the Pharisees, you certainly will not see the kingdom of Heaven".

"Woe to you, teachers of the law and Pharisees, you hypocrites. You give a tenth of your spices, but you have neglected the more important matters of the law: justice, mercy and faithfulness. You are like whitewashed tombs, which look beautiful on the outside, but which are filled with dead men's bones and everything unclean. In the same way, on the outside you appear as righteous, but inside are full of wickedness and hypocrisy".

It can be a galling thing to listen to Christians today who justify their ambivalence towards modern-day events by making the ridiculous claim that their Master was not interested in politics and who maintain the indefensible position that he was concerned only with saving men's souls. It betrays the fact that not only do they suffer from the effects of shallow thinking, but as well that they have adopted the image of their Master that has been deliberately molded for consumption by the Jewish supremacist agenda, the image of the effeminized Christ who did nothing more than to say nice things and who encouraged his followers to surrender themselves to the designs of evil men. And yet, it is obvious that within the pages of the story recounting the contention that existed between him and the leaders of Israel at that time — the Sanhedrin — that no such foolish claim can accurately be made.

To those who have not allowed the leaven of the Jewish supremacist agenda to cloud their comprehension of Christ's war of liberation, it is obvious that there were *many* aspects to his 3 year fight with Zionism's founding fathers, and that there existed many practical concerns which he had hoped to accomplish. *In addition* to desiring the salvation of man from the Hell of the next world, he wished to save man from the Hell of this world as well. This should be a no-brainer, particularly when considering the manner in which he went about curing the sick and alleviating the suffering of those around him. But it should also be apparent to those with eyes to see that he had more serious plans which encompassed long-range issues as well, something that he obviously tried to make clear during the week of Passover when he warned anyone who would listen what kind of monster was dwelling amongst them. It is clear as well that he did not waste anything, whether it was the leftover fishes and loaves or whether it was his words.

Therefore, when we consider the warnings he left for mankind concerning the personages of the Sanhedrin who were chasing an agenda which he viewed as dangerous, there is no reason for us to assume that he was overreacting, nor that he was just using poetic language. More importantly, this very fact defeats the notion held by many weak-willed and weak-minded Christians that their Master was not involved in nor concerned with political events. When he warned everyone that the individuals making up the Sanhedrin were the descendants of Cain and that they were the children of the Devil who could do no more than to lie and fulfill the agenda that their father desired, it should be obvious to all with eyes to see that it was his intention that mankind take these words seriously. When he surrendered himself to their agenda and thus allowed these individuals to display the methods of their madness—the use of political corruption, lying, false-witness, torture and murder—in seeing their supremacist agenda realized, he obviously hoped that mankind would learn an important lesson from this. His goal was to prevent a political, cultural and sociological disaster from happening, accomplished in part by replacing it with a system that would serve the interests of humanity by creating a vibrant, healthy civilization wherein mankind could eventually learn to live as brothers. Had he been interested *only* in saving men's souls, as intellectually lazy Christians try to claim today, there would have been no political contest between him and the founding fathers of the Jewish supremacist agenda known as the Sanhedrin. Had he not been on a mission to thwart those embracing the logic of Cain, he would have steered clear from them during his three years, and left nothing for mankind to consider but a few nice words and a few good deeds. It is obvious that from the beginning, even before Christ entered in on the scene personally that a political contest was brewing, as evidenced by the words of his cousin John, who, in preparing the people for his cousin's mission, opened this war with the salvo he launched against the Sanhedrin. In calling them a *"brood of vipers"* (the exact terminology used by Christ himself) John the Baptist set the political tone for what was to become a 3-year war of liberation. Certainly it was obvious to his *enemies* that political issues were involved, a reality that screams out from their own words when they plotted to rid themselves of this pesky revolutionary.

"What are we accomplishing?" they asked. "Here is this man performing many miraculous signs. If we allow him to go on like this, everyone will believe in him, and then the Romans will come and take away our place and our nation". Then one of them named Caiphas who was High Priest that year spoke and said "You know nothing at all. Do you not realize it is better that one man die than that the whole nation perish?"

Therefore, when today's Zionized Christians defend the manner in which they have supinely surrendered the inheritance that was left to them by their Master (as well as what was accomplished by the freedom fighters who followed in his wake) by viewing what took place in purely spiritual terms, they are trying to construct a model that cannot withstand the crushing weight of reality. Like all coins upon which are found two sides, so likewise it is that there were (are) two sides encompassing Christ's agenda, involving the concerns of both this world and the next. The agenda for which he labored and which cannot be rationally denied was his desire to make this world as conducive to and as cooperative with mankind's transition to the next plane of existence as possible. By creating a civilization in which evil and the vice that his enemies peddled were contained and by promoting goodwill and justice among all peoples, what he attempted to do was to build a very short bridge between these two worlds, and an indispensable part of doing this resided in warning mankind as to what kind of evil seeds the disciples of the Jewish supremacist agenda were planning to sow amongst them.

In sum, what this means is that in warning mankind in the manner he did during Passover week, as well as in allowing the real nature of his political enemies to be revealed, what he was trying to prevent was the very situation as it exists today: *The establishment and entrenchment of the gangsterism of the Jewish supremacist agenda, an agenda that, having clawed its way to the top, has imposed a political situation upon mankind in complete variance to that which Christ envisioned, that being a brotherhood of nations acting in cooperation with each other and based upon the precepts of justice, compassion and humility towards fellow man.*

Today, due to the fact that this criminal mindset has been set free from its cage and has firmly ensconced itself in the most powerful positions on earth, what we find is that vice and evil are celebrated and that the virtues of justice and compassion are slowly but surely being systematically slaughtered on a minute by minute basis. And the people who were supposed to bring the situation as Christ envisioned it to its completion, the ones who were supposed to continue his war of independence and to act as a natural, organic barrier to this dangerous agenda rooted in the poisonous sentiments of Jewish supremacism were those in the Christian world. They were, in effect, supposed to be the Jedi knights of the Star Wars saga, who wisely and courageously kept order for the benefit of mankind against those who were organized around the forces of darkness. Tragically, what must be acknowledged is that not only did they *not* prevent this disaster from occurring, but that in addition they have allowed themselves to be co-opted into seeing it take root and flourish as it has today.

Dancing with the Devil

Doubtful it is today that a Christian in today's world would see him or herself as an integral component as to why the world is in the mess that it is. The truth is though, sadly, that this is the case, and undeniably so. Were it not for them and the position that they occupy in the world today, the present state of affairs with regards to this poisonous ideology known as Zionism, an ideology that poses the most serious threat that mankind has ever faced would not exist today nor be doing so in its present condition.

This is a peculiar thing to note, particularly since there are many Christians who can be found from time to time who, in lamenting over the ever-increasing destruction of their culture throughout the world, make the pretenses of accepting the blame in some of the clichés that they periodically use. It is impossible by now to compute how many times it has been said by many of today's Christians in the most solemn tones that *"All of the evils in the world are due to the easy-going attitude of Christians"*. And yet what is so painfully obvious about all of this is that what they really mean to say is that all of today's troubles are the result of the easy-going attitude of *other* Christians, not themselves. However, play the devil's advocate with them in these cases, and agree with them on their position and apply it in a very personal way — that the world finds itself in this present mess *as a result of their own failures* — and the entire position they maintain on the matter alters itself dramatically.

By doing such — this attempted charade at self-deprecation — what individuals such as these hope to accomplish is the casting of themselves in the favorable image of the humble Christian servant, without really being subject to the consequences that would logically follow if their sentiments were real. Such an act of voicing empty sentiments is an easy thing to do when the person doing it knows that there are no consequences that will follow in its wake, and such it is with today's Christians who make the *pretenses* of piety in wailing about the state of the world but who refuse to do anything about it. What has become apparent is the fact that when such discussions between Christians take place, wherein they beat their breasts over the destruction of their culture and wail the inevitable "mea culpa, mea culpa," what is taking place is an unspoken agreement among them whose program is well-rehearsed and studied. This vignette (within which I used to be a player on many occasions in the past) is one that I have witnessed now almost with as much frequency as I have heard the phrase concerning charity.

"Let us engage in this little drama together here, but without going too far. Let us be actors in this play wherein we assume the roles of the tragic heroes who flagellate themselves over having not done enough to save some noble institution, but remembering all along that we are only players, and that this is but a drama".

As I said, this is tough stuff to say, and the reader should understand that I derive no pleasure in saying it. And I realize that these are generalities that I am making, and I recognize as well that there are exceptions to the rule. Unfortunately, however, the exceptions are so rare nowadays as to almost be, statistically speaking, non-existent.

In considering this monstrous problem of the Jewish supremacist agenda and the choke-hold that it enjoys over the world' affairs today, there can be found some weight, albeit artificial in its nature, in the argument that today's Christians in the West offer in attempting to defend their sense of complacency, namely that little can be done to reverse the mechanics of this situation. What must be understood though is that the *only* reason that they are willing to make such an argument is due to the fact that they are still holding onto some kind of comfort that precludes them from actively doing anything that may endanger it. Rather than admit that they have been infected with the same corrupting influences that Western life offers its members on a daily basis, rather than admit that in many ways they are no better than their fellow countrymen who have completely abandoned the idea of living a life of principle and of self-sacrifice in exchange for a life of luxury and immediate gratification, such hypocritical Christians attempt to maintain their sense of superiority by making the claim that their hands are tied. But regardless of this, of whether or not there *could* be found some weight in the argument that "nothing can be done," it still does not offer any justification for the disinterest that they have nursed for this issue, a disinterest which they have allowed to dominate the manner in which they now live their lives. This is indeed a damning indictment that reveals the manner in which the Christians of the West have become like the harlot of the Apocalypse, who have dressed themselves up in gold and purple and who care nothing about their duties with regards to the issues of justice or compassion.

By contrast, no such reasoning will be heard from the mouths of Christians (nor from those of any other faith for that matter) whose comfort has become a thing of the past, and who do not have the luxury of deluding themselves and those around them in such a disgraceful manner. No such excuses will be heard from those living in Palestine or Iraq who are fighting with their very life's blood, nor from those in any of the other areas that have become the buffet table for the beast of the Jewish supremacist agenda. No such excuses would have been heard coming from the mouths of the 60+ million Christians who perished under the boot of Jewish Bolshevism in the early part of the 20th century. No such arguments would be heard coming from the mouths of the *hundreds of millions* of unborn children who have been murdered in their sleep while in the wombs of their mothers, an unprecedented abomination that is but *one product* of the moral rot injected into the societies of the Christian West by the Antichrist Jewish supremacist agenda. Were today's Western Christians one of *these* individuals who were fighting for their very lives against the beast in a manner *up close and personal*, then the mendicancy that they maintain with regards to their duty in resisting this animal would certainly change its tune rather quickly. Suddenly, the whole issue of the Jewish supremacist agenda would take on a theme of the utmost urgency and seriousness, and those individuals (who now scoff at what has been said up to this point) would tell anyone with ears to hear exactly the same message that is being argued within the pages of this book.

The real tragedy is that this is exactly what *will* happen to many of them in the not-too-distant future, individuals who will find themselves in the same position as today's victims, at which time they will be left to ponder the terrible knowledge that when they had the opportunity to fight—of fighting when they had a better chance of victory—instead they sat by and carelessly watched as helpless others were devoured, digested, and discharged. All the make-up which today's Christians use in masking the fact that they have acted like cowards in the face of their eternal enemies will pour off of their bodies as rivers of sweat flow forth from their pores resulting from the terror they will be experiencing in those moments. Of course, as that time approaches, all the disgusting displays of the narcissism that has infected the Christian West will be boldly displayed in its various themes, and better so than if neon signs had been employed. *"Something must be done, before it's too late, before it's too late!"* they will say, forgetting of course that for many, it was already too late decades ago. What they will mean by saying this is, *before it's too late for them*—as well as for the comfortable lifestyles that they have always known.

What these individuals fail to consider is the fact that it is *already* too late for the quarter-million Palestinians who have been murdered by the Zionists, as well as for the millions who have suffered lifetimes of watching their family members being slaughtered, not to mention enduring a lifetime of living intimately with the terrorism of the Jewish supremacist agenda. It is *already* too late for the million + Iraqis who have been murdered as a result of America's wars fought for Israel's benefit, and too late for the millions more whose lives have been reduced to a carbon copy of that which has been inflicted upon the Palestinians. It is already too late for the unborn children in the West who were abandoned by their "Christian" societies and who were fed to the pagan god Moloch through the institution of abortion, just one brainchild of many such barbaric institutions injected into the cultural lifeblood of the West by the Jewish supremacist agenda. It is already too late for the hundreds of millions of young people who, although fortunate enough to have made it out of the wombs of their mothers in one piece, nevertheless have been exposed to a lifetime of the intellectual and moral rot that has been poured into the wellspring of Western culture by the Jewish supremacist agenda, and who are, spiritually and intellectually speaking, the walking dead. And of course, by the time that today's "soldiers for Christ" realize that *their heads* are next in line for the chopping block, those in Syria, Iran, Jordan, Libya, Saudi Arabia, and Lebanon will have already had their turn in tasting the bitter fruits of the thorny tree of the Jewish supremacist agenda.

Every Idle Word...

In general, today's Christians, (if indeed they are even paying attention to the manner in which their culture is being destroyed as a result of the leaven of the Jewish supremacist agenda) will ascribe the degeneration of their world in such non-descript, shallow and for the most part *safe* statements such as "war is caused by sin" as well as the unavoidable diagnosis concerning "man's fallen nature," etc, etc, etc. Such statements, while they may carry a certain *outer veneer* of piety and wisdom in their application are, when all is said and done, nothing but dribble, given the seriousness that encompasses the events taking place today. Such statements are tantamount to saying that "disease is caused by germs," something of such obviousness as to preclude the need of mentioning. Those who wish to enjoy all the emoluments that are associated with the vocation of being doctors of philosophy and who resort to such kindergarten level explanations of modern day tragedies deserve to be rewarded with trophies for their foolishness, and surely not for any sense of wisdom that they presuppose themselves as possessing.

In truth, this tendency towards a shallow understanding (as well as the even more superficial *expression* of this understanding) is the product of the fact that most of today's Western Christians live comfortable lives, and more importantly, possess as well the fear of losing that comfort lest they delve too deeply into these matters. Their bellies are full of food, their houses are warm, and they do not *directly* suffer any direct, tangible effects of this poisonous agenda rooted in Jewish supremacism. They sit by and watch as, day by day, minute by minute, the order that used to encompass and stabilize their societies is worn away and replaced with moral chaos, yet because of the fact that, *as of this moment,* they have yet to suffer from it in any real manner, they are able to philosophize about the destruction of their Christian culture in a very dispassionate and detached way. And if this aspect of their complacency — the fact that they suffer by virtue of their leisure and luxury — can be accurately said to be one of the skeletons in the collective closet of the Christian West, the other skeleton (and definitely the more ugly of the two) is the fact that they have come to such an unenviable position as a result of their fear of the Jews.

Anyone who has involved him or herself in this topic knows intimately what is being discussed here. Talk about all the ills that are dissolving the connective tissue of Western Civilization in a general, safe, and above all in a manner *non-too-specific,* and all goes well. Begin discussing however the real source of these ills, that all is the product of a concerted, organized effort on the part of the Jewish supremacist agenda, and such "soldiers for the faith" go scurrying away to their intellectual caves just as the Apostles did on the night that their Master was arrested by the high priests of this same agenda. I myself have participated in discussions with fellow Christians who were willing to discuss anything that pertains to this situation — the destruction of the Christian West — up and until the moment in which the discussion takes the unavoidable dangerous detour towards criticizing God's chosen people. Of course, they will attempt to pretty-up this evasion of the truth with high minded principles-an aversion to racism, an abhorrence to Hitler's crimes, etc, etc, etc, blah, blah, blah, but what is really at work here is the fact that they fear for their comfort and for their livelihoods, and for good reason. It is no secret what happens to those who wrestle with this alligator, a reality that was made apparent during the course of the last year with what took place regarding Mel Gibson's movie *The Passion.* This fear is understandable, as it is an unavoidable consequence of the human condition, but when those who attempt to paint themselves as "warriors for justice" don the masquerade of "rationalizing" or "spiritualizing" that fear with feigned principles such as "prudence" or "humility" the entire charade becomes sickening. This was clearly the case when Christ singled out the Pharisees for their hypocrisy, and so we should not make the mistake of thinking that 2,000 years later it is a characteristic that is any less unattractive. I actually listened in shock as one friend, a devout Christian, said that if the situation ever came into being in which it became illegal to criticize the existence or mechanics of the Jewish supremacist agenda, that as Christians we would have to obey such laws, defending this position with the phrase, and I kid you not, *"Render unto Caesar the things that are Caesar's"*.

And if this weren't bad enough, (the fact that today's "soldiers for the faith" have become an army of complacent, stupid and cowardly collaborators who by their actions are assisting in the fabrication of the same supremacist agenda that their Master gave his life tearing down 20 centuries past) what is worse is the manner in which they envision themselves as possessed of all the strength that will be needed when the *real battle* begins and the moment in which their own personal "moment of truth" arrives.

For anyone who has participated in these discussions with today's apocalyptically-minded Christians, individuals who are anticipating at any moment the arrival of the Antichrist, rarely is there to be found an individual among them who doubts that his or her faith will get them through the future trials that are forthcoming. Whether they are Catholic or Protestant matters little in their insistence that they will stand under the weight of all adversity that Christ's arch-enemy will be throwing at them. They envision themselves in the same imagery of Christianity's former freedom fighters and who will be bravely facing down the barrel of a gun and saying without reservation that they stand by their Master, knowing what lies ahead within the next few seconds as a result.

The problem for many of them lies in their apparent inability to employ a requisite amount of abstract thinking, something that should not be that difficult, considering how abstractly written the prophecies concerning the end times really are. After all, are they really expecting to see a beast with 7 heads and ten horns, with blasphemies written on each head? Are they really expecting to see a dragon spewing forth water from its mouth to drown the mother and her son, as well as sweeping a third of the stars out of the sky with its tail? Understanding the vision that John had on the island of Patmos should be, if they knew their own roots better, not that difficult. His vision of the beast was nothing more than the re-emergence of the same Jewish supremacist agenda that opposed Christ, that put him to death and which hunted down and persecuted his followers. His vision of the beast who was *"wounded in the head and yet lived"* perfectly conforms to the re-creation of the state of Israel in the 20th century and the deification of the Jews as God's chosen people, circumstances that are in absolute variance to the message of universal brotherhood that was preached by Christ. The depiction of the false prophet, as well as his now infamous 'mark of the beast' go hand in hand with an accurate understanding of those who, either actively or passively, assist in and acquiesce to the demands of the Jewish supremacist agenda in elevating such individuals to a position far above the rest of humanity.

None of this should be a surprise to those Christians who make all the pretenses of being watchful for the return of their Master, and who wear an air of smugness about them that betrays their own sense of undeserved self-confidence, individuals who are quick to assert that they have remained as *"wise as serpents"* in these heady days. For most of them, they have spent a good portion of their time in recent years awaiting the arrival of the storm that was predicted some 2,000 years ago, but who now are to be found in the midst of it and yet who are too blind to recognize it for what it is.

In addition to being a maddening thing to watch, it is an embarrassing thing as well, as these individuals run like frightened mice in the face of even a *private* discussion of the Jewish supremacist agenda, but who puff out their chests and claim that they will possess all the strength they need when the expression of their faith is required of them in a manner open, blatant and bold. They claim by such an argument to possess all the faith necessary to order mountains to hurl themselves into the sea with but a word, but yet who do not now possess enough faith to hurl a small stone at the Goliath of the Jewish supremacist agenda that is responsible for destroying all that was their culture.

And in such a way, today's Christians who refuse to stand against this beast known as the Jewish supremacist agenda have become the same followers of the beast that were predicted would arrive in the end times.

It is for this reason therefore that we can justly entertain more of an expectation that it will be those in the Muslim world who will be rewarded with the proverbial Medal of Honor for having resisted the Antichrist than we can for today's Christians. Events have a funny way of working themselves out in reality, and just as in the time of Christ, in which the Jews who were originally chosen to bring the message of justice to the world rejected all the sacrifices that such a mission entailed, so too are today's Christians found occupying a similar position. And in the same manner, just as the honor and duty of bringing that message was handed over to the Gentiles during Christ's time, so too today does it appear that will it be done with those in the Muslim world.

Critical Mass

If such a futile argument *could* be made with regards to what is taking place today, that little there is that can be done to effect the situation in any substantive manner, then certainly no such argument can be made as it pertains to what was taking place a century ago, when this beast still remained in its cage, but who was then set free upon mankind with the active participation of the Christian world. Today's situation as it pertains to the Jewish supremacist agenda and the destructiveness that is its undeniable by-product is a classic case wherein the sins of the father are handed down and placed upon the heads of his children, who bear the brunt of his foolishness and who are left with the task of cleaning up the mess that he has created.

If there is one dictum in history that will remain a constant, it is that people never learn from it. There has never been a civilization that has been able (with any authority) to make the claim that they were the exception, although many today foolishly attempt to do so. And so it is with those in the Christian West, who a century ago forgot who they were and what they were about, and thus allowed the seeds of their own destruction to be sowed by their enemies.

Given that the talk around town these days concerns "weapons of mass destruction" and "so and so's nuclear program," etc, etc, all done for the purpose of justifying a continued state of war in the Middle East as well as in keeping the masses distracted as to what the *real reasons* for these wars are, then it is perfectly appropriate therefore that we remain within the scope of this theme, albeit in a somewhat tangential manner. And given the fact that the West is about to begin phase two of the war for the Zionist Empire, the invasion of Iran and Syria (which will of course be preceded by some terrorist incident, and assisted no doubt by America's best friend in the region, Israel) it then makes perfect sense that in maintaining this theme, we discuss one of the most important components to this type of weaponry that exists, that component being something known as critical mass.

In its essence critical mass is the process by which an exponential increase of energy takes place when enough individual components of nuclear material are gathered together. Simply explained, what happens is that as a result of the close proximity each shares with the others, they begin energizing each other with electrons that are perpetually escaping by virtue of their radioactive nature. What results is a nuclear reaction, whose destructive capabilities should by now be understood by all.

This is exactly what mankind is facing today, in that we are experiencing the results of critical mass — not of nuclear material — but rather of this poisonous and dangerously destructive element found within the periodic table of human sentiments, the ethno-religious political ideology known as Jewish supremacism. The manner in which Western Civilization is being destroyed is the product of the fact that there has been an accumulation of various entities whose "radioactive nature" is such that they possess a proclivity towards devouring and replacing any existing order with the supremacist schedule that they have envisioned. Although these properties have existed for the last 2,000 years, this agenda has posed only limited danger by virtue of the fact that the various entities remained scattered and separate, although obviously they have succeeded from time to time in "sickening" to some extent the communities within which they were to be found. However, now that they have been gathered together again, (and have done so within the protective confines of a nation-state no less) what we see taking place is the process of critical mass, and with it the exponentially explosive and dangerous effects to surrounding living tissue.

The "living tissue," about which we speak allegorically are the cultures and peoples of the world who have had to suffer the brutality of the Jewish supremacist agenda in a direct way now for the last century. The first of these, the peoples and cultures of the Middle East can be accurately said to occupy ground zero, where the most immediate and dramatic results of this nuclear reaction are taking place. They are the ones suffering from the literal application of violence on a daily basis as represented in the bombings, shootings, and all the other manifestations of modern warfare. But they are by no means the only ones who have been adversely affected by this situation.

Just as in any literal nuclear incident, there are others who have been sickened as well from the "radiation poisoning" that has been released into the air as a result of this critical mass, and when we speak of these victims, the entity who has obviously suffered from these effects the worst are the members of the Christian West, who have drunk from the spiritual, intellectual and sociological well that has been deliberately poisoned by operatives within this agenda. As opposed to the dramatic, immediate effects that have characterized what has taken place in the Middle East, by contrast that which exemplifies the terminal condition of the West has been more slow and gradual. The effects suffered by the West of this type of radiation poisoning are similar to that which are produced by the real thing, in that their societies have been physically and intellectually weakened and thus easily led by the nose into executing whatever actions they have been ordered to perform by overlords whose immune systems are not effected by such toxins. They are listless, docile, incoherent, contradictory, and in some cases, as can be easily ascertained by the behavior exhibited by those in the Christian Zionist community, mad.

Thus it becomes easy to see then why the Jewish supremacist agenda has been absolutely maniacal in maintaining a program of propagandizing those in Christian West in favor of Israeli interests, as well as in pouring into their thinking the poisonous elixir of Jewish supremacist sentiments, a love potion designed to induce the members of this civilization into adopting the dogmatic theme that such individuals are "God's chosen people". Were it not for the active (and passive) support of the Christian World, there would be no such thing as Israel, and thus no such thing as critical mass of Jewish supremacist interests. It has been a coin with two sides, a scheme that was brilliantly conceived and executed with even more brilliant precision, the poisoning of a civilization that has been marked for death while using that civilization and its resources to do all the dirty work in the process. A more relevant comparison would be the instances during the previous century wherein the thugs of Jewish Bolshevism had their victims dig their own graves, and having completed this, shot them in the back of the head. Likewise, by adopting this "most favored nation" status in the human realm, what the Jewish supremacist agenda has done is to induce the Christian world into participating in its own program of suicide, although scarce few realize this to be the case, even though the evidence of their culture's terminal condition is displayed right before their eyes on a daily basis.

What must be remembered though is that such fantastic leaps into this realm of unreality, this deification of the Jewish people, could not have taken place until the thinking processes of those in the West had been degraded and corrupted to the point wherein they were reduced to that of functioning idiots. In accomplishing this, what has been done has been to implement a process of degrading the intellectual and spiritual health of those in the West through constant exposure to violence, pornography, forced acceptance of the sodomite lifestyle, the defiling of women and marriage, slaughter of the unborn, and in all other ways, the destabilization of the moral order upon which their collective mental health was firmly rested, an accomplishment that has been realized over the course of the last half century through the influence of those who have been operatives within the Jewish supremacist agenda. And what we must keep in mind is that this thing which began as a voluntary program of acquiescing to the demands of this agenda soon will become, if indeed it has not already, a *forced* program of acceptance and acquiescence, the proverbial *"mark of the beast,"* about which the Christian Zionists seem to dedicate so much of their energy towards discussing, the refusal of which will result in imprisonment or death. It is this fact with which those in the Christian world must come to terms before it is upon them in an unavoidable way, for as this storm approaches, it is but sheer foolishness that is entertained by those in the Christian world that somehow or another this system will shift course or in some other way be rendered harmless. The point is, they need to prepare themselves, either by battening down the hatches or by fleeing, but believing that they will survive this thing in tact is a vision of things to come that has little chance of bearing itself out in reality.

Cause and effect

In coming to terms with the nature of historical events and their origins, those studying such items look at them not as entities in and of themselves, but rather as chemical compositions that are the results of other combined entities. As such, when an individual considers the history involving the manner in which Western Civilization was formed, those studying this socio-political compound must look at what went into its composition in determining the recipe that was used in making up its existence. And for all the arguments that many ir-religionists may offer about the importance that was offered by the Greeks and the Romans and the other secular ingredients making up the West, the one component whose absence in the mix absolutely changes the nature of this civilization in an undeniable way is the religion of Christianity. Christianity was as indispensable in this mix as yeast would have been in making bread, and if the absence of Christianity would have resulted in something else having been created, than what needs to be considered is the importance of those events which were the turning points in the creation of this history. Having said this then, one can easily make the argument that had it not been for the events that took place in 70 AD, Western Civilization as it has been known might not have been born, or at least not in the way in which we have come to know it over the course of the last 2,000 years.

The reason that 70 AD is and has remained a watermark event is for the simple reason that this struggling new resistance movement to the Jewish supremacist agenda, Christianity, was given a long-needed and well-deserved break. Up until this point, things were looking rather bad for this band of 1st century freedom fighters from Palestine, who, on a regular basis were being hounded, chased, arrested, beaten, tortured and put to death. What they were up against was the most powerful military and economic entity in the world at that time, the Roman Empire, whose political machinery was bit by bit being co-opted into serving the interests of the Jewish supremacist agenda. The emperor Nero had himself converted to the religion of Pharisaical Judaism, and he along with his wife Poppea, was heavily under the influence of the rabbis who sat in his court and advised him. The infamous persecutions that were inflicted upon nascent Christianity were the result of this influence, as evidenced by the manner in which the rabbis suggested that, after Rome was burned to accommodate the construction of Nero's new palace, the Christians be blamed for this act, along with the inevitable campaign to hunt them down and destroy them. Given the fact that the precedent had been set and that Nero, being the madman that he was, would have, (just like the new Roman emperor, George Bush) most likely ceded over to the rabbis in his court more and more influence, it is more than mere conjecture to say that Christianity, the *salt* that brought flavor to the world in the form of Western Civilization, would have been wiped out in due time.

What changed all of this was what took place in 70 AD when the members of the Jewish supremacist agenda (who have always suffered by virtue of overreach when it comes to implementing their schedule) bit the hand that fed them and began a campaign to rid Palestine of Roman occupation. What resulted was an overwhelming invasion by the Romans who dispersed the various parts of this entity to the farthest reaches of what was at that time the known world. Besides their dispersion, the centerpiece of their identity and source of the Sanhedrin's power, the Temple, was destroyed completely, not one stone having been left upon another, just as Christ predicted would take place.

And thus, what we as students of history see having taken place was the prevention of this "nuclear reaction" of the Jewish supremacist agenda, for by breaking up its critical mass, the various entities could not energize each other in pushing forward what was a dangerous agenda for mankind.

"We have now what we have always wanted..."

It is not surprising that those in the West would completely miss the historical significance of the previous discussion as it pertains to the concentration of power in the hands of a few individuals possessed of what is by any measurable standards a criminal mentality. For all the noise that those in the "enlightened West" make over what they perceive to be their intellectual and political heritage; namely an inherent distrust of the concentration of power in the hands of a few individuals who seek it, nevertheless what must be remembered is that they are nothing more than *heirs* to this legacy, and rarely can there be found an heir who was the equal of his forefathers. In general, heirs have been fools who did not possess the mental energy or character sufficient to create a fortune on their own, and who in most cases have acted as the prodigal son in squandering whatever it was that they were given.

Likewise in the West, it is obvious how much these individuals value this thing called "freedom" today as well as how much distrust they maintain towards those who thirst for power, a reality that is impossible to deny when considering the manner in which they have allowed the most power-hungry among them, the fanatics of the Jewish supremacist agenda to ascend the highest positions that are attainable in their respective societies. Therefore, it only makes sense then that such individuals would miss the significance of the previous discussion concerning critical mass. However, what we must remember is that this tendency is but one aspect of the overall intellectual breakdown that has afflicted the greater part of those in the West, and which is, in this case, merely a manifestation of denial.

The tendency in the West towards this denial of what in the best of terms is gangsterism, pure and simple, is something that is a curious thing to watch, particularly since the very theme of gangsterism has occupied such an important place in Western media and journalism. It seems that every ethnic group has a particular gangster theme in its own culture that is put before the consideration of the public on a regular basis. The Italians, Irish, Chinese, Colombians, Russians, etc, etc, all have some legacy of gangsterism attached to their identities whose unflattering implications are discussed without any concern paid to what kind of defamation such a discussion may bring to the rest of the group. The only group who has escaped being the subject of such an unpleasant discussion has been the Jews, even though their place in this lineup is, comparatively speaking, more justified and noteworthy than any of the others. After all, the rest of the ethnic groups can only boast of *wielding* influence from time to time, and usually in a very limited political location such as a city, whereas the gangsters of the Jewish supremacist agenda can brag of *possessing* a nation-state of their own, that being Israel. And, again, unfortunately, there are few in the West who will appreciate the importance of this item, and particularly those afflicted with the mania of Christian Zionism who will look upon the re-creation of the state of Israel in the 20th century as a direct manifestation of God's goodness to mankind.

What we must remember is that these individuals, the followers of the beast, are the fulfillment of the dire warnings that were uttered by the fathers of the early Christian church. They are the 'ignorant and unstable individuals' who were predicted would be arriving towards the end of time bringing with them a program of destruction for everyone else. They are 'conflicted in everything that they do,' and suffer from as much myopia as did the Jews of Christ's time in seeing that he was the fulfillment of the promise they had been given generations past. The hysteria that the adherents of this oxymoronic religion known as Christian Zionism maintain over the return of Christ that accompanies all the support that they give to the state of Israel would be laughable were it not attached to such serious issues. Were it not for the fact that they drone on and on about the manner in which they are going to be sucked up into heaven prior to all the tribulations that are going to befall mankind one would have real trouble understanding the processes at work within their minds. But it is this thing, the *rapture,* as they describe it that offers the best explanation for all of it. It, like all others mechanisms of corruption wielded by the Jewish supremacist agenda, paints a perfect picture as to why individuals such as these can hold two contradictory pieces of information simultaneously and still manage to function. This promise of reward, the rapture, is the modern-day equivalent of the 30 pieces of silver that Judas accepted in betraying his Master and which rendered him senseless by its allure. Likewise, those calling themselves Christian who are possessed with the mania of the worship of the Jewish people have been rendered senseless as well, and blind to the reality that the re-creation of Israel in the 20th century was from its inception not an act of God, but rather an act of his nemesis, and for reasons that we will discuss now.

In the film *The Godfather II*, the sequel to the first film, the fictional gangster Hyman Roth (whose character was based upon the life of real gangster Meyer Lansky) was celebrating the fact that his crime syndicate had just completed a deal with the government of pre-Castro Cuba. He ended his celebratory words with something that had ominous implications to it, although many in the West would not grasp these implications even though they have been drawn out and realized in the real-life events of today.

"What I am saying is that we now have what we have always wanted...Real partnership with a government".

The implications attached to these words are simple yet extremely dramatic:

Individuals such as these, possessed with a gangster mindset and criminal agenda can do whatever they want by virtue of the fact that they enjoy the protection and insulation afforded to them by their partnership with a nation-state.

And if mere *partnership* with a nation-state can be a dangerous situation, just imagine then how dangerous it is when these individuals *become* the nation-state, and possess not only insulation, but the sovereignty and power to enforce their agenda, backed up with an arsenal of nuclear, chemical and biological weapons.

This is the situation as it exists today with regards to the physical manifestation of the Jewish supremacist agenda, the state of Israel, and is the very scenario whose existence was prevented by the destruction of the Temple in 70 AD. As a result of the *scattering* that took place of these radioactive elements making up this agenda to the farthest corners of the known world at that time, in breaking up the cohesiveness of this gangster agenda and by destabilizing it in such a way that it could not attain the power for which it hungered, the world was given a respite, the absence of which would have changed things dramatically. Had the Jewish supremacist agenda succeeded in firmly entrenching itself within the power structure of the Roman Empire at that time and remained there long enough, then the last 2,000 years would most likely have been a completely different story. After plugging in all the variables of this situation, what the student of history is left to reasonably conclude is that the Roman Empire would have been co-opted into implementing this supremacist agenda to the detriment of Western Civilization, and we need look no further than at what has taken place with regards to present circumstances in validating this theory.

Today, as this agenda has wormed its way like a cancer into the new Roman Empire (America and the rest of the Western nations whom she drags along with her on her expeditions) it has made her an instrument in satisfying the demands of this agenda and of dispersing its poisons throughout the world. In such a situation, war, pornography, abortion, economic exploitation, the destruction of the nuclear family and of all God-centered religions and morals takes place in the interests of erecting a humanist, materialist plantation ruled by overlords who espouse the sentiments of greed, hedonism and viciousness...and all of this has become the duty that the West in general and America in particular have been consigned to execute for the interests of Israel and for her philosophical lifeblood, the Jewish supremacist agenda.

Conversely, it was those who were charged with preventing this scenario from re-emerging who, in complete disregard for history and for the lessons that it has tried to impart, allowed the reversal of this situation to take place and who have thus endangered the world in a manner never experienced before. The Christian world, *who knew better than anyone else* what kind of danger existed in the re-emergence of this criminal agenda and who therefore possessed the greatest reasons for preventing this from taking place, instead sat back and allowed the cage that had housed this beast for 20 centuries to be unlocked and by doing so cooperated with the business of setting him loose upon humanity. Now, the Christian West, a hull of what it once was, sits back and wails over what has been the inevitable product of this foolish and tragic mistake, the destruction of her civilization, and thus the sins of the father are handed down like any other inheritance into the lives of his children.

In sum, what this means is that when Christianity's founding father counseled his followers the week in which he was murdered concerning the future of mankind, he was not speaking metaphorically when he depicted the founding fathers of the Zionist ideology as the physical embodiment of the Devil sent to implement his agenda. It is but a fool who considers the warnings uttered by the Palestinian freedom fighter known as Jesus of Nazareth as something that was meant only for that time period, a situation that clearly is not the case today.

"When you see standing in the Holy Place (the holy land) the abomination that causes desolation spoken of through the prophet Daniel, let the reader understand...for then there will be great distress unequaled from the beginning of the world until now, and never to be equaled again".

And if this weren't enough, then what should have complimented his first words was his warning that

"The day will come when your enemies will build an embankment against you and encircle you in on every side. They will dash you to the ground, you and the children within your walls. They will not leave one stone upon another, because you did not recognize the time of God's coming".

In more plain and down-to-earth terms, what this means is that the Christian world, in allowing the descendants of the Sanhedrin to regroup in Palestine, and by assisting in undoing that which took place 2,000 years ago and which saved them from certain destruction, have facilitated in bringing about this process known as critical mass that we see today...and in assisting in the entrenchment of this gangster ideology known as the Jewish supremacist agenda as it is manifested in the state of Israel, what they have done is to assist in the return of the very same Antichrist, the beast of the apocalypse whom they were charged with keeping locked up 20 centuries past. And thus, in so doing, tragically they have become one of the heads of this beast, and absent that, have become an army of his followers.

And thus we see why the Christian world, Western Civilization, has been destroyed in all but name, *not one stone having been left upon another,* as well as the manner in which the West has been encircled from every side by its mortal enemies. It is for this reason that the children of the West have been *"dashed to the ground"* through the systematic process of their physical murder by infanticide and abortion, and why it is that those who have escaped the abortionist's knife walk around as the spiritually and intellectually limbless, a tragic result of the slaughter that has taken place upon their minds and hearts. It is because of the carelessness of those in the Christian world that today their children are found murdering each other in their schools and neighborhoods and why they have embraced all the characteristics of the gangster lifestyle—prostitution, pimping, pornography, promiscuity, violence, hedonism and all the other ugly fruits of this existence that have been celebrated through a media run by the Jewish supremacist agenda. And, lest we forget, there are the wars, both the present and future to be fought for the Jewish supremacist agenda that are only in the beginning stage and which promise the deaths of even more, given the scope and the ambitiousness of this agenda's desires.

When considered in this light, it is apparent now just how backwards is the depiction that is entertained by maniacal Christian Zionists as they view the return of Christ for the defeat of his enemies. His return, in whatever manner it takes place, will not be some kind of beneficent incidental, but rather the precursor to a punishment of sorts upon those who foolishly loosed this animal known as the Jewish supremacist agenda upon humanity. Rather than jumping up and down like a nation of idiots, such individuals, and indeed the entire Christian West should be trembling with fear, and particularly so when they consider the manner in which they themselves have assisted in the creation of this Antichrist agenda known as Zionism and its physical manifestation in the state of Israel.

****

In closing let me say that my one great hope is that all my analyses, predictions and worries turn out to be unfounded. My sincere desire is that the picture that is being painted here of the times in which we find ourselves today and tomorrow is but the product of an overactive imagination. I would gladly endure the public ridicule of being wrong, of being laughed at and of possessing no credibility on anything for the rest of my life in return for the peace that such a situation would create. To awaken from this nightmare and find out that truly things are all right, and that I can go back to the business of raising my family without needing to watch the horizon would be a dream come true.

Conversely, my great fear is that none of these reversals will bear themselves out, and that in the end I will be proven correct.

As so, as the issue comes full circle and all is brought to completion, let us end this voyage by saying that what the world needs, and more importantly what the Christian West needs to do is to embrace in a *complete* way the idea that charity begins at home, understanding by such that their very existence depends upon them applying this sentiment with all the militancy that they are capable of mustering. Their lives, as well as the lives of those whom they love—their children, families, nations and the civilization that was founded upon the teachings of Palestine's first freedom fighter—all these stand at the precipice of destruction, and destruction in a manner *"unequaled from the beginning of the world until now, and never to be equaled again"*.

Having embraced this idea, may this frank discussion we have had serve as one small stone cast at the Goliath of the Jewish supremacist agenda. May this stone cause such waves that others will be motivated to do the same, and that by such a campaign, we may be rewarded with liberation from those espousing the logic of Cain who have so infected the world with this diseased thinking. The fruits of this liberation; goodwill, justice, mercy, the appreciation of innocent life—all these things are precious beyond measure, despite the fact that they have been devalued by this brood of vipers who feast off of the destruction of all that is good and decent.

And in this way, let us cry out with one voice, understanding what is at stake for humanity, motivated by, if for no other reason, the fact that charity does indeed begin at home.

"And the Jews said in boasting "We killed Christ Jesus, son of Mary, the Messenger of Allah.' Nay, Allah raised him up unto Himself, and Allah is exalted in power and in wisdom. And there is none among the people of the Book who may not believe in him, in Jesus son of Mary before his death, nor on the day of Judgment, for He will be a witness against them."
– The Qur'an, Islam's most holy book, Surah IV

"I still remember old Jews spitting while passing by a church, and cursing the dead while passing by a Christian cemetery. Last year in Jerusalem, a Jew decided to refresh the tradition. He spat at the Holy Cross carried in the procession along the city. "

"Last year, the biggest Israeli tabloid Yedioth Aharonoth reprinted in its library the Jewish anti-Gospel, Toledoth Eshu, compiled in the Middle Ages. If the Gospel is the book of love, Toledoth is the book of hate for Christ. The hero of the book is Judas. He captures Jesus by polluting his purity. According to Toledoth, the conception of Christ was in sin, the miracles of Jesus were witchcraft, his resurrection but a trick."

"Even today, Jews in Israel refer to Jesus by the demeaning word Yeshu (instead of Yeshua), meaning "Perish his name". In a similar pun, the New Testament Gospel is called "Avon Gilaion", the booklet of Sin. These are the endearing feelings that the friends of Christian Zionists maintain towards Christ."

– Israel Shamir, Israeli Jew turned Christian writer and anti-Zionist

----

"Hassidic Jewish children called Jesus 'Yoshke' a mocking name meant for the village idiot; some grown-ups called him the Yimach Sh'moinick, the one whose name should be blotted out, the traitorous Jew who had brought disaster upon his people."

– Yossi Klein Halevi, author of "Memoirs of a Jewish Extremist."

"Israel is able to stifle free speech, control our Congress, and even dictate our foreign policy."
– Paul Findley, former US Congressman and author of the book "They Dare to Speak Out."

The Rest of the Story

"Mary, God has chosen thee, and purified thee. He has chosen thee above all women. ....Mary, God gives thee good tidings from Him whose name is Messiah, Jesus, son of Mary. High honored shall he be, in this world and the next, stationed near to God. He shall speak to men in the cradle and of old age, and righteous shall he be."
"Blessed has he made me," said Jesus, "wherever I may be, and He has enjoined me to give alms, so long as I live, and likewise to cherish my mother. He has not made me arrogant or unprosperous. Peace be upon me the day that I was born, and the day that I die, and the day that I am raised up alive."

Most Americans reading the above passages would assume that they were written by a Christian, or that it was to be found in some kind of Christian literature. The fact is, (surely to the surprise of many) that it was taken from the Qur'an, Islam's most sacred book.

It certainly would be a surprise to most Americans, considering the fact that they have been fed a smorgasbord of propaganda concerning the religion of Islam and its adherents for the last 2 years that conspicuously has made no mention of how Mother and Son are so revered by those in the Middle East whose culture has now been scheduled for destruction. To the opposite, the racists who run our media and, who by default have assumed the power of doing our thinking for us have painted the religion of Islam as something organically inimical to Christianity and Christian culture. One in particular, and lately much discussed is the rabid Zionist extraordinaire and racist of no apologies Daniel Pipes (recently appointed by Bush to sit in on the Board of the United States Institute of Peace) who has made his living and his fame over the period of the last decade with publications whose one and only purpose has been to slur the peoples of the Middle East.

Also a part of his repertoire in Muslim bashing has been his refusal in attempting to hide the fact that his primary reasons for doing so have been for the purpose of benefiting his co-religionists in the nation of Israel, whose racist ideology he seems to embrace without any detectable reserve. Were any other person foolish enough to voice only some of the opinions that Pipes has been bold enough to put down on paper, they would have been run out of the business, if not worse. The fact that he has endured and has in fact been rewarded for such sentiments speaks volumes about what is the double standard which exists in the United States today as pertains race and religious issues, particularly when they are applied to the situation involving Israel and the Middle East.

For those who are still holding out on whether or not to accept the "conspiracy crackpot theory" that the US government and media have been captured and are dominated by racist ideologues who worship before the golden calf of Zionism, consider some of the following quotes which Pipes has authored, and allow reason to weigh in on the fact that this man has not endured the standard treatment that others receive when they voice sentiments that only *appear* to be racial in nature.

"All immigrants bring exotic customs and attitudes, but Muslim customs are more troublesome than most. West European societies are unprepared for the massive immigration of brown-skinned peoples cooking strange foods and not exactly maintaining Germanic standards of hygiene."

A quick translation of the above statement would read like this: Muslims are the worst of immigrants, who, smelling bad and having an unusual palate, are not welcome in societies of superior white people.

The Golden Boy of the Zionist establishment has not limited his remarks to only these mentioned. In other writings he accuses Muslims of being parasites on society, being disproportionately engaged in criminal behavior, (most notably the crime of rape) of having unacceptable customs and seeking to take over the country.

In short, this is the stuff of the infamous Ku Klux Klan. Replace the word "Muslim" with "black" or "nigger," and the comparison is without equal.
How then is it possible for such men to possess the amount of

prestige and influence as he does, without being subject to the same backlash that would result from someone else engaging in such behavior? Quite simply, he is an example of the "politically correct" racist, meaning, a racist in favor of Israel and Judaism, and, unfortunately, he is only one of many who work diligently in keeping Americans from hearing the rest of the story.

Only in a nation whose government, media, and culture have been hijacked by the interests of an ideology so naziesque in its nature such as Zionism could such statements have been made by an individual without any resulting serious repercussions. In a nation where someone is attacked in an overtly coordinated effort for merely speaking out against the verifiable history of Israeli violence and duplicity (or for that matter, simply making a film concerning the crucifixion of Jesus Christ) the fact that individuals such as Daniel Pipes could get away with saying such things speaks volumes about what is the deplorable state of intellectual dishonesty in American society. Thus has the ability for intellectual discourse degraded to such a point that to engage in any discussion which only *slightly* whiffs of criticism against the biggest practitioner of terrorism in the Middle East results in a society of unthinking, uninterested reactionaries who will, like Pavlov's dogs, jump up and start barking the mantra of "anti-Semitism" for the sole purpose of quieting their opponents. Had he not been a stalwart supporter of Israel and said the same thing about any other group of people, (and especially if it were said *against* his cohorts in Tel Aviv) he would have received a one-way ticket down the infamous memory hole, never to return, as have all those who have committed the unforgivable crime of not bowing down before the Balaam of Zionism.

The recent outrage over Bush's nomination of Pipes for a seat on the United States Institute of Peace is quite a telling event as well, especially when viewed within the context of the now obvious double standard applied to others not so favored. Consider how the Bush Administration (and in fact the Republican Congress in general) reacted to the media-managed frenzy swirling around former Senate Majority Leader Trent Lott for having attended a gathering in honor of a white segregationist. They wouldn't touch him with a ten-foot pole for fear of the obvious tainting they would acquire by association with him. Now comes forth a man such as Pipes, whose overt bigotry makes the implied bigotry of Lott look pale by comparison, and yet where are the hourly news stories? Where are the interviews, wherein Pipes and others like him are stuttering and stammering for an answer which they hope will pacify a society nurtured on the religion of anti-racism? Where are all the individuals from the ADL and other like-minded groups calling for Pipes' resignation? Where is the distancing of the Republicans from such a man? In this light, the favoritism afforded to politically correct racists as well as the complicity that exists in the outlets of mass information in the proliferation of such sentiments becomes clearer. Besides the fact that Pipes did not get the ax (as so many others have and do to this day) whenever they utter phrases as outrageously racist as were his, conversely he has been rewarded for such statements, as evidenced by his recent nomination. But even more telling is the fact that Bush, who most assuredly was briefed by his advisors on what was the background of Pipes and his writings, obviously saw nothing to fear in associating himself politically with such a reprobate bigot, and his insistence upon putting this man in such a position speaks loudly not only about his own fearlessness concerning what would most assuredly be the backlash to such an event, but as well about his fear of what would happen to him politically if he didn't. In short, Bush was assured by his hirelings that there would be no negative fallout from such an appointment, due to the fact that it would get little to no coverage by a cooperative media, but as well that there would be serious consequences to face if such an appointment were not forthcoming. How else are we to view his willingness to nominate such a man who once agreed with the notion originally espoused by a spokesman for the KKK that "if we fail to stop the Muslims now, the sixteen million niggers of America will soon be Muslims, and you will never be able to stop them."

The nomination of Pipes to sit in on the United States Institute of Peace, having justifiably caused a firestorm among Arab and Muslim groups here in the US, nevertheless must be tempered in view of the fact that Pipes is just one man in an army of like-minded ideologues who occupy seats of power in the United States. They are individuals who have gotten away with this very same thing for not just years, but rather for decades, and who in citing the Qur'an have squandered no opportunity in fitting whatever text may be used to portray the religion of Islam in the worst light, even if it means taking passages completely out of context. They understand their audience well, knowing that here in the United States few Christians have ever read the Qur'an and know only what is alleged to be contained in it from the likes of pseudo right-wing talk show hosts and fundamentalist maniacal Christian Zionists, who on a daily basis hurl ethnic, religious, and cultural slurs towards a group of people whom they are paid to demonize. Those individuals in media and academia who shape America's thinking (and by default America's policies) are capitalizing on the abysmal ignorance of the average uninformed American as to what comprises not only the religion of Islam, but Middle Eastern culture in general. In addition, these peddlers of men's souls have successfully decoded just how to utilize the bitterness that has grown over the last few decades in conservative-minded Christians whose religion and whose values have been attacked by these very same degenerate elites who now have decided to target the Muslims. Hoping that no one noticed the slight-of-hand, the secular atheists who have for decades worked tirelessly in deconstructing what was the Christian social order of America were removed from the suspicious role they had justly occupied, and through their own concerted efforts had themselves replaced with the same "brown-skinned peoples" named by Pipes and others like him, whom he and his fellow gangsters now seek to marginalize in the interest of bringing Israel's enemies to heel.

Besides the fact that these individuals obviously enjoy the protection of a media which applaud their sentiments and their agenda, they can also rest well at night knowing that not too many people will hit the books and check out their facts. This is unfortunate, since the Qur'an is not very long, nor is it difficult to read. Equally unfortunate is the fact that were Americans better readers, they would find an entire world of information that would prove to be quite a stumbling block for the arguments offered by those seeking to misinform America about not only her relationship with Islam, but as well about her relationship with Israel. And while it is true that there have been liars, propagandists and slanderers in every age, it is true as well that only in an age wherein the intellectual capacity (or rather intellectual willingness) of the people has been reduced to the level of an unthinking mob of Roman spectators can such a program of mass-hypnotism take place. After all, had Americans been skeptical about the information they were fed about the Middle East situation after September 11, they might have read the passages in the Qur'an which have never been mentioned by a Zionist controlled media who have conspicuously told only a small part of the story.

The small part told has been that section dealing with the darker history of Islam, which, as religions go, has no more skeletons in its closet than do any of the other religions of the world. What has not been mentioned (as it was in the commencement of this discussion) is the manner in which Muslims hold Christ and his mother in such high regard, nor has been mentioned anything concerning the accomplishments which Islam has been responsible for bringing to Western Civilization. In effect, the bringers of mass information have scoured the photo albums of Islamic history for snapshots of those unfortunate moments which have occurred, and in the interest of misleading an uncritical public mind have presented these snapshots to the world as being the entirety of its history. A discerning people should have suspected this, but, as can be expected in a civilization which has surrendered its soul and intellect to the idols of materialism and self-gratification, thinking past these idols proved to be too expensive.

The rest of the story that has been cleverly been kept out of public view (and therefore out of public consideration) is the amount of influence that the interests of Israel (once described by a prominent Jewish-American reporter as the "elephant in the room which no one wants to acknowledge") have played in the whole equation. In the days and weeks following the tragedies on 9/11, the discussion of the relationship between the US and Israel and its relevance to the day's events were carefully kept out of the media mainstream. Anyone at the time who (rightfully and logically so) brought it up for discussion was quieted down in a hurry, for fear that people may begin to question the propriety of an alliance that has up to that day been kept sacrosanct. Had Americans began to consider their association with Israel and the cause and effect circumstances as pertain to that day's events, they might also have learned of important events in the history of that relationship, such as those concerning the attack on the USS Liberty, Israeli espionage against the US for the benefit of America's enemies, and a whole host of other embarrassing tidbits that may have jeopardized the stability of what has been (at least to Israel) a fruitful and lucrative situation. But on a more simple level, Americans who took their Christian faith seriously might have also run into upsetting items involving religious sentiments, a topic willingly discussed when it demonizes

THE REST OF THE STORY

Muslims, but carefully avoided when it embarrasses Jews. However, given the willingness of the Ministry of Truth to discuss religious sentiments so as to better understand the mindset of America's "enemies," by the same standard a similar discussion should take place when it comes to understanding America's "friends," even at the risk of sacrificing sacred cows.

"Miriam, mother of the Nazarene, was the descendant of princes and governors who played the harlot with carpenters." *Sanhedrin 106a*

"Jesus the Nazarene practiced sorcery and black magic, and led Jews astray into idolatry. He was sexually immoral, worshipped statues of stone, was cut off from the Jewish people, and refused to repent." *Sanhedrin 107b*

"The books of the Christians must not be saved from fire." *Shabat 116a*

"The best of the Gentiles should be killed." *Soferim 15, rule 10*

For the uninitiated, these few passages are excerpts of the Talmud, a book considered to be as sacred to Judaism as the Qur'an is to Islam. These excerpts are but a few of the many passages which speak with an unmistakable and undeniable invective against the same Jesus and Mary who are so honored by the Muslims, but which have suspiciously escaped being mentioned in the discourse concerning religious hatred and its relationship to terrorism. In addition to these items mentioned, there are passages which permit the rape of children, (particularly non-Jews) as well as a whole host of other religious/racist sentiments which, if made public to the audiences of Jerry Falwell, Pat Robertson, Limbaugh, Hannity, et al, may cause quite a bit of trouble for groups such as AIPAC and others like them who make it their business to promote the lie that Israel is America's "lone ally in the Middle East". In light of this, it should also be remembered that barely an instance goes by when in the context of discussing the religion of Islam by major media outlets that it isn't alleged the adherents of this religion are pedophiles and enemies of Christians.

This is the other half of the story which Americans have not been and are not told. From the mouthpieces on the right such as Limbaugh, Liddy and Hannity, to the mouthpieces on the left who have their hands spread across all channels of information, this dirty little secret has been completely left out of the equation when people such as Pipes and his ilk begin quoting religious texts of Islam, a grandstanding done for the sole purpose of furthering the cause of murdering, dispossessing, and robbing the peoples of the Middle East. In defense of the adherents of Judaism, fairly it can be argued that such racist and abominable statements cited above do not represent the sentiments of all followers of Judaism. In fact, it can be justly said that many are not and have never been acquainted with them at all. In like manner, perhaps this caveat should be applied to the Muslims as well, who in general harbor no ill feeling towards Christians or their religion.

One should not be naive enough to think that the bringers of information are not aware of the rest of the story, and with this in mind, the American public who will be the ones paying the highest price for the war against Islam must ask the logical and, considering the high stakes involved, fair questions of Mr. Pipes and those standing behind him:

"In your discussion of the ugly side of Islam, why did you leave out the ugly side of Judaism? Why were relevant passages of the Qur'an cited, but not of the Talmud? If religiously inspired sentiments such as those cited by you concerning Islam are relevant towards understanding the war on terror, then why aren't those sentiments harbored by the religion of Judaism relevant as well?"

After, all, the noble mission that men such as he are professing to realize is the awakening of the average American to the dangers of religious fundamentalism, and surely that would include everything, wouldn't it?

How then, does one account for this obvious duplicity? What is one to make of those who deliberately refuse to cite those passages of the Qur'an which speak well of Christianity, and who at the same time refuse to reveal those notable sections of the Talmud which speak so hatefully against not only the personages of the Christian faith, but of its followers as well?
The answer is not difficult to grasp. In its simplest explanation, its

understanding resides in the fact that the people in charge of disseminating information to the American public do not have Muslim names. By and large they are Jewish, and as a result promote information from a decidedly biased viewpoint in favor of Israel. The obvious importance of these circumstances should lead the average American to approach information as pertains the Middle East with a certain amount of healthy skepticism, but then one must consider the times in which these events are all taking place; It is the age of a commercial mindset, where, like the fast food business, everything is prepared quickly and likewise quickly consumed without much thought as to what is in it or what it may do to its consumer.

A further explanation of the reason for this duplicity resides in understanding that there are those whose raison d'être is the state of Israel and that which benefits her. These individuals portray themselves as loyal Americans, but who seem not to be bothered by the long list of ill effects which have resulted from American association with the Zionist state, an association which, in addition to the incontestable history of espionage and subterfuge against America and her interests, has also resulted in the acquisition of new enemies which threaten her safety in demonstrably new and dangerous ways. Men like Pipes, Perle, Wolfowitz, Limbaugh, and others who hold fast to the religion that the welfare of Israel supersedes in relevance and importance the welfare of the United States are not true Americans, for if they were, they would put America and her interests (particularly her national security) first. Being true patriots, (as well as educated and intelligent men) they would acknowledge the fact that by this *dangerous liaison* America has signed on to a mortgage whose heavy price will be American blood, sweat, and tears for the benefit of another entity whose interests and loyalty are self-serving and one-sided. But it must be understood that these wolves in sheep's' clothing already know this all too well, and as a result, quake in fear of the inevitable domino effect that would result from Americans being given the whole truth concerning the Middle East, a domino effect that would lead to the deconstructing of a dangerous and unprofitable business relationship 50 years in the making.

The day that America discovers that the entire "war on terror" is and has been from the beginning a concerted, coordinated effort brought about by individuals whose only concern is that which benefits Israel, and that it has been waged for the purposes of facilitating murder, racism, and genocide, thus begins the day that the apocalyptic dream of Zionism comes tumbling down like the Tower of Babel, and to some, this is truly a nightmare too horrible to consider. As such, individuals such as Pipes et al, in the spirit of duplicity and corruption, willingly and deliberately tell only that part of the story which serves their interests. They can be likened to the schoolyard bully, who after being pounced upon by his victims in retribution for the injustices he has wrought against them over an extended period of time, goes crying to the principal about his aggrieved status, feigning his innocence and crying his crocodile tears. They are like the parents of a girl who have entered their daughter in a beauty pageant, a girl who has neither talent nor good looks, and in the interest of calculating a victory for their daughter, bribe the judges while calumniating and intimidating the other contestants, for fear that a fair contest untainted with corruption would frustrate their hoped-for victory. In like manner, those whose sole objective is to see the racist ideology of Zionism triumph to its apocalyptic conclusion will tell only those portions of the story which will further their mission, even if it means killing millions of people in the process.

For many years, Americans have been fed half the information, information which has resulted in momentous policies and incalculable human suffering, and it is only the beginning.

Perhaps now, in a country which boasts of its hard won freedom and Christian conscience, as well as in the interest of knowing what kind of liabilities they face in this process, they should be told the rest of the story.

"When we, the followers of prophetic Judaism, returned to Palestine...the majority of the Jewish people preferred to learn from Hitler rather than from us."
— Martin Buber, Jewish philosopher and author

"Jewish villages were built in the place of Arab villages. There is not one single place that did not have a former Arab population."
— Israeli General Moshe Dayan, 1969

"Between ourselves it must be clear that there is no room for both peoples together in this country. We shall not achieve our goal if the Arabs are in this small country. The only solution is Eretz Israel, or at least all the land west of Jordan River without Arabs. There is no room for compromise on this point ... There is no other way than to transfer the Arabs from here to neighboring countries - all of them. We must not leave a single village, not a single tribe."
— Joseph Weitz, head of the Jewish Agency's Colonization Department in 1940.

"The present map of Palestine was drawn by the British mandate. The Jewish people have another map which our youth and adults should strive to fulfill — From the Nile to the Euphrates."
— David Ben Gurion, Israel's first Prime Minister

"We have to kill all the Palestinians unless they are resigned to live here as slaves."
— Chairman Heilbrun of the Committee for the Re-election of General Shlomo Lahat, the mayor of Tel Aviv, October 1983.

"The Palestinians should be crushed like grasshoppers, their heads smashed against boulders and walls."
— Israeli Prime Minister Yitzhak Shamir.

"I took the Palestinian girl captive. On the first night the soldiers pack-raped her and the next day I saw fit to remove her from the world. I had the soldiers dig a shallow grave, and then I killed the 12 year-old girl with a burst from a sub-machine gun."
— 'Moshe,' a Second Lieutenant in the Israeli army.

Grabbing a Wolf by the Ears

Thomas Jefferson, co-writer of the American Declaration of Independence and 3rd president of the United States once remarked that the introduction of slavery into a society was akin to "grabbing a wolf by the ears," in that the person grabbing the wolf must never let go for fear that if he did the wolf would devour him. Jefferson should not have limited his statement merely to the crime of enslavement, but rather, should have expanded the idea to include the crimes of oppression and systematic brutality of people as well. After all, enslavement could be argued to be any system wherein one person or a group of persons imposes their will upon others, which in its most common form is recognized as government, and that therefore enslavement as a word by itself does not suffice to explain the hideousness of the situation imposed upon its victims. Rather, the stigma of enslavement, that thing which makes it odious and which has earned it its rightful place in human understanding as a crime which calls out to heaven for justice is to be found in its oppression of people and in their subjugation to a life of violence and indignation. And he was right; one dare not let go, for if you do you are dead.

In essence what Jefferson (a slave owner himself) was saying is that human nature is such that people have long memories and that they are all imbued with the instinct to survive. Therefore, when someone or a group of people are subjected to oppression for any extended period of time, they will remember with perfect clarity the circumstances surrounding what was done to them and by whom it was done. Human nature, also imbued with the need for justice, will at sometime come calling for it, and given the level of violence with which the life of an oppressed individual was marked, it is safe to say that one can expect the same to be meted out in return, or put in simpler terms, "an eye for an eye and a tooth for a tooth." History has born the obvious proof of this out in the various slave revolts that have occurred from the time of Rome to the post-colonial age areas wherein Europeans were responsible for subjugating indigenous peoples to lives of oppression.

If examples from the past do not convince the reader of the truth in Jefferson's prediction, than the present should, in examining the relationships that exist between white Americans and those whose ancestors were the victims of the kind of oppression which he names. Beginning with the Native Americans, it would be difficult if not impossible to find any sense of overall favorable sentiments by the majority of them towards white Americans, and how could one expect otherwise? They, the Native Americans, are today a group of people whose ancestors were forced out of their lands, starved, shot, and lied to at almost every turn by a group of people intent first upon enslaving them and later on stealing their lands. To say that the white Americans of today do not bear any responsibility for the suffering of those in the past holds obvious merit in its most basic sense, but at the same time, means nothing to the average Native American who today is born on a reservation in circumstances of poverty and want. If the aforementioned relationship exemplifies the tendency of a formerly oppressed people to rely on long memories and the mistrust that these long memories create, then as well there is no better proof of the accuracy in Jefferson's predictions than in examining the situation that exists today within those communities of black Americans who, just like their Native American counterparts, are born into circumstances of poverty and violence and who inescapably direct their gaze towards the whites of the past who were and are responsible for their present condition.

All this discussion about oppression and long memories couldn't take place at a better time than now, given the items in the news concerning the events in the Middle East and in particular Palestine. Bush's "Roadmap for Peace" and all the extolling of a "liberated" Iraq are events that are inextricably entwined within Jefferson's remarks, despite the fact that they are taking place thousands of miles away and concern peoples who have never set foot on American soil. And while those in the US may (at the prodding and insistence of their programmers in the media/government complex) look with hope towards those ideas which are being discussed in bringing the current situation to a peaceful end, perhaps they should also factor into the equation the inescapable truth that these people also have long memories and that they thirst for justice, and that their captors know this all too well. And if the first step towards bringing an end to the violence of the region resides in Jefferson's symbolic act of letting go the wolf's ears, it is then safe to say that those parties who have been holding the ears understand better than anyone what it is that they stand to lose by so doing, and with this in mind, it should then be concluded that there is no intention of bringing any peace to the region, whether it involves the Americans or the Israelis.

Despite the public relations circuses that have taken place recently with various leaders smiling, shaking hands and making promises, there is no intention of giving Iraqis their freedom nor the Palestinians their land. In the first case, Iraq and her oil are now the defacto property of Bush & Co, a conglomeration of business interests whose existence is denied only by the most naive or the most intellectually dishonest. The program of bringing "liberty" to the Iraqis is identical to the program of bringing liberty to the former slaves of the American south by unscrupulous Northerners who sought their own personal gain in exploiting the unfortunate situation that existed in Reconstruction-era America. The Americans, through their corporations and threat of military force, are re-shaping Iraqi society and her infrastructure to suit their own purposes of extracting her wealth while at the same time keeping her people pliant. They will talk of freedom, but only the kind of freedom that suits American purposes, and in like fashion, just as the blacks in America were moved from one form of enslavement to another, the Iraqis now are graduating from one form of oppression to something new and more efficient, but enslavement, exploitation and abuse nonetheless.

The Israelis, despite the tactical use of promises which are nothing but repeats of the same lies which they have employed for purposes of deflection in the past, have no intention of giving up one inch of ground that they consider to be rightfully theirs by virtue of the violence they expended in acquiring it. Theirs has been a history of expansion in the region, not contraction, an expansion fueled by many interests and ideologies, not the least of which have been religious in nature, and which has been shown by history to be the most powerful of all prime movers. They would just as willingly part with some of their booty as would any pirate or predator, whose driving force is not justice and equity, but rather the law of the jungle or of the streets. Were the Palestinians fortunate enough to acquire some power or influence which would bring about a leveling of the situation, the Israelis would simply bide their time until some future event would present itself in such a way as to allow them to gain the upper hand again. Apologists for Israel would attempt (in common and predictable fashion) to argue away this assertion by attacking it as an ideologically-driven diatribe, however, unfortunately for them and for their argument, the history of how Israel has conducted business in past situations similar to these is the best indicator of how she would do things in the future, and given this history, there is no reason to suspect that the leopard has suddenly changed her spots. Furthermore, it should be remembered that many Israelis, including Ariel Sharon and others like him who hold the seats of power there, believe in the "biblical borders" concept concerning the area known as Eretz Y'Israel, an area which in their estimation includes not only the post 1967 borders, but as well the areas of Lebanon, Jordan, Syria, and parts of Iraq and Northern Saudi Arabia. This concept of "biblical borders" is but another example of the Manifest Destiny ideology first adopted by the Americans and now adopted by the Chosen People, and with this in mind, one should not contemplate with too much gullibility the idea that Israel is intent upon giving the Palestinians their land back in any permanent fashion.

However, the biggest reason for a discerning person not to surrender to any undue optimism concerning the peace process lies in the understanding that people have long memories, and there certainly are a lot of memories for those in the Middle East to consider when everyone gets together to talk about peace. When considering those living in the Occupied Territories, optimists who wait with baited breath over the possibility of peace should remember that every inch of the territory in which the Palestinians now exist is a shouting testimony of the 50 years in which they have been shot, blown up, poisoned, and bulldozed out of their homes. Every child who has been maimed by Israeli bullets or bombs is a prosecutorial witness to the nightmare that has been the minute-by-minute oppression of these people. Every picture of a dead relative on the mantle in each home is a roadblock to the roadmap. And if these items do not serve as any indicators as to why the peace process cannot take place as long as the present situation in Israel exists, then perhaps those who are gambling on this hope should consider the fact that Israeli violence against the Palestinians (as well as the deliberate destruction of any infrastructure that they manage to achieve) continues unabated while these talks are taking place. With this in mind, it is safe to assume that the most important component of any discussion or negotiation, trust, is absent, and that therefore the vehicle necessary for bringing an end to hostility is absent any fuel.

Bush and Sharon know perfectly well what awaits them by letting go of the wolf's ears. They realize that despite whatever promises are made by their victims to "forgive and forget" that nevertheless memories of people being killed by occupying armies (whether in Iraq or in Palestine) will override any sense of amnesia which their oppressors hoped their victims would develop. After 50 years of systematic brutality against the Palestinians and over 10 years of the same for the Iraqis, to expect that suddenly everyone would decide to just "get along" is folly. As well, the two leaders can forget about any help from neighboring countries in that region, as they have witnessed for themselves what has been done to the subject peoples of Iraq and Palestine, and who therefore have no reason to trust that there is any genuine desire for peace and justice on the part of the Americans or the Israelis. It is for these reasons that Bush and Sharon, despite their public display of devotion to the peace process, nevertheless have no intention of letting these people go. Instead, they will draw things out, making demands which are impossible for their victims to meet, and will blame the unavoidable violence that takes place upon an unbending, unreasonable mindset that they assert their victims possess. And if the violence is not forthcoming in such a way as to bolster their position at the appropriate time, they will see to it that something manages to "pop up" through their own channels of influence.

One would think that educated men had considered the domino effect of history and the violence that is produced whenever a people are oppressed before engaging in brutal behavior. There simply are too many instances throughout history that confirm this tendency for one to assume that it would be any different today. An intelligent person at some point must ask the question "Why do they do it? They know they can't hold on to the wolf forever, and they must know what awaits them when they let go." The only answer that suffices in understanding this condition lies in the age-old saying about vice and greed breaking down the intellect. Whether it is the sudden, short-lived violence perpetrated by a rapist or an assailant upon an individual, or the prolonged, systematic application of violence and oppression upon a group of people, the root cause of this willingness to inflict the worst upon mankind is derived from the individual's surrender of his own sense of humanity over to the lower passions of greed and malice, and the willingness to believe that he can get away with it indefinitely.

In the interest of tempering our optimism about the proposed solution for the problems in the Middle East, we must remember that history is the best teacher of all, and that she has already spoken about what is sure to be the present outcome in some varying degree. The wolf will not go away quietly, and there is no reason to suspect that her captor will be able to outrun or outfight her. Therefore, with this image in mind, one should assume that the peoples of the Middle East who are and have been subjected to an existence of oppression and violence must either resolve to stay that way indefinitely, or else turn violently upon those who have oppressed them in such a way lest they themselves be completely destroyed by their captors.

"In the summer of 1983, this same informant told the Mossad about a large Mercedes truck that was being fitted by the Shi'ite Muslims with spaces that could hold bombs. Now, the Mossad knew that because of its size, there were only a few logical targets, one of which must be the U.S. compound. The question then was whether or not to warn the Americans to be on particular alert for a truck matching the description. Admony, in refusing to give the Americans specific information on the truck, said, 'No, we're not there to protect Americans.' At the same time, however, all Israeli installations were given the specific details and warned to watch for a truck matching the description of the Mercedes."

"At 6:20 a.m. on October 23, 1983, a large Mercedes truck approached the Beirut airport, passing well within sight of Israeli sentries in their nearby base and turning left into the parking lot. A U.S. Marine guard reported with alarm that the truck was gathering speed, but before he could do anything, the truck roared toward the entrance of the four-story reinforced concrete Aviation Safety Building, used as headquarters for the Eighth Marine Battalion, crashing through a wrought-iron pate, hitting the sand-bagged guard post, smashing through another barrier, and ramming over a wall of sandbags into the lobby, exploding with such a terrific force that the building was instantly reduced to rubble."

"The loss of 241 U.S. Marines, most of them still sleeping in their cots at the time of the suicide mission, was the highest single-day death toll for the Americans since 246 died throughout Vietnam at the start of the Tet offensive on January 13,1968. The general attitude at Mossad about the Americans was: "As far as the Yanks go, we are not here to protect them. They can do their own watching. They wanted to stick their nose into this thing, so let them pay the price."
– – Ex-Israeli Intelligence officer Victor Ostrovsky, describing in his book **By Way of Deception** how the Mossad knew of the impending attack upon the American Marine base in Beirut and refused to warn them about it.

"The individual is handicapped by coming face to face with a conspiracy so monstrous he cannot believe it exists."
– J. Edgar Hoover, Director of the FBI

With Friends Like These...

They get together once or twice a year to smile and shake hands in front of the cameras in their desire to keep the outside world in its 50 year long state of delusion. The actors in question are the leaders of Israel and the United States, celebrating a friendship which has existed since the days of Harry Truman, a friendship which they extol as vitally important to the other's interests as well as to the safety of the free world. The truth is though, that these exhibitions are nothing more than cheap perfume which are used to mask the stench of their combined hatred for America and for her people. These leaders, (Mafiosi whose hands drip with the blood of American patriots, patriots whose lives have been snuffed out in the service of Zionism) are nothing more than vampires who have profited off of the blood of innocent American citizens for 50 years. The obvious examples proving this hatred are so numerous as to be mind boggling, but empirical and undeniable facts of history they are nonetheless. And now, as America and her people face the calm before the storm, a storm which threatens her possible annihilation, it should be recounted who has, time and again, put her head on the chopping block, and who has been engaged in a plan of systematic mass murder of the American people since her inception in 1948.

The recent news concerning President Lyndon Johnson's order to cover up the murder of 35 American sailors aboard the USS Liberty by the Israeli government should come as no surprise to anyone who has followed the history of the American/Israeli relationship. The sailors whose lives were stolen by Israeli pilots that day, pilots who, (after noting to their command headquarters that the ship was American) bombed, machine-gunned and napalmed the ship for 90 minutes are, tragically, only a few of the thousands of Americans who have died and will continue to do so because of America's friendship with Israel. The history of Israel's relationship with America is replete with examples of similar incidents, up to and including the murder of over 3,000 Americans on September 11, 2001. And with this in mind, any levelheaded and patriotic American must ask him or herself at some point the rhetorical yet prophetic question, "With friends like these, who needs enemies?"

The Liberty incident, kept barely alive in public discourse by those who survived the 90 minute attack, is, (albeit one of the most glaring examples of Israeli duplicity and treachery against the people of the United States) nevertheless by no means an isolated event. The war waged by Israel against the American people, in military action, espionage, and erosion of freedoms and security is as ingrained in the decades-long relationship as the color red is ingrained in the American blood she has shed. The concerted effort by the long arms of Zionist power in media, government and finance to keep a lid on this easily verifiable history of treachery has succeeded to the point that to this day a thorough investigation of these events by Congress has yet to take place. The lies surrounding the murder of America's young men aboard the USS Liberty, as well as those Americans murdered on 9/11, are so thick and so brazen in their audacity that it has long since surpassed being surreal. And as much a revelation as it may be concerning that murderous, duplicitous nation founded in 1948 by many who were atheistic communists from what was then the Soviet Union, it also speaks volumes about who are the traitors occupying the seats of power in the US government, who for 35 years have not sought an ounce of justice for the American people out of their fear of Zionist power.

For those who now, wide-eyed and incredulous, ponder the ridiculous "how did this happen?" question, consider this: It is only one instance in a mountain sized heap of similar instances. The Liberty, as awful as it is, is only one of many times in which the Israelis have deliberately harmed or put in harm's way the American people for their own benefit. And let the American people not fall victim to the propaganda surrounding what has been an acquittal of the Israelis in these situations. The evidence proving willful intent of malice is so prevalent that an individual whose only legal training was watching Judge Joe Brown on daily TV could put the pieces together with the competence of a trained lawyer.

Besides the acts of overt warfare against the people of the United States, the Israelis have for generations now employed agencies such as the ADL, AIPAC, JINSA, and the JDL as outlets in facilitating for their purposes the prosecutable acts of espionage, bribery and sometimes outright murder and terrorism. The ADL, which champions itself as a defender of those who suffer from racial persecution (except when it comes to Arab-Americans) has been on the front lines in deceiving Americans about what has been the parasitic relationship Israel has enjoyed with the US since its creation. The ADL has boldly lied about every instance of verifiable treachery in that history, maintaining in the process a network of spies and disinformation agents (who share files with the government of Israel) concerning Americans who dare to exercise their 1st Amendment right in criticizing this dangerous relationship. This has been validated recently in the fact that the ADL has been busted several times for illegally wiretapping the phones of American citizens, and for which has recently lost a $10,000,000.00 lawsuit brought by an American citizen in pursuance thereof. In addition, the ADL is and has been actively involved in an overt attempt at de-Christianizing American society to the point that now the most successful actor in American society, Mel Gibson, cannot make a movie about the death of Christ without having the heat brought down upon him and upon his family by the Jewish lobby.

Besides the spying they have perpetrated, the ADL has labored without pause in its interest of destroying the protections that the American people have enjoyed under the US Constitution for 200 years. Just as Israel in 1967 attacked the USS Liberty in furtherance of her desires, in like manner today she (through her interlocking networks in the US) time and again attack US Liberty in her outright contempt for the freedom by which America has been made great. The Israeli spy network known as the Anti-Defamation League works night and day to erode the rights of gun owners, property owners, the rights of parents and homeschoolers, and has in effect used its very powerful influence in having police-state legislation introduced and implemented into the fabric of American life. It was the ADL who pushed for "Anti-Terrorist" legislation six months before the bombing in Oklahoma City, and who steered the US Justice Department into initiating the events which led to the murder of US citizens at Ruby Ridge and Waco. And besides using their power to see to it that Americans are not afforded the right to express their religious sentiments, (as in the case of Mel Gibson and Judge Roy Moore) at the same time Israel's Spymaster Abe Foxman sees to it that public funding is used to denigrate and degrade every religious sentiment held dear by the same American people whose money has been the lifeblood of the Israeli state. It is no surprise therefore to see the ADL coming out and supporting the use of taxpayer dollars in promoting "art works" such as those depicting a crucifix immersed in a jar of urine and pictures of Christ's Holy Mother covered with elephant dung.

The JDL, the more "action-oriented" of Israel's defenders operating in the US, (and the more willing of her organizations to get its hands dirty) to this day continues to occupy its well-deserved place on the FBI's list of most dangerous terrorist organizations. In 2003, 2 of its members were convicted for attempting to blow up a Mosque in the state of Florida. Prior to this, the group's former leader, Irv Rubin, was "suicided" in prison the day before he was to go on trial for his role in the planned bombing of the office of California Congressman Daryl Issa, an American of Middle Eastern descent. There are several other instances of violence in their history, including attempted arsons, bombings, bricks thrown through windows, not to mention the obligatory death threats for which they claim credit, revealing a characteristic cleverly kept hidden from Americans who still believe that Israel is their best friend.

If the ADL and JDL attempt to hide their agenda of supporting Israel through their use of spying and threats, AIPAC, the American Israel Political Action Committee, makes no such attempt. It is the largest political action committee in the US, and literally decides who wins government offices at the State and Federal level. If an individual, (incumbent or not) is not looked upon favorably by this Israeli lobbying group, all the stops will be pulled out in making sure that he or she doesn't get into office, and along with a Zionist controlled media, this organization will make sure to run at break-neck speed and efficiency in sabotaging such a campaign. In this way, the nation of Israel, not the American people, decides who runs the nation.

In further consideration of this friendship under which Americans have suffered and continue to do so, perhaps a further review of that friendship's history is also in order.

Lest it be forgotten, it was Israel who, in 1983, knew of the planned assault on the Marine barracks in Lebanon, an assault which resulted in the deaths of 241 Americans, and about which Israel refused to warn the US. Consider the words uttered by the same intelligence officers in the Israeli government who watched as the explosives-laden truck met its final destination with American lives:

WITH FRIENDS LIKE THESE . . .   151

"As far as the Yanks go, we are not here to protect them. They can do their own watching. They wanted to stick their nose into this thing, so let them pay the price."

Lest it be forgotten, it was Israeli intelligence operatives, dressed as Arabs who blew up American buildings in Egypt, done for the purpose of blaming the Arabs in an event known as the Lavon Affair.

Lest it be forgotten, it was Israel who sent a team of covert operatives into Libya, rented an apartment near Khaddafi's headquarters, and broadcast radio messages in Arabic to make it sound like terrorist cell planning in what was known as Operation Trojan Horse. As a result of this, air strikes were launched against the Libyans under completely false pretenses for Israel's benefit.

Lest it be forgotten, it was Israel, through her intelligence agency Mossad who was plotting to have President Bush assassinated following the first Gulf War, in the interest of blaming the Palestinians and bringing the Americans in to help fight her wars.

Lest it be forgotten, it was Israeli intelligence who was handling the Monica Lewinsky affair for the purposes of blackmailing then president Bill Clinton. Having, as Clinton admitted, tapped his phone, "America's only ally" in the Middle East held a gun to the head of her leader and blackmailed him into dropping his support for a peace plan between Israel and the Palestinians.

Lest it be forgotten, in a theme similar to that which involved Monica Lewinsky, the whole business involving Chandra Levy and Congressman Gary Condit was managed by Israeli Intelligence. It is now postulated by investigators that their affair and her subsequent disappearance were done in an attempt to blackmail him into revealing what information his Intelligence Committee had on the bombing of the Murrah Federal Building in Oklahoma City and how much his committee knew of Israeli spying done on America in the months before 9/11.

Lest it be forgotten, Israel, now the headquarters of the Russian Mafia, is the biggest trafficker in the drug Ecstasy, which plagues American society and preys on American youth.

Lest it be forgotten, Israel is now and for some time has been involved in the sex-slave business, as well as snuff-pornography involving children. Several Americans have been indicted for acting as "mules" for the Israelis in bringing these vices into American society and acting as marketing agents.

Lest it be forgotten, in the days and weeks after 9/11 the largest spy ring in American history was busted up by the FBI. The events that led to this were the arrest of 5 Israeli intelligence agents who were seen videotaping the planes crashing into the Twin Towers while cheering in the process. Another team of intelligence operatives was arrested in New York while driving a van containing Palestinian-looking clothing, and who upon arrest were quoted as saying "We're not the enemies. Your enemies are the same as ours, the Palestinians!" Since that time, there have been several teams of Israeli operatives arrested carrying false passports, and within several of the vehicles they drove were found traces of explosives. All in all, over 100 intelligence agents have been deported back to Israel since 9/11. It is to be assumed then that upon this basis was the assertion by Senator Bob Graham of Florida made that a foreign government was involved with the attacks, as well as Fox News' statement that "all material linking Israel to the events of 9/11 was classified".

Lest it be forgotten, it was Israel who employed the American Naval Officer Jonathan Pollard to steal over 500,00 pages of ultra secret documentation concerning America's most high tech weapons, documentation which was then turned around and sold to America's enemies, including the Russians and the Chinese.

Lest it be forgotten, it was Israel who in the year 2001 scoured the downed US Spy plane in China of all its technological secrets. It has been revealed that the reason the Chinese held the plane (as well as the American servicemen) for the duration of time that they did was to facilitate this scouring at the behest of "America's only ally in the Middle East".

Lest it be forgotten, it was Israel who stole American nuclear material and technological wherewithal from the Nuclear Materials and Equipment Corporation located in Apollo, Pennsylvania. FBI agents literally stood and watched, helpless to do their jobs under orders from their superiors, as nuclear material was packed in boxes marked "diplomatic" and loaded on a ship sailing for Haifa. The Israeli Embassy threatened to make trouble if the US Government interfered.

Lest it be forgotten, it was Israel who sold the computer software known as *Promis* to the Chinese government, who then used that software to hack into the computers at Los Alamos Nuclear Laboratory, enabling the Chinese to advance their nuclear capability (and thus advance the danger posed to the American people) by a quarter century.

Lest it be forgotten, Israel is the biggest violator of US Patent laws, particularly those which involve military technology and encryption. There are several recorded instances of Israel directly breaking into or penetrating sensitive American military installations in the interest of stealing such technology, and afterwards selling it off to America's enemies.

Lest it be forgotten, the main suspect in the Anthrax attacks which occurred in the weeks following 9/11 is an ardent Zionist and political friend to Israel. It is alleged that his reason for doing this was to frame an Arab-American who worked in the Army Weapons Lab with him.

Lest it be forgotten, Islamic Fundamentalism, which as been blamed for the 9/11 attacks and against which the war on terror is being fought, is the product of Israel's murderous policies against the peoples of the Middle East, and in particular Palestine. Her stated desire to rebuild Israel to its "biblical borders," encompassing all the lands within Jordan, Lebanon, Syria, Iraq, and the northern part of Saudi Arabia is the greatest source of the violence against her main supplier of weaponry and funding, the United States. Prior to her creation in 1948, Islamic Fundamentalism did not exist, and the countries of the Middle East were friends who wanted to emulate the United States.

Lest it be forgotten, it was Israel who created Hamas, the organization blamed for terror attacks against her own people. Hamas was created by Israeli intelligence for the purpose of drawing support away from the PLO and Yassir Arafat.

There are other disturbing pieces of information as well. For those who are still unconvinced of the danger which is posed to America and her people by her relationship with Israel, the following items should be considered also:

*At least one Congressman who has sat on several intelligence committees, Paul Findley, has voiced his suspicion of Israeli involvement in the death of President John F. Kennedy. It is a well-known fact that David Ben Gurion, then Prime Minister of Israel, was infuriated with JFK for his refusal to allow Israel to develop nuclear weapons. A detailed account of the evidence supporting Congressman Findley's suspicion is outlined in a book by Michael Collins Piper entitled *Final Judgment.*

*Much evidence exists implicating Israel in the death of Clinton Administration Official Vince Foster. It is suspected that he may have been involved with passing on the launch codes of America's nuclear arsenal to Israel in return for monetary contributions to Clinton's presidential campaign. In the hours following his death, Mossad agents scoured his apartment in search of something which, in this light, was deemed of obvious importance.

*Within moments of TWA Flight 800 exploding over the Atlantic Ocean after leaving New York, the Israeli Government (through her agents in the US media) put the blame for the atrocity on Islamic Fundamentalists. This fact, coupled with the 100 or more persons who have sworn in public testimony that they witnessed a missile hitting the aircraft leaves troubling questions about who actually engineered this act of war against America. Given Israel's history of perpetrating similar atrocities, (known in Israeli Intelligence parlance as "false flag operations,") concerned Americans are left with troubling conclusions.

Based on this short list, it should be obvious to anyone with an ounce of sense that America's only ally in the Middle East is the kind of friend she would be better off not having. She has murdered American citizens, lied in every instance and occurrence, and deliberately placed America and her people in the gravest danger as it has served her own purposes. And now, in the calm before the storm, she is preparing (facilitated by the Neocons in the Bush Administration and disinformation agents on the talk show circuit)

WITH FRIENDS LIKE THESE . . .

the next event which will send American men and women off to the sands of the Middle East to fight and die for her. It is possible that it is too late for America to disentangle herself from such a bad friendship, as the inference has already been made that in the event that America puts the Jewish state in danger, she (Israel) would resort to the "Samson Option" which entails the use of nuclear weapons against anyone termed an "unfriendly".

It should be clear to all Americans who love their country that the "friendship" they enjoy with the terrorist state of Israel is the most perverse notion of an alliance that has yet occurred in the history of the United States. It has been a one-way friendship from the beginning, as is that enjoyed by some parasitic tick on the back of a dog. Like any parasite, this tick, as it draws the life-blood out of its healthy host, at the same time introduces various diseases and maladies that will one day sicken that host. In like manner, the American body is beginning to show serious signs of such sickness and weakness, to the point that her very survival is threatened. And were she, America, fortunate enough to survive for a short time in this unenviable state, it would still be the slow, agonizing death of watching her freedoms torn asunder as a result of Israeli influence over the American legislation process, influence which has already brought forth such abominations as the Patriot Act and other like minded assaults on US Liberty.

The time has come (much too late) for America, and for her freedom loving/justice hungry/ patriotic citizenry to take a good look at the Beast which masquerades itself as her friend, and at the same time eye with commensurate suspicion and anger those elected officials who have sold out America in what have been the greatest acts of treason and treachery in her history. Americans who truly love their country should, in all justification, feel the bile rising in their throats and view with nausea those leaders who make a mockery of their duty to protect America from her enemies, those self-serving traitors who heap derision upon the very nation whose flag they dare to sport as lapel pins for all the world to see. A responsible America must not lazily allow the interests of a terrorist nation such as Israel to do her thinking for her when it comes to meting out justice against her enemies, nor to allow this parasite the power to decide who her enemies will be.

A new American Revolution is drastically needed, the origins of which must be born in that question which (with God's help) will burn in the hearts of an outraged American people who have considered such treachery in light of the danger which they now face. That question, simply put, is this:

"With friends like these, who needs enemies?"

"You brood of vipers! Who told you to flee the coming wrath? The ax is already at the root of the trees, and every tree that does not produce good fruit will be cut down and thrown into the fire."
– John the Baptist addressing the Sanhedrin.

"And when the chief priests heard the news of Jesus' resurrection, they devised a plan to give the soldiers guarding the tomb a large sum of money, telling them 'You are to say that His disciples came during the night and stole his body away while you were asleep. And if word of this gets to the governor, we will satisfy him and keep you out of trouble.' So the soldiers did as they were instructed and this story has been widely circulated among the Jews to this very day."
– **Book of Matthew**

"Christians and others who reject the Talmud will go to hell and be punished there for all generations."
– **The Babylonian Talmud**, Judaism's most holy book, Rosh Hashana, 17a.

"Woe to you, teachers of the law and Pharisees, you hypocrites. You shut the kingdom of heaven in men's faces. You yourselves do not enter, nor will you let those enter who are trying to."
– Jesus of Nazareth addressing the Sanhedrin

"Jews feel towards Jesus today what they felt in the 4th century or in the Middle Ages. For centuries, Jews concealed from Christians their hatred towards Jesus, and this tradition continues even now. Jesus is revolting and repulsive, and this repulsion passed from the observant Jews to the general Israeli public."
– Rami Rozen, writer for the Israeli daily newspaper **Haaretz**

"So when the crowd had gathered, Pilate asked them 'Which one do you want me to release to you, Barabbas or Jesus, who is called Christ?' for he knew that it was out of envy that the Jews had handed Jesus over to him...and the Chief Priests and the elders persuaded the crowd to ask for Barabbas and to have Jesus executed."
– **Book of Matthew**

The New Sanhedrin

"What are we to do with these men?" they asked among themselves. *"We must warn them not to speak anymore in his name."* The problem for those who were debating this question of "what to do with these men" was that many miracles had been performed by them in the plain sight of the whole community, and there was no arguing against it. What was even more vexing to them was the boldness of these former fishermen in going forth fearlessly like first century renditions of William Wallace and his band of Scotsmen, refusing to knuckle under and abandon their War for Independence in the face of so many threats. And it was due to these reasons that their opponents were gathered that day, and understandably anxious about handling this problem without too much attention being drawn to it.

Those who were gathered together pondering this troubling question were the members of the Sanhedrin who had just recently put that ambitious and pesky carpenter from Nazareth to death, and who now were in the business of persecuting his followers, stoning them, having them thrown into prison, and in general bringing to bear all of the mechanisms of coercion which were available to them at the time. Clearly, the business of bringing to an end the boxing match that took place over the course of 3 years between the Nazarene and the most esteemed and honored members of the religious leadership was not as finalized as they had thought it was. In killing him, they had opened up a can of worms that appeared to be almost uncontainable, and now, in utter desperation, they were attempting to stop a fire that appeared to be unstoppable.

Thus were the events which gave birth to the Christian faith as recounted in the Book of Acts, a heart-pounding, heroic tale in which a band of revolutionaries defies the powers that be in their desire to live as free men. As such, there are to be found in this story all the elements which have encompassed other tales of similar theme, including the evil tyrants who oppress and weigh down the people, and the heroes who, having been struck with the idea that it is better to perish as free men than to live as slaves, bravely go forth lighting the fires of revolution and justice in the process. Most of those who call themselves Christians today, while acknowledging their respect for these events, nevertheless seem to have little understanding as to where the importance of such events lie in the present. To those who pay some lip service to the freedom fighters, (Peter, Paul, et al) the events are simply occurrences of a bygone history, as was General Washington's crossing of the Delaware or Patrick Henry's speech to the Virginia House of Burgesses. Little do they appear to realize that they are living in the midst of this event, an event which was only part one in the War of Independence which Christianity declared against Pharisaical Judaism in the tiny town of Jerusalem nearly 2,000 years ago. The danger to this inaccurate understanding of the event is lethal, both spiritually and physically, for in the process of getting bad intelligence reports much of what calls itself Christianity has made fatal errors in terms of logistics and planning, and as such now stands poised to be overrun by the enemy, if indeed this has not already happened.

"What are we to do with these men?" they ask on a daily basis today, and have now, for at least one century, possibly two. Those who are gathered together today, pondering this troubling question are the modern day descendants of the same Sanhedrin who had put that ambitious and pesky carpenter from Nazareth to death, and who now are in the business of persecuting his followers, killing them, having them thrown into prison, and in general bringing to bear all the mechanisms of coercion which are available to them at this time. *"We must warn them not to speak anymore in His name."*

The average Christian contemplating who such persons might be today, (and inevitably falling back on the propaganda which has been poured into his or her consciousness by a Zionist media) would invariably arrive at the conclusion that what was being discussed was some form of religious extremism emanating from the Middle East, which would be partially correct. Where clarification is needed though, is in recognizing that in this case the real threat existing today to the religion of Christianity and its adherents is not posed by Islamic Extremism, but rather is to be found lying within the sentiments of Judaic Extremism, The New Sanhedrin, and never before has it been more apparent than now.

THE NEW SANHEDRIN

As much as the American media, (for decades now a mouthpiece for the interests of Marxist Zionism) has propagandized America since the fateful day in which the Twin Towers came down concerning the "hatred for Christianity" that it alleges is the defining characteristic of the Islamic religion, nevertheless from time to time the mask comes off the Beast and gives the observant spectator a glimpse of what better constitutes reality. Whether such sloppiness is the result of laziness on the part of those weaving the spell or whether it is the product of divine providence makes little difference in the fact that the world should be grateful that it happens, even if it is only too infrequent. In such instances, the act of the Beast in revealing itself allows truth, (if even only for a brief moment) to have an opportunity in dispelling the clouds of confusion under whose cover an agenda is permitted to operate. It is understandable how sloppiness like this can exist, since maintaining a deception is a full-time job, much akin to keeping a dead corpse alive through artificial means. As such, from time to time the hypnotists managing the delusional state of American Christianity are not as diligent in covering all their tracks and tying up all the loose ends with respect to the propaganda they peddle which fuels American involvement in the Middle East.

The double-sided justification for this involvement, after all the polemics and flowery arguments are removed can be reduced to two main ideas, the one being that Muslims hate Christians, and the other that Americans who consider themselves to be Judeo-Christian in their orientation owe their allegiance to the Marxist state of Israel. In furtherance of this agenda, Israel's propaganda infrastructure in America has hidden not only what are the easily verifiable sentiments of respect and veneration which Muslims maintain towards Christ and those who follow him, but as well have kept hidden the malicious sentiments held by adherents of Judaic extremism which can be verified with equal ease.

This cover-up has been accomplished by what has become a fast moving shell game in which the Muslims, who hold and always have held Christ in the highest regard, have been inaccurately portrayed as his enemies, while the real villains have gone unsuspected and unmentioned throughout the entirety of the discussion. This is tragic on several levels, not only in the fact that a decades-long war has now been launched against almost a billion people under completely false pretenses, but as well in the fact that it illustrates what has become the intellectual capacity of the average American Christian Zionist in his or her blind support for the interests of Marxist Zionism. The average American who has swallowed the bait put forth by a Zionist media that the religion of Islam is inherently anti-Christian in its foundations could have easily become better enlightened in an afternoon of reading, not The New Republic or the other rags that are nothing more than rolls of toilet paper passing for Zionist propaganda, but rather passages of the Qur'an, a process by which much if not all of the negative notions which have been put forth concerning the religion of Islam and its adherents would have been reduced to the meaningless dribble that they are. By doing so, the curious American would have found out that he or she has much more in common with the adherents of Islam than has been revealed, including a shared belief in Christ as the Messiah, his miraculous works, and that he is favored in the eyes of the creator. In addition to this, it would have been discovered as well that Christ's mother is revered as the highest woman ever to have walked the face of the earth, and that his Apostles are held in the same esteemed positions of honor that they occupy in the religion of Christianity.

By the same notion, the average Christian, spending an afternoon reading (instead of watching some foolishness designed to reduce his or her intellect to that of a drooling, sexualized adolescent) might find disquieting pieces of information concerning the religion of Judaism and its extremist elements in Israel whom Americans subsidize to the tune of over 6 billion dollars a year. In the great shell game of propaganda which has fueled American Christianity's support for the war in the Middle East at the behest of Israel, with deafening silence has been discussed how Christ and his followers (including his mother) are viewed by adherents of modern day Judaic extremism, the members of the New Sanhedrin. Amidst all the programming which has appeared on mainstream television and radio, whether such programming has featured paid polemicists for the Zionist agenda like Daniel Pipes, Richard Pearle, Dore Gold, et al, or whether they are the Zionists wearing the garb of Christian sentimentality as personified by the likes of Falwell, Robertson, Limbaugh, Hannity, or Lindsay, not a mention has been made concerning what are the blatant anti-Christian tenants as practiced and preached by Talmudic Judaism or its extremist adherents. One would think that such items which include Christ being depicted as a sorcerer and a mamzer (bastard child) who suffers in Hell by being boiled in excrement would arouse some suspicion among a rightly (and hopefully, genuinely) outraged Christianity. One would hope that religious sentiments depicting his mother Mary as a prostitute who mated with carpenters and Roman soldiers would spark some sense of curiosity to find out more. And finally, in the interest of learning all there was to know concerning religious extremism and how it has played itself out in the events surrounding 9/11, one would expect that the average Christian in America would like to understand better who is and who is not the real enemy, particularly when his hard-earned livelihood is sent to prop up a nation which has been billed as the only ally to Christian America in the Middle East. Sadly, this has not taken place, even when there are glaringly obvious reasons to do so.

All this talk about religious extremism (particularly when it takes place within the context of an anti-Christian agenda) couldn't occur at a better time than the present. Besides the war taking place in the Middle East, (which Christians in America are told is a war fought between a religion of terror and a religion of freedom) the culture war in America is raging at full throttle, even if unbeknownst to many. The culture war, whose victims include the most basic precepts with regards to decency and morality have been and are being attacked by a Zionist agenda which never seems to pause for a breather. Pop idols who have more influence over America's youth than people would like to realize or admit are now publicly engaging in acts of lesbianism, simulated sex, and parading themselves nude on stage under the direction and protection of a media intent on destroying the moral underpinnings of an entire nation for the furtherance of the Israeli agenda. Unfortunately, Americans who have since 9/11 effected a sense of outrage over what were attacks against a Christian nation seem to be bothered more by the crumbling of America's concrete pillars than they are bothered by the crumbling of America's moral pillars which are of far more importance to her stability and survival. Even more so, those in America who boldly put themselves before America's television and radio programs and who earn a living by professing their Christianity, while showing outrage over such attacks against America's morals, nevertheless refuse to reveal that such attacks are the product of a Zionist agenda which rules America's airwaves and by default America's sentiments. And if there existed in the past a gray area in which Christianity in America could be excused for such shortsightedness in not recognizing what forces have been behind the destruction of America's moral foundations, there is no such gray area now, and particularly with regards to the current controversy surrounding Mel Gibson's movie *The Passion*.

Unfortunately for the bulk of American Christianity, the significance of the controversy surrounding the movie which depicts the murder of Christ at the hands of Jewish extremists 2,000 years ago has been lost. This is due in large part to the fact that American Christianity (like much of mainstream America) has been robbed of the ability to think for itself outside of the totalitarian box which has been fashioned for it by a Zionist propaganda infrastructure. What ability for independent thought which hasn't been torn to shreds by the Zionist agenda in mainstream media like some intellectual abortion has been accomplished by the seduction of Christian Zionism, whose false prophets are given all the leeway they need in manipulating what remains of independent thought. If the American intellect were in tact, able to think for itself critically about the current controversy surrounding the movie and its content, then what would inevitably result would be the dissonance and cacophony of the crashing together of contradictory statements, leading inevitably to a series of questions and debate. Tragically, the fact that organized Jewish groups, (most notably the ADL) are those who are spearheading the attack on Gibson's film has barely caused a blip in the American consciousness or curiosity, even though the relevance in this fact is of momentous importance. In an America which has been warned to "watch out for the adherents of Islam who are out to destroy Christianity and its followers" by the propaganda which it has been force-fed on a daily basis by a Jewish owned media to not take note of the importance of the current controversy only portends the worst. One can imagine the campaign that would be launched by a Zionist media upon a complacent and intellectually compliant American public if the opponents to the film were Muslims instead of Jews. Rather than getting the sanitized coverage that it has received up to now, such opposition to the film would make headline news every hour on the hour and would be the subject of talk-shows designed to raise the ire of American Christianity. Such coverage would without question incorporate in its content the message concerning the dangerous existence of religious extremism and how it threatens

THE NEW SANHEDRIN   165

the American way of life, and used to bolster the Zionist agenda of wiping out Israeli's enemies in the process.

This event brings to clarity what is the unfortunate status of American intellectual decay which can only be accurately described as in an advanced and possibly irreversible stage. And despite the fact that Christian Zionists (not only the religious but irreligious as well) are making at least the pretense of defending the movie, nevertheless they are complicit in covering up what are the true roots of the peculiar brand of religious extremism which is driving the opposition to it. One must wonder whether or not their motives for defending the movie are rooted in general sentiments which are favorable to Christianity, or whether instead they find themselves in the frightful position of possibly having their carefully constructed masks ripped off, revealing them for the frauds that they are. Certainly, it has been a difficult juggling act for them, calling themselves Christian while at the same time supporting the most anti-Christian agenda which has ever been hatched in the last 2 millennia, that being the agenda of Marxist Zionism as managed by members of the New Sanhedrin.

"We gave you strict orders not to teach in his name, yet you have filled Jerusalem with your teaching and are determined to make us guilty of this man's blood." Acts 5:28

The above quote, although 2,000 years old, nevertheless encompasses the agenda which has been feverishly and mercilessly enacted in America today against the religion of Christianity and its adherents. In the process, the Christian faith which is day by day assaulted and regulated by the legal process and made to be the butt of jokes on prime time television has been harrowed and hushed over the course of the last 30 years through the efforts of Zionist groups operating under orders from their corporate headquarters in Israel. Whether such an agenda has been realized through the dizzying number of lawsuits brought to silence and remove the effervescence of Christian sentimentality from American society or whether it has been accomplished through the efforts of a Zionist media and its immoral programming, nevertheless the message which has been imparted upon American Christianity has been a decisive warning "not to teach in His name". It is within this context that the lunacy and duplicity of Christian Zionism becomes all too apparent. For all the grandstanding that such groups do in challenging the secular attack on Christian sentimentality in America, nevertheless they refuse to reveal the identity of the groups orchestrating these attacks for the Israeli agenda, including the ADL, JDL, and others of similar stripe who collectively represent the membership of the New Sanhedrin.

The well-publicized argument being put before the consideration of Americans by the likes of Abe Foxman at the ADL and others concerning *The Passion* that the movie will create anti-Semitic reactions in American Christians is revealed as the falsehood it is when considered next to the mountains of contradictory evidence readily available to anyone with eyes to see. For groups such as the ADL, JDL, and all the other friends of Israel, anti-Semitism is as vital to their survival as lawsuits are vital to lawyers. They fear anti-Semitism the way that a dentist fears tooth decay, or the way in which an abortionist fears unwanted pregnancies. These groups, all managing multi-million dollar budgets and enjoying the pretension of respectability and influence which has been conferred upon them by their siblings in the media would be out of business permanently were it not for the hysteria that they create over alleged acts of Jewish persecution. They were founded on such occurrences and need them to continue if they are to remain in the positions they now enjoy. Therefore, in considering the arguments which they put forward for their opposition to the movie, the world would have to conclude that such groups are either very honest or very duplicitous, and humanity would be wise to assume that it is the latter. They thrive on anti-Semitism the way that a weed thrives on manure, and like their Marxist cousins who in the past instigated acts of anti-Semitism for propaganda purposes in the early years of Israel's founding, it must be assumed that such groups today, if finding themselves without the necessary fuel for their machinery, would be willing to author or sponsor in some manner similar acts against their own Jewish constituency for the same purposes.

But what should be more revealing to American Christianity than this is the fact that the same Zionist groups who today are screaming passionately over *The Passion* and the anti-Jewish feelings which they claim it will produce are the same groups who are now and have been on the front lines championing every abomination that comes forth from the Zionist agenda which defames Christ, the religion of Christianity and its followers.

If ever there were items which such groups needed to worry about in terms of anti-Jewish backlash, then certainly there are none which would be more worrisome than those which a Jewish run media commits on an hourly basis in America. It is reasonable to assume that if anti-Jewish feelings are going to erupt, that they will do so over the blatantly anti-Christian programming which the media under the direction of the New Sanhedrin vomits out on a daily basis. The thoughtful spectator witnessing the present circus and soap opera must ask at some point where the same concern for anti-Jewish backlash is to be found when movies such as *"The Last Temptation of Christ," "Dogma,"* and *"Priest"* are made available for public viewing, in addition to all the daily assaults to Christian morality which are found on primetime television. Certainly, were the arms of the Zionist propaganda machine worried about anti-Jewish feelings, they would step away from supporting the regular attacks on Christ and his dignity, recognizing that in the process of associating themselves with such bigotry, they would cause the age old spectre of anti-Semitism to flare up again. And yet, in perfect intellectual contradiction, they are to be found on the front lines of every instance in which the religion of Christianity is degraded and defiled, proudly asserting their Zionist sentiments in the process without fear of the same ensuing backlash which they predict will result from the release of a movie depicting Christ's dignity. Their fear that Christians will be angered over seeing a film concerning the murder of Christ is conspicuously absent when art exhibits go mainstream which depict a crucifix immersed in a jar of urine as well as those of Christ's mother covered with elephant dung. Such concerns over negative stereotyping of Jews, resulting in vindication of what have been age-old negative attributes unfairly applied to the entire group are not present whenever these same organizations publicly associate themselves with attacks on the family values which have formed the strength of American society for 200 years. In every instance wherein a radical program for elevating some form of degeneracy in American society makes the news, the members of the New Sanhedrin can be found offering their support both financially and philosophically without a trace of the same fear which they presume to possess now over the release of *The Passion*. In such a circumstance, American Christianity doesn't need to have a degree in Psychology to see that such contradictory reasoning is nothing more than a mountain sized sense of hypocrisy whose tip is barely visible above the water's edge. The trouble is that she doesn't see it, which truly portends a worse condition for her intellectually than was imagined.

A better understanding for the reasons behind all the growling and snarling which the Zionist groups have put forth concerning *The Passion* lies not in their fear of anti-Jewish backlash, but is to be found rather in the anti-Christian extremism which forms the philosophical underpinnings of their organizations. By definition, these groups are conglomerations whose members are devoted to religious extremism and who attempt to hide their particular brand of bigotry and racism behind noble sounding terms and titles. In such a way, they attempt to cover the ugliness of their religious extremism in the same manner that an individual attempts to hide what is a hideously bad odor with perfume or some other device of distraction. In any case, the mixture of the two, nobility and duplicity, stench and perfume, is a nauseating combination which makes its presence known within the shape-shifting characteristics of their contradictory arguments. The Zionist groups who make the pretense of combating religious extremism are in reality there to combat only those sentiments which thwart or threaten the will of their parent organization which is the Marxist state of Israel. As such, they have done absolutely nothing in exposing or combating the anti-Christian, anti-Gentile sentiments which are the lifeblood of Talmudic Judaism, sentiments which are driving their opposition not only to *The Passion*, but indeed every instance which serves to reveal the dignity and worthiness of Christ and his message of liberation.

American Christianity would be wise to consider what is the real animus driving the opposition to this movie. In reading between the lines of their arguments, it is revealed that what the New Sanhedrin fears more than anything else is a reversal of fortune for their agenda. *In truth, the reason for the current apoplexy over the release of The Passion is rooted in the fact that such a work threatens to undermine much of the success they have achieved in the last few decades in demoralizing and de-Christianizing American society.*

It is obvious to those who have not been lulled to sleep that there is and has been a concerted, in-your face effort over the last 30 years to bring low not only the personage of Christ and his followers, but the moral underpinnings of Western Civilization as well. The Zionist octopus, with all its tentacles spread across the avenues of influence and power has on a daily basis either through law, academia, or media, reduced the dignity of Christ and Christianity to a group of buffoons who should be shuffled off towards the hinterlands of societal organization and left to die. As such, the interests of Zionism stand to lose much if such a movie and its message succeeds in reawakening in a slumbering humanity what were at one time positive sentiments with regards to that pesky Carpenter who condemned the same race-conscious bigotry which the practitioners of Marxist Zionism embrace today. And with this in mind, it is therefore not difficult to understand why all this has taken place, as well as what is to come later.

An honest examination of the philosophical roots of Marxist Zionism reveals an unbroken chain of connecting sentiments hovering around the idolatry of race-worship and derision of outsiders. As much as detractors from this argument may try to deny the existence of such sentiments, nevertheless they are as easily verifiable as the phrase "We hold these truths" is visible in the American Declaration of Independence. In reading the Talmud, (considered to be the "holy of holies" in modern Rabbinic Judaism) one finds within its pages the blueprints for radical societal reorganization so as to benefit and elevate the practitioners of Judaic extremism, and in particular those enjoying the positions of leadership. This reorganization is achieved through the process of undermining by any means available the moral fiber and stability of all existing societies for the purpose of supplanting them with an oligarchy rooted in Jewish supremacy. As such, in assaulting Christian morals over the course of the last 3 decades, Israel and her infrastructure of propaganda have succeeded in reconfiguring and rearranging Western morality so as to put it in alignment with her policies in the Middle East that would otherwise result in moral condemnation. As a result of such a process, the objective laws of right and wrong as recognized by the adherents of Christianity have had an asterisk placed next to them, noting that certain exceptions to these laws exist when they apply to the machinations of the Zionist agenda. Therefore, murdering Palestinians and reducing their existence to that of concentration camp victims is no longer murder and genocide, but rather an exception to the rule. Imperialistic ambitions, revealed in the long dreamed of Zionist plan of creating a Greater Israel which would encompass the lands of Jordan, Lebanon, Syria, Iraq and Saudi Arabia are given a pass as well. Modern day Christianity (and in particular in America) has, through the Zionist agenda of obliterating the personage of Christ and his religion, suffered the obliteration of her moral compass as well. As a result, her morality remains in a state of flux, constantly changing to suit the needs of those who dictate what is considered to be of benefit or of liability to Israel's agenda in the Middle East. And it is for these reasons that American Christianity, having had its moral foundations made unstable through concerted attacks on its dogmas and sentiments can be seen embracing contradictory principles in today's age, and most notably in its support for the murderous and duplicitous state of Israel.

Christians around the world, but particularly those in America, would do well to take note of the current controversy surrounding *The Passion* and to consider it well. The fact that the Zionist organizations have revealed themselves for the hypocrites that they are in their arguments should induce what remains of Christianity to ponder what the real reason for such opposition is. The reality of the situation is that what is fueling this vitriolic opposition is nothing more than the same ugly, bigoted, religious extremism encompassed within the Pharisaical mindset which Christ himself condemned. The modern day remnants of Pharisaical Judaism, the New Sanhedrin, whose great great grandfathers waged a war of oppression against Christ and his band of freedom fighters have never forgiven them for having won their independence and as such are now in the process of undermining all that the war for liberation has produced. In the same manner that they plotted and schemed, bribed and threatened to erase from society the pesky and ambitious carpenter from Nazareth and his message of liberation, so too today do they attempt the same through the use of similar tactics.

As such, those who consider themselves Christians today and who are supporters of the Marxist state of Israel would to well for themselves by arriving at the inescapable conclusion that through their support they are helping to raise up a Beast which will at the most propitious moment devour them and their sentiments. Christianity today must (if indeed it is not too late) wake itself from the delusion known as Christian Zionism, an unholy marriage which has been consummated in the wedding ceremony of two contradictory ideologies through an unnatural intellectual process. As such, let what remains of Christianity and its legacy of liberation from Pharisaical Judaism realize that despite all the flowery talk which the paid mouthpieces of Marxist Zionism preach with regards to the strength of the Judeo-Christian alliance, that no such alliance exists in reality. In truth it is nothing but a ploy, a Trojan Horse designed to penetrate Christianity and subvert it from within, using it as a mechanism for empowering the terrorist state of Israel while at the same time planting the seeds for Christianity's destruction, an event which will be realized when it is no longer of any use to the Marxist agenda of Zionism.

Americans who consider themselves Christian and who stand with Israel and the Mafia families which control her must at some time recognize that they cannot serve two masters. The Zionist infrastructure of propaganda in America, personified by groups such as the ADL, JDL, World Jewish Congress et al are, (if even only unofficially) arms of the same Marxist octopus which Americans support with their tax dollars and now with the blood of their young men and women in the military. It is the same octopus which has been working diligently over the course of the last 3 decades to obliterate America's moral foundations, and is the fountain from which all the poison which presently infects her society has flowed. And finally, it must be recognized that this Beast which today enjoys the adulation of Christian Zionists is the same which is now attempting to prevent the release of what portends to be a spectacular film celebrating the dignity and divinity of the only King which America has had in her 200 year history, Jesus Christ. And let not American Christians be so naive as to try to separate the sentiments of the various Zionist groups in America from the Zionist agenda in the Middle East, for in reality they are both limbs of the same tree.

As such, let what remains of not only Christianity, but indeed the world at large, view with honest consideration what has been laid out before them and their future. Humanity is being marched into the gulag camps of apocalyptic suffering and despair, a feat accomplished only through what is willful ignorance and evasion of the truth. For Christianity, this present circumstance holds particular relevance, as it is but the continuance of events which began in her War for Independence against the tyranny of Pharisaical Judaism 2,000 years ago. As such, let a slumbering world come to the inescapable conclusion that there is no beauty in the beast known as Marxist Zionism, and that if it is not slain it will succeed in devouring all of known creation. Let the revolution not begin, but rather continue as was intended by the Author of liberty who lit that fire 2,000 years ago in the town of Jerusalem. And in the process of awakening from the delusion, let what remains of humanity nod their heads reverently towards the precepts of justice and righteousness, and begin again the struggle to live as free men, taking the first step in this revolution by asking out loud that most important and desperate question as concerns today's members of the New Sanhedrin:

"What are we to do with these men?"

"Four Israeli soldiers caught this Palestinian minor, Imran Abu Hamdeieh, 17 years old, as he was standing in front of his house. The situation was very quiet, no clashes, no violence, no actions in Area H2 of Hebron, where the Israelis have full security control. The soldiers beat Imran in a corner near his house. Then they took him to their military Jeep and continued beating him. The soldiers drove off at very high speed on road 60 and threw Imran out of the Jeep. His head exploded on the road, his brains spread everywhere. One of the soldiers filmed these horrible scenes with his video camera."
— Excerpt of "**Israel is an Anti-Semitic state...the Daily life of Kawther Salaam,**" written by Palestinian journalist Kawther Salaam.

"When the heretic Herzl invented his ideology of Zionism and a "Jewish state," his supporters embarked upon a huge campaign of libel and slander against the Jewish people before the other nations of the world so as to enhance anti-Jewish feelings and enable those nations to expel their Jewish citizens. The Zionists wrote articles about this, as did the newspapers of the day. The entire campaign was designed to coerce Jews into moving to the Holy Land to enable the Zionists to accomplish their nefarious goals. The heretic Herzl wrote in his own abominable diary that increasing anti-Semitism would be of great help to his movement."
— Vayoel Moshe, Israeli writer and commentator

"I don't know this thing called 'international principles.' I vow that I'll burn every Palestinian child that will be born in this area. The Palestinian woman and child are more dangerous than the man, because the Palestinian child's existence infers that generations will go on, but the man causes limited danger. I vow that if I was just an Israeli civilian and I met a Palestinian I would burn him and I would make him suffer before killing him."
— Israeli Prime Minister Ariel Sharon

"If I knew that it was possible to save all the children of Germany by transporting them to England, and only half of them by transferring them to the Land of Israel, I would choose the latter, for before us lies the historical reckoning of the people of Israel."
— Israeli Prime Minister David Ben-Gurion

One Less Than Six Million

It was the event of the 20th century, at least according to the history that was written by the conquerors. It has pervaded Western thinking and morals for over 50 years now, and those in the West (particularly in America) are not spared a day wherein they are not reminded of its importance. It is the subject of literally hundreds of films, from *Schindler's List* to *Sophie's Choice* to the obligatory programs appearing on public television. It has been raised in the consciousness of the Christian West as the ultimate act of savagery and brutality, an act that has never and will never be surpassed in its inhumanity. It has become the grain of sand around which the black pearl of collective guilt has been formed, and it is the weapon whose brandishment elicits the Pavlovian response of a conditioned populace whose sentiments are used for the furtherance of public policy. It has become the new religion for many, a blank check for a few, a slavemaster to others, and it is known as the Holocaust.

Not since the 2,000 years following the Crucifixion of Christ has such infamy been placed upon a single event. Whereas the murder of Christ by the leadership of Israel formed the basis around which the religion of Christianity would be formed, now the murder of the descendants of those leaders at the hands of those professing to be Christians has supplanted what was the religion which helped to create Western Civilization. In some countries it is illegal to challenge the dogmas of this new religion, and in other countries where it may still be legal, an individual engaging in any scholarly study that wanders outside the parameters that have been rigidly established by the High Priests of Holocaustism is sure to be victim to an inquisition of sorts. It may result in something as dramatic as losing one's livelihood or even losing one's life. One thing is for certain though, which is that there will be Hell to pay for the individual who jeopardizes the ground which the bludgeon of Holocaustism has gained for Israel and for the interests of Marxist Zionism. To lessen the seriousness of the crime, to cause others to forget what plight and tragedy happened to its victims is to commit a capital offense that will be avenged at any cost. To bring it into relative terms, showing its diminutive stature in comparison to the Holocausts authored by the other siblings within the Marxist family results in one being branded an enemy of the people. To cause others to deflect their attention towards the plight of others, to cause them to shift their gaze towards injustices wrought against someone else is a mortal sin of the highest order. To reduce its size by even one less than six million will result in organized fits of apoplexy of the most maniacal version, and understandably so, particularly when it becomes apparent what is to be gained and what is to be lost because of it. It is the goose which lays the golden egg, the key which locks and unlocks all gates to the centers of power for those who brandish it, and it is as feared in intellectual circles today as was a knock on the door in the middle of the night in Stalin's Russia. Presidents, kings, writers, academicians and all others who occupy some position of importance in the effluent society of the formerly Christian West today bow their intellects reverently, if not fearfully, towards this golden calf, dutifully acknowledging in the process that they owe their lives and livelihoods to his good graces. But in all respects, the entire process is wrought with hypocrisy, which is the only genuine article that can be found in the whole sordid affair.

The ugliness of this particular brand of hypocrisy can be said to be such not only in its inherent sense of dishonesty, but also due to the contempt with which it holds its victims. In its application it betrays the fact that the perpetrators consider the rest of humanity to be so stupid as to be easily fooled by their sense of false values by which they have gained their ascendancy and respectability. Clearly, for Christians, this discussion should have particular importance, particularly when considered within the context of the dramatic events that surrounded their Messiah and the Pharisaical hypocrisy that he so clearly condemned. And if today's world can be said to be infected in a full-blown way with this particular virulency known as hypocrisy, then verily it reveals itself in the religion that has been formed around the suffering of Hitler's victims, (and in particular the Jews) during the Holocaust. Even its title, "Holocaust" (meaning sacrifice) carries with it the implication that the crime of murdering the Ashkenazim lambs of Europe serves as a replacement and antitype to the murder of the Lamb of God around whom the religion of Christianity has been formed. In essence, the final solution which the proselytizers of the new religion of Holocaustism have sought and nearly accomplished has been the replacement and reconfiguring of Western morality so as to align it in such a way as befits the agenda of Israel, as well as in silencing dissent towards her actions.

There are several tragedies which are associated with this new religion, one of which is that those who were Hitler's victims, who suffered and deserve what is a rightly earned sense of compassion from history and from humanity have been made showpieces in a spectacle which has defiled and degraded the solemnity and seriousness of their plight. The badge of honor which they earned by virtue of the nightmare that was inflicted upon them, a badge which they justly deserve to wear has been, due to the adventurism and ambitiousness of the more profligate among them, tarnished and made to appear cheap and whorish. The other victim of this tragedy, and probably the most serious aspect of the whole affair, can be said to be the assault on the intellectual process that formulates public policy, and in particular in America. The daily reminder to American Christianity concerning what is alleged to be its collective guilt is like the proverbial salt rubbed into the wound of American intellectualism, and as such has rendered her without the ability to think reasonably as regards her policies in the Middle East, and in particular Palestine. The results are, needless to say, tragic on several levels.

In the first case, the suffering of the Palestinian people, now almost a century long in its duration, has been completely cast aside as a necessary evil in redressing the crime committed by the National Socialists of Hitler's Germany. In such a way, the pimps of Holocaustism (manifested in the out-in-front/in your face stance of those who shape American sentiments towards Israel and by default public policy) have revealed what are the undeniable dogmas upon which their new religion is founded. For them, the fact that the murder of six million, or six thousand, or sixty million, or whatever number in actuality it is, takes on a more sober, somber, serious tone when it happens to fall upon their particular group, reveals in and of itself what are the racist, exclusivist, self-absorbed sentiments which form the operating ideologies of their agenda. In their insistence, (particularly with regards to the Holocaust of Nazi Germany) to focus only on the suffering of the Jewish people, grabbing the limelight as it were from the others who proportionally suffered more (including those who were Christian and who have received little if any attention) exemplifies what is on their part an irrational mindset which forms the philosophical underpinnings of an agenda which they attempt to masquerade as a religion of morals. The fact that hundreds of movies have been made by an entertainment industry (for decades now firmly in the hands of Zionist interests) and as of yet there have been few if any movies made which depict the horrors of Stalin's death camps or what was endured by the Christians at the hands of Jewish Bolshevism in relatively the same time period exemplifies what are sentiments rooted in self-absorbed racial narcissism of titanic proportions. The message which is constantly pounded into the conscious and subconscious intellect of Western (and in particular American) Christianity is one of shameful reflection, which amidst all the films, lectures, books, museums and whatnot all revolve around a set of fixed questions:

"How could you do this? How could you let this terrible thing happen? Where are your morals? Where is your sense of compassion? Where is your decency? If this event, the killing of six million Jews at the hands of Christians is but the logical outcome of a religion which is anti-Semitic in its essence, perhaps then you should abandon such a religion, and choose instead to work out your penance for such an infamous act by raising up our suffering as the ultimate act of inhumanity, and consider no other suffering for all eternity."

If these individuals, the pimps and whores who worship the golden calf of the Israeli state and her agenda were truly the humanitarian individuals they pretend to be (a pretension which they effect by their condemnation of Hitler's atrocities) they would not single out those instances in which they suffered, but would instead condemn all human suffering, including those Holocausts which they or their kin have authored. How conspicuously silent are their voices when a discussion takes place concerning the holocaust of 50 million Russians at the hands of Jewish Bolsheviks, as well as the Holocausts which they have effected against the peoples of the Middle East. Were the peddlers of Holocaustism genuine in their sentiments, if they were truly possessed of the humanity which they have accused the rest of the world of not having, then they would abandon what has been the welfare system of human sentimentality, a process of exploiting in a parasitical way the goodwill of American Christianity and its willingness to make reparations for the suffering of Hitler's victims.

ONE LESS THAN SIX MILLION   179

For the rest of the world not under their spell, the real lesson of all the Holocausts of the 20th Century has not been lost. To the rest of the world not held under the spell of the magicians of Holocaustism, the lesson learned has been that irrespective of whether atrocities were committed by Marxist Christians in Germany or by Marxist Jews in Russia, what truly matters is that the blood of humanity which has been rendered so worthless does not appreciate or depreciate in value depending upon its racial origin. As such, for the gangsters at the ADL, JDL, AIPAC, JINSA, and all the other crime families of Marxist Zionism whose job it is to elevate the Jewish blood shed in WWII to a level of superiority over all others, (and in particular over that blood which their cousins in Israel shed in Palestine) such a willingness betrays what are the detestable traits found in the practitioners of master race ideology, an ideology which they in perfect hypocritical fashion condemn in others who oppose their agenda. And as sickening as such convoluted and contradictory logic is, it is worse when considered that many of the individuals who make the pretense of fighting for the interests of their people, individuals who have been inflicted with what is best termed *racial narcissism* have themselves been willing participants in bringing to bear the same Holocaust whose historical importance they now use as a vehicle for their own enrichment and empowerment.

"The anti-Semites will become our most loyal friends, the anti-Semites nations will become our allies."

For those who have been given an extra sized serving of Holocaust History over the period of the last 4 decades, the above quote would appear to have originated with Hitler or one of his fellow travelers. The reality of the matter, however, is that its origin resides with the godfather of the Zionist movement, Theodore Herzl.

The reader should not be surprised to see that Herzl, (considered by many in modern Jewry to be a greater savior of the Jewish people than Moses himself) would author such sentiments. His statement reveals what has historically been a secretly nursed hatred for the Jewish people that has been entertained by those occupying positions in their leadership for the last 2,000 years. Historically, they are individuals who have schemed and plotted for their own benefit, using those under them as stepping-stones in their ascent to power. Whether their leadership has been religious or secular in nature, they have over the centuries of the Diaspora planted the seeds of suffering which would later blossom into the same anti-Semitic persecutions by which they have advanced in their power. Tragically, those who have drunk from the poisoned well of Zionist Marxism and who have elevated men like Herzl and others to positions of sainthood and respectability do not realize what an injustice they are doing to themselves and to those who follow after them. If the members of modern day Jewry were truly concerned with isolating what have been the root causes of their persecutions and suffering, they would then come to the undeniable conclusion that it has been their leadership which has been the source of their suffering for the last 2 millennia. From the Pharisees of the Sanhedrin to the Pharisees at the ADL, it has been the racist, exclusivist mindset entertained by those in leadership positions which has been the cause of friction between Jew and Gentile and which has led to anti-Semitism. Being that, historically speaking, persecution of the Jewish people has been good for business for the likes of Herzl and others, therefore it should come as no surprise to find them rubbing their hands greedily in expectation of what has been for them a reliable source of enrichment and propagandistic revenue. And as diabolical as such scheming appears to be when it exists merely in the theoretical stages, more so is it when it is moved from the drawing table to the production line, for in addition to those who theorized, such as Herzl, there are those as well who were directly responsible for the same suffering and persecution which has become the lifeblood of the Holocaust religion.

Besides those ardent Zionists who helped finance Hitler's rise to power (exemplified by Jewish banking interests, including those of the Warburgs, Rothshields, and others) more dastardly is the history of those who refused to help those Jews who were suffering under the Holocaust as it was occurring.

"About the cries coming from your country, we should know that all the Allied nations are spilling much of their blood, and if we do not sacrifice any blood, by what right shall we merit coming before the bargaining table when they divide nations and lands at the war's end? For only with blood shall we get the land."

The cold, calculating, ambitious words of the above quote illustrate what was the willingness of Zionist interests to participate in the suffering of the Jews for the purpose of furthering their cause. These demonic sentiments are none other than those that were enunciated by representatives of the World Zionist Congress, the most powerful Zionist group in the world at the time. These damning words were part of a response sent to Michael Ben Weissmandl, a Rabbi who, after being taken prisoner by the Nazis in Slovakia, worked out an arrangement with his captors for the release of tens of thousands of Jews upon payment in the amount of $50,000.00 to officials of the Third Reich. The response he received from Nathan Shwalb, representative of the World Zionist Congress, clearly shows what was a deliberate effort on the part of Marxist Zionism to participate in the suffering of European Jewry for the purposes of increasing their leverage and power. In addition to this, it has been chronicled with equal clarity the cooperation that took place between the Third Reich and the leaders of the Zionist movement, namely Dr. Rudolf Kastner, for the transfer of almost 1 million Jews to the now infamous death camps in return for the release of a few thousand who were ardent followers of Zionism and considered to be good prospects for the future state of Israel. In addition to these and other nauseating depictions of betrayal and duplicity, the history of the event also reveals what was the involvement of Zionism in acts of terrorism and murder, manifested in the bombings of Synagogues and assassinations against anti-Zionist Jews, acts which were then exploited for their propagandistic value in driving Jews into the protective, loving arms of Zionism.

The instances of Jewish leaders executing violence and subterfuge against their own for the purposes of furthering the interests of Zionism are too numerous in number to discount. And as surely as Hitler's remaining henchmen were rounded up and subjected to the justice of the Nuremberg Trials, so too should have been those individuals who held the seats of power in the Zionist organizations and who (for the purposes of consolidating power among themselves) conspired to subject world Jewry to the now infamous instances of inhumanity and suffering. And yet, these historical accounts and many others of similar stripe are conspicuously not mentioned when the ghouls who operate the ADL, JDL, and other organs of espionage and propaganda for Israel's benefit maintain what has become a state of heightened hysteria concerning the ever looming spectre of anti-Semitism and its history. And if a seldom mentioned history has now indicted those individuals who have acted as cannibals upon the suffering of their own people, reducing their victims to a state of sub-humanity who are of no worth outside of that which brings political power, it should then be easy to see how the same individuals would be willing to inflict misery upon those not of their own family as well.

It is within this context therefore that one comes to grasp what is the sickeningly apparent reality concerning the peddlers of Holocaustism and the disciples over whom they hold sway. The picture that is fleshed out in clearly discernible images is one of duplicity, avariciousness, and hypocrisy of apocalyptic proportions. The truth is that the lessons of the Holocaust have been lost on these individuals, and their presence in the dialogue concerning human rights and persecution is as out of place as would be the presence of the Ku Klux Klan in a forum concerning the civil rights of African Americans. As such, society must conclude that all their public displays of outrage over inhumanity and suffering are nothing more than scripted words that have no sincerity behind them, which is revealed not only in the history of what they have done to their own, but as well in the racial hatred they have nurtured against the Palestinians whom they view as impediments in their ascent to power.

"One million Arabs are not worth a Jewish fingernail." —Rabbi Yaacov Perrin, Feb. 27, 1994

"May the Holy Name visit retribution on the Arab heads, and cause their seed to be lost, and annihilate them." It is forbidden to have pity on them. We must give them missiles with relish, annihilate them. Evil ones, damnable ones." During a sermon preceding the 2001 Passover holiday by the influential Israeli Rabbi Ovadia Yosef: Ha'aretz April 12, 2001

"The Palestinians are beasts walking on two legs." Israeli Prime Minister Menachem Begin, speech to the Knesset, New Statesman, June 25,1982.

"The blood of the Jewish people is loved by the Lord; it is therefore redder and their life is preferable." Rabbi Yitzhak Ginsburg, head of the Kever Yossev Yeshiva (school of Talmud) in Nablus. He was later quoted in praise of the infamous machine-gunning to death of 40 Palestinian

worshippers by Baruch Goldstein, that it was *"a fulfillment of a number of commands of Jewish religious law...Among Goldstein's good deeds, as enumerated, are...taking revenge on non-Jews, extermination of the non-Jews who are from the seed of Amalek...and the sanctification of the Holy Name."*

"There is no such thing as a Palestinian people... It is not as if we came and threw them out and took their country. They didn't exist." Golda Meir, in a statement to The Sunday Times, 15 June 1969.

In the post Holocaust age of sensitivity to political speech that even whiffs slightly of what is the ugliness of racist sentiments, the fact that members of Israel's ruling classes are and have been able to utter such abominations and not be called to account for them betrays what is the hypocrisy that flows like rivers through the veins of today's Zionist organizations. More outrageous is the fact that these same individuals who have brought themselves to the centers of political power by riding atop the waves of condemnation for the inhumanity of Nazi racism are willing to embrace the very same Beast which they now make a show of despising. In the above quotes, (which are but a small sample of what exists) a simple rearrangement of the wording to indicate that the authors were Germans talking about Jews would have resulted in world-wide condemnation by the very same Zionist organizations who today have enshrined and lionized those among them who were bold and brash enough to voice the same sentiments in public. To simply designate this as hypocrisy is not sufficient, for in reality it is criminal, and on the scale that deserves the same condemnation from history as was showered upon those who were the infamous henchmen of the Third Reich.

The statements, as ugly as they and the sentiments that they betray are, can be said to be merely the tip of the iceberg when compared to the actions that have accompanied them since the birth of Zionism. The list of war crimes perpetrated by the New Third Reich, Israel, wrought against the peoples of the Middle East are crimes which date back to the early years immediately following the Balfour Declaration up to the present, and are clear examples of a nation and its people who are afflicted with the same poison of race-conscious Marxism as existed in Nazi Germany. In the same manner as the deluded people of Germany sat back and justified the actions taken by their government with regard to the extermination of the state's enemies, in like manner so do the citizens of Israel and her supporters abroad in their justification of Israel's extermination of the Arab peoples who dare to sit on the land which was given to them by divine mandate 2000 years ago. Today's disciples of Zionist butchery, who have made as a pillar in their discipleship the condemnation of the defense given by the German people following WWII that "if only we had known, something would have been done," cannot make the same claim concerning the plight of the Palestinians whose concentration camp existence is visible for all to see today. In allowing the men, women and children of Palestine to be degraded to the status of untermenschen as were many of the present inhabitants of Israel in WWII Europe, they have ignored what were the lessons which history has painstakingly sought to impart upon humanity concerning racism and the persecution which inevitably accompanies it. In such a manner, by facilitating the extermination of the "cockroaches" and "beasts" of Palestine as well as subjecting them in the meantime to a daily life of sickness, starvation, violence and fear, they spit on the graves of all those who perished in the Holocaust at the hands of thugs who have worked in concert for the furtherance of bloody Marxism, whether it was in the form of Nazism or Zionism.

Those who today are riding atop the Beast known as Marxist Zionism, and who imagine themselves as occupying a place of such power that is impervious to defeat should think again. This hypocrisy which manifests itself by those who are forced and pretend to worship Israel and her people (as personified by those nations of non-Jewish lackeys who today bow reverently before the history of their suffering) is a tenuous and transitory condition. With this in mind, everyone involved who has, for the purposes of furthering the interests of Israel, exploited the event known as the Holocaust and the infamy that it represents should recognize that at some point the clock will run out on them, and along with that their luck. Being that everyone involved has by virtue of their self-interested motives long ago shed any sense of honesty or integrity, (be it in their words, deeds, or sentiments) it can be therefore safely said that their sentiments are unreliable at best. Given that today's policies that are propped up by what is in reality a forced sentimentality towards the people of Israel and her suffering means that at some point the world will abandon those sentiments that are not rooted in genuine concern. As such, the wider the war becomes between Israel and her enemies, the more havoc which is wrought upon the world as a result of her belligerent behavior, the less willing will her supporters in gentile nations be willing to run to her defense. And with this in mind, those who use the charge of anti-Semitism and the suffering of the victims of the Holocaust as a bludgeon to silence critics of Israel should recognize that inevitably the value of their currency (the charge of anti-Semitism) will eventually lose all its purchasing power, at which point they will then be left to the tender mercies of those whom they have bullied now for 5 decades with its use.

Let the world hear no more from the mouths of the Zionist organizations that bewail the death of six million Jews and at the same time cheer the Holocaust of the Arabs in the Middle East. They have demonstrated themselves by such contradictory sentiments to be the dregs of humanity, without an ounce of the same decency which they accuse their critics of not having, an absence of which they attempt to conceal by their pretended condemnation of Hitler's atrocities. In truth the tears they pretend to shed over the murder of millions in WWII might as well be tears of joy for all the sincerity that is behind them. In their insistence upon elevating the suffering and well-being of their cousins in Israel over the rest of the peoples in the Middle East (and in the rest of the world, for that matter), they have revealed themselves to be vampires and ghouls without an ounce of soul left in them, dispossessed of the qualities of compassion and justice which separate man from beast. In their insistence upon sanctifying the violence and duplicity with which the humanity of the Middle Eastern peoples is violated, denying in the process the existence of their suffering and misery, the High Priests of Marxist Zionism have become carbon copies of the same Holocaust deniers whom they castigate today through their effective infrastructures of propaganda. In the meantime, the world might as well prepare itself for the new era which is quickly approaching as a result of Zionism's hatred for mankind, an era in which will be asked the same questions concerning the Holocaust of the Arabs (Muslim and Christian) as were asked concerning the Holocaust of the Jews:

"How could you? How could you just sit by and do nothing? Where is your humanity? Where is your decency?"

At which point the world, condemned by its foolishness in allowing the vampires of Marxist Zionism to again drown humanity in its own blood will have to sit there, unable to say anything in its defense other than *"I was just following orders."*

If it should be said that the lessons of the Holocaust should be reduced to one, all encompassing, non-discriminating dictum, it is that human suffering at the hands of a group of thugs who stand to gain by such suffering is a crime. The type of blood that flows in the veins of brutality's victims should not have an exchange rate attached to it by virtue of which race it designates. The one truth that should be enshrined forever in monuments and movies should be that misery that has been authored by racism or political ambition is a crime anywhere and at anytime. And with this in mind, those who would raise the importance of Jewish suffering over the suffering of others should be seen as the frauds that they are, and therefore let the world disregard without hesitation all the feigned sentimentality that they make in their passionate yet disingenuous condemnation of crimes against humanity.

As for the rest of the world, it should begin the long overdue abandonment of the system of weights and measures that it has adopted with regards to human suffering. Such a system is nothing more than a convoluted violation of the laws of decency, a backwards attempt to quantify and qualify human suffering through the use of maniacal formulae, genetic calculations and other methods of junk science. The followers of such a system, despite their perceived power and respectability, are by definition nothing more than academicians in the now defunct Flat-Earth Society who deserve neither consideration nor respect. Amidst their outrageous exhortations for the execution of violence upon all those whom they have deemed to be "beasts walking on two legs," let what remains of humanity understand that blood is red everywhere, without any respect paid to the veins which carry it.

As such, let the world finally rid itself of the sickness of racial narcissism, and its ugly twin sister, racial hatred, which has been the author of so much suffering. Let humanity once and for all drive a wooden stake into the heart of all political thought that embraces the heresy of master-race ideology, and let mankind finally grasp the reality that all holocausts and institutions of human suffering are vile, even those which bear the distinction of being one less than six million.

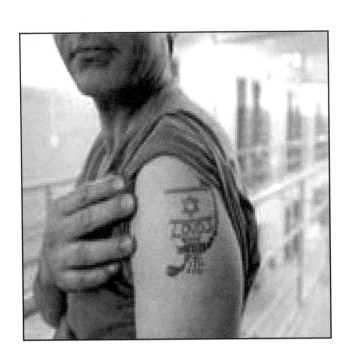

"I encourage my soldiers to rape Arabic girls, since the Palestinian woman is a slave for the Jews, and we do whatever we want to her and nobody tells us what we shall do but we tell others what they shall do."
— Israeli Prime Minister Ariel Sharon

"Here in the United States the Zionists and their co-religionists have complete control of our government, and they rule these United States as though they were the absolute monarchs of this country."
— Benjamin Freedman, author of the pamphlet "**A Jewish Defector Warns America**"

"I was in tears. These guys were joking and that bothered me. These guys were acting like, 'Now America knows what we go through.'"
— An American commenting on the manner in which his Israeli co-workers at Urban Moving Systems (a Mossad front company operating in the United States) reacted to the attacks of September 11.

"In the southern part of Hebron, the Israeli soldiers caught a Palestinian shepherd on the top of a hill. They checked his ID, and then they kicked and beat him. The Israeli soldiers, these "nice civilized soldiers" ordered the Palestinian man to bring his donkey. They ordered the poor man to strip, and then they threatened to shoot him if he disobeyed their orders. The poor man stripped, and then the Israeli soldiers ordered him to have sex with the donkey. 'I couldn't refuse, the soldiers were ready to shoot me,' he later reported. 'The soldiers were spitting and cursing at me the whole time. I am so ashamed and disgusted,' the poor man said."
— Excerpt of "**Israel is an Anti-Semitic state...the Daily life of Kawther Salaam**," written by Palestinian journalist Kawther Salaam

---

"At Deir Yassin, all of the killed, with very few exceptions, were old men, women or children. The dead we found were all innocent victims, and none of them had died with a weapon in their hands."
— Eliyahu Arieli, member of the Jewish Haganah who arrived at the Palestinian village of Deir Yassin shortly after the massacre committed by Zionists.

Birds of a Feather - Israel and America

As America seems to be going through the motions of squirming uncomfortably over the Iraqi prisoner abuse scandal, there are many who are not squirming, and are asking the question "why is anyone surprised?"

It's not that these individuals are comfortable with the situation, but rather that it is the anti-climactic result of having foreknowledge of the event, as much as one could expect to hear a clap of thunder following a bolt of lightning during a rainstorm. Those who have been following the Middle East situation for some time could have, and indeed in many cases have, predicted that this would arrive at some point. Other Americans, who today stand wide-eyed with gaping mouths at the situation, asking that completely out of place question of "how could this happen?" should really just keep quiet. It's not as if they weren't warned. The signs for something like this happening have been screaming out at them for the last 3 years, if not for the last 3 decades.

The fact that a good portion of Americans are showing shock and dismay at this situation can only result in making those around the world hate the United States more than they already do. Watching this spectacle is like watching an individual suffer the shock of finding out that he or she has just come down with a sexually transmitted disease after having lived a life of promiscuity for years. In watching such an individual, the world cannot even muster pity at such stupidity, particularly when the stakes are as high as they are concerning the present war in the Middle East.

Had they been listening and paying attention to more than just the foolishness that passes for political commentary on talk radio and mainstream news, they would have seen that this situation was as predictable as would be old weather in January. After all, in the United States of America over the course of the last three years, talk show hosts and other outlets of information have repeatedly crossed the lines between constructive political discourse and outright hate mongering in their insistence for various pogroms against Middle Easterners. Such individuals, considering themselves and their agenda as testimonies to the precepts of morality and justice have suggested time and again that this situation in the Middle East would be best solved by "killing all the Muslims," or some variation of that theme. Short of calling for their extermination, these individuals have, without an ounce of reserve, referred to them disparagingly as "ragheads," "sand-niggers," "Hajis," as well as a whole host of other eloquences, and have in general created an air of racial and cultural hatred towards them that has helped to bring about this current situation. On a seemingly daily basis in America over the course of the last 3 years, Muslims, both men and women, have been attacked physically, had beer bottles thrown at them from moving vehicles, had their Mosques set on fire, had bullets fired into their homes, and been the recipients of telephone death threats without any substantive media coverage nor law enforcement reaction. Muslim children have been taunted, beaten up, and in some cases, sent to the hospital as a result of the injuries they have received at the hands of "freedom-loving, God-fearing Americans". In what is an obvious testimony to a smothering sense of hypocrisy in America, there has yet to be found any morning news programs devoted to exposing these outrages, and why would one expect that there would be, particularly when it is considered who owns the airwaves and what agenda is being pushed? After all, how many movies and television programs have been made over the course of the last 3 decades by a Zionist owned media which have depicted Arabs and Muslims as violent, vicious fanatics who only understand the language of brutality and deadly coercion?

What those who are standing amidst this scandal, shaking their heads in bewilderment should realize is the fact that these American soldiers are only doing what they have been programmed to do from birth. In America over the course of the last 3 decades, the Zionist control over all outlets of media, and most importantly television, has resulted in a daily barrage of programming designed to obliterate the moral foundations of American society and to supplant this morality with a way of thinking that benefits the Zionist agenda. By the time these soldiers were 18, statistically they had witnessed over 20,000 acts of simulated murder on television, many of which were directed against those being of Arabic descent or of the Islamic religion. Over the course of the last decade, close to a dozen blockbuster movies have been made carrying such a theme, from *"True Lies"* to *"Executive Decision"* to *Blackhawk Down,"* not to mention the barrage of television programs dedicated to the same plot line. The whole business of murdering people, and more importantly, exterminating the enemies of the state of Israel, in an American media dominated by Zionist interests has been turned into a cavalier act with no bothersome after-effects. It is for this reason that America's children are taking weapons into schools and murdering people en masse, and this being the case, why therefore should anyone expect that any different behavior would be found among those soldiers whose very existence is concerned with the business of killing? They are merely doing exactly what they (and all Americans) have been programmed to do by the Zionist agenda. Through the daily drip by drip application of programming designed to desensitize Americans towards violence, a nation of mindless, bloodthirsty automatons has been created for the purposes of fighting a "decades-long war" for Israel's benefit in exactly the same manner as was promised by George Bush. In addition, in an America where the average time spent in prison for killing another individual is only 18 months, and the average time spent in prison for rape is only six months, why would these soldiers fear any justice that might come their way as a result of such behavior? And the fact that many of these abusive acts had sexual themes attached to them should surprise no one either, since America is now awash in a flood of sexually explicit programming and propaganda. America of 2004 is, whether in its media or real life, a bordello and a bloodbath, and why then should anyone be surprised to see American soldiers bringing these themes to other lands when it is all they have come to know in their lives here?

The Zionists who 80 years ago embarked upon the program of fulfilling the divine mandate of Eretz Y'Israel knew that such an ambitious program could not be done without the assistance of a rich and powerful ally such as America, and that the business of conquering the entire Middle East in a campaign rooted in injustice could not be done by an American people who still possessed any moral reservations. In this light, it becomes perfectly clear then why such a program for removing any religious or moral precepts has been fanatically employed by the Zionist agenda in America. In such an agenda's view, the only morals that matter are those which benefit

BIRDS OF A FEATHER

Israel, and in this way, all others must be rooted out, which is exactly what has taken place through its influence over media, academia and law.

Of course, this speaks only of those Americans who are outraged over the abuses. There are plenty of them out there who think nothing of it, or who are even cheering over it. One need look no further than America's most popular unconvicted felon, Rush Limbaugh, for validation of this theme, who jokingly referred to the outrages in the Abu Ghraib prison as no more serious in their nature than mere "fraternity pranks." This is a situation that was equally predictable as well, particularly when it is considered how many bumper stickers can be found placed on the backs of cars that summed up America's role in the Middle East with base suggestions such as "nuke their ass and take their gas." Driving these cars are individuals sporting t-shirts and hats that depicted Saddam Hussein or Osama Bin Laden on the front with some four-letter expletive solution in dealing with the Middle Easterners. The fact that this torture and abuse has taken place, and that it has taken place because of the massive propaganda campaign that has been nursed along by the Zionist agenda and that no one recognizes this to be the case only confirms just how advanced is the state of intellectual and moral decay in the US. Following this will be instances that will make the current goings on pale by comparison, at which point, there will again arise a befuddled and quizzical American population.

For those Americans who still have a spark of decency left in them, as well as a remaining grain of independent thought, perhaps an old adage should be considered.

"Birds of a feather flock together."

And if this still makes no sense, then perhaps

"Lie down with dogs, wake up with fleas."

If there are two birds who are flocking together these days, without a doubt it is Israel and America, who have adopted this symbiotic relationship, one a bird of prey and the other a bird of carrion. In determining which is which at this point it is hard to say, since the one seems always eager to outdo the other in nefariousness. One thing is for sure though, (and this was something about which those who understood the realities of the Middle East situation were warning as well) which is that this conflict, being a war fought for Israel's benefit, indicates that it will be done under her direction and by her methods. The pictures that have made their way into the press, along with the descriptions of the torture that took place are of no surprise to those who know anything of Israel's history and methods of abuse and torture against the Palestinians. These acts of abuse in Iraq over which Americans now are in a state of mild shock have been and are today common fare in Israel. Executions of Palestinian men and boys, simply by virtue of their age and physical fitness is and has been a daily occurrence, coupled with the now 50 year history of Israel's use of torture. And yet, those in the information business, (whether they are left wing mainstream media or pseudo-right wing pundits) refuse to acknowledge that these recent instances of Iraqi abuse are just an application of methods adopted by Americans doing the bidding of Israel. This assertion is easily validated by the fact that these media outlets have stubbornly refused to report the fact that many Mossad agents were present in these prisons when these activities took place. Equally silent has been the press coverage detailing the way that American troops have been receiving training of this sort from Israeli intelligence officers for exactly this type of business, a fact that has not been missed by the foreign press over the course of the last year.

Those who have been warning about this most assuredly would like to say "I told you so," except that to do so would be pointless in a country as brainwashed as America has become. The fact that the world is seeing these predictions validated today in the Iraqi prisoner scandal will have little effect on the average American whose view of the Middle East has been shaped by Ariel Sharon's friends and cousins in the media. And as much a tragedy as this is, this blind, cooperative stupidity, it is nothing compared to the tragedy that is to come. It is entirely possible that the whole reason that the Zionist media in America has chosen to expose all of this business is to further desensitize Americans to the more outlandish war crimes that are scheduled to take place in the near future.

Given the fact that America is even reacting to this scandal is a testimony to her pitiable stupidity in and of itself. The current issue of whether or not members of the US Military subjected a dozen or so Iraqi men and women to the humiliating and degrading treatment that has been reported in the news is secondary to what has taken place over the course of not just the last year, but indeed the last ten years. The real scandal here is the fact that tens of thousands of Iraqis have been murdered in a war that was fought on Israel's behalf, and that millions of them have had their lives ruined by a war fought on completely false pretenses. Besides this, over the course of the last decade more than a million Iraqis have died as a result of the sanctions that were placed upon them, preventing many necessary food and medicine items from getting to those who needed them. If the pictures of these abused prisoners cause America's stomachs to do somersaults, how much more so should this take place when considering the thousands of Iraqi children who were born terribly malformed as a result of the radiation poisoning they received during the first Gulf War. If Americans are bothered by the images of Iraqi men being forced to climb on top of each other in the nude, then equally bothered they should be when viewing the pictures of 11-year old Iraqi boys whose arms and legs have been blown off by American bombs, as well as the pictures of those whose heads are missing and their guts lying all over the ground. The sheer scale of difference between these injustices, and the fact that Americans are easily led by the nose into focusing on and fretting over the one and not the other reveals the intellectual and moral prison within which their political and sociological existence is constructed, these people who boldly and brashly call themselves "free."

One must question at this point where the media's interests lie in reporting on this issue so heavily, since they have kept the truly horrifying aspects of the war hidden from the American people. Only time will tell as to whether it is being done as if to say "See, we can report the news, even when it is ugly," or whether it is being done merely to inflame the Arab world and thus widen the war. One thing is for certain though, which is that if the Zionist agenda which so thoroughly controls the American media saw something in this scandal which posed a danger to its plans, that this information would not be receiving the airplay that it is getting. And one can forget about the argument that maybe the individuals who control the flow and flavor of information may have suddenly been smitten by a sense of right and wrong, as well as having all at once adopted a genuine concern for the ethics that are supposed to guide journalism—it is way past that point. Were they truly dedicated to bringing the truth of the situation involving the Middle East to the American people, the media would have from day one made sure to point out what everyone else around the globe already knows, namely that this war was and is being fought solely for the benefit of Israel and her interests. After all, extremely explosive information concerning Israeli involvement in acts of war against the American people, from the murdering of 34 sailors aboard the USS Liberty to Israel's involvement in the events of 9/11 have been kept under wraps in a most efficient and comprehensive way. With this in mind, one should not assume that there is something so explosive about this current situation involving the abuse of Iraqi prisoners that makes it uncontainable. This is something that those who are "in the know" should consider when pondering the real motives behind what has been this controlled release of information.

For those others, the ardent Zionists (either Jewish, Christian, or whatever) who are feeling that twinge of nervousness over the amount of news coverage that this event is causing, such worrywarts should put their fears to rest. The waves that are being produced by these revelations will be calmed down soon enough by those who have kept America asleep on this subject for decades, so your little project in the Middle East is in no way threatened in any substantive manner. Those who have a vested interest in keeping America uninformed about the truth will leave nothing to chance, and indeed will pull out all the stops in seeing to it that a sleeping giant goes back to what he does best, which is sleeping. When a few concerned Americans begin to rouse themselves from their hypnotic stupor by considering the importance of that now infamous comment made by Ariel Sharon in 2001 about the "Jewish people controlling America," the anesthesiologists whose job it is to keep America asleep will be there to do their job. When college professors or journalists begin delving into the story of the Israeli intelligence officers who were arrested in the days following 9/11 for videotaping the planes crashing into the buildings and cheering for a job well done, the ADL, JDL, AIPAC, and JINSA will do their best to shout down any pertinent information and in the process get these rabble rousers fired from their jobs. Americans will not note the fact that many of George Bush's closest advisors hold dual citizenship in Israel and at times have worked for her as lobbyists. Americans, desperate to avoid facing the humbling experience of recognizing their folly in fighting Israel's wars will pay little mind to the

BIRDS OF A FEATHER

mountain of evidence that exists indicating the involvement of Israel in the blackmailing of President Clinton during the Monica Lewinsky affair, the blackmailing of Representative Condit through the Chandra Levy affair, the 9/11 tragedy, the anthrax attacks, and a dozen more infamous instances of treachery and betrayal. And finally, in putting your fears to rest, when something goes "boom" in America, (a low-yield nuclear weapon or some type of biological attack) everyone will assume, (with the assistance provided by a Jewish owned media in America) that it was perpetrated by a bunch of swarthy, third world Islamic extremists from the caves of Afghanistan, or, in the case of the next theater of war, Syria, Iran, or Lebanon.

For those who are optimistic that the current scandal may be successfully used to awaken the bulk of Americans into recognizing the danger that the friendship between Israel and America has caused, such optimism should be tempered as well. It is way past the time for anything taking place that would allow America to extricate herself from this parasitic relationship without serious harm being done to her. Besides the fact that every member of Congress was bought off at least 3 decades ago, America must come to the realization that there are very dangerous consequences that would result from such a divorce. The marriage between Israel and America is exactly like that between an abusive husband and an abused wife, a wife who, after years of being beaten up decides to leave him, and he, in his desperation to prevent her from leaving, has the last say on the matter by killing her and then himself. Israel's parasitic relationship on America is rooted in a psychosis of sorts, a situation that screams out a madman's warning to the rest of the world that "If we can't have her, no one can." Israel has already hinted at this in her long standing military policy known as "the Samson Option" which would entail the use of nuclear weapons against anyone, including her most lucrative spouse America, who in any way threatens her existence in a serious manner. Considering the parasitic relationship that exists between Israel and America, the fact that America is the lifeblood of Israel and the means to her realizing her 2,000 year dream of global hegemony, what then could be more serious to her existence than having America cut off all aid to her, without which she would cease to exist?

Those who are just now realizing the fact that the current scandal with the Iraqi prisoners can be said to be the product of America's friendship with Israel can now better understand why there has been a very vocal minority warning about such a situation for decades. Perhaps now they will better understand why there are those who have risked life and limb in order to expose the danger of this relationship, true patriots who foresaw the manner in which America's decency would be tarnished through such an unhealthy friendship. Whether or not this parting of ways can be done without leading to her complete destruction is a matter for fate to decide. But those who are wetting their pants in fear over coming to terms with this reality shouldn't blame fate either. If it can be said that birds of a feather flock together, than America, understanding the nature of Israel's history and the ideology that propels her forward in the world, should have stayed as far away from her as possible from the beginning. This was the recommendation that was made by virtually every foreign service officer in the United States government at the time when President Truman was pondering whether or not to accept that big bag of cash by Zionist agents in return for his endorsement of the Jewish state.

In truth though, the recommendations of the US State Department should be seen as secondary arguments as to why America and her integrity would be compromised by such a friendship. After all, more potent an argument than that is the fact that many of those who embarked upon this adventure called Zionism were the cousins of those who butchered tens of millions of people in Bolshevik Russia. With this in mind, one should ask the prudent and prophetic question, "does a leopard ever change its spots?" Logic should tell the world, and more importantly America, no, and therefore, what benefit would there be in forging a relationship with such an animal as this? America has lied down with the dog and has now woken up with fleas, and in choosing bad company, has allowed what goodness existed in her character to be corrupted.

In practical terms, all that remains for the rest of the world to do is watch in horror as these two birds of a feather go about the business of plunging the world into an orgy of warfare and inhumanity, whose end result one need not be a prophet to envision. This orgy will be but another instance of madness that will one day be studied and weighed by historians who will shake their heads in bewilderment, asking the same unanswerable question being asked by Americans today over the Iraqi abuse scandal, which is "how could this happen, and why?"

"When the Israeli occupation soldiers left after three days, the El-Najjars went to see what happened to their apartments. They couldn't believe what they saw. The Israeli soldiers stole everything that they could take with them, particularly jewelry, about $1,000 (which is a fortune for the residents of Rafah most of whom are unemployed now), cellular phones, and anything they could carry with them. The most disgusting thing was that they urinated and defecated on the beds in all of the apartments."

"Seventy-year old Muhammed Mustafa El-Najjar couldn't take the horror of having six enemy soldiers staying with his extended family for 72 hours at gunpoint, frightening the children and humiliating the adults. Whenever he would open the window for some air the Israeli soldiers would scream at him not to. He needed heart medicine. Using a cellular phone his sons called for an ambulance to come to take him to the hospital. When the ambulance came it was fired upon by the Israeli soldiers who refused to even let the driver bring the medicine to Muhammed. He had several heart attacks and two days after they had left, Muhammed Mustafa El-Najjar died. His death was not counted in the official statistics as one of the victims of the Israeli horror campaign in Rafah, but it was absolutely related to that savage campaign."
– Dr. Hassan El Najjar, editor of www.Al-Jazeerah.info relating what took place during the Israeli siege of the Palestinian town of Rafah in 2004

"While in Israel, the tourists, Jews and Gentiles alike are carefully watched so that they do not stray and happen to see the sordid side of Israel-the true Israel. Like in Soviet Russia and other communist countries, visitors to Israel are taken on carefully planned guided tours. They are shown the religious sites, the lush orchards, the technical accomplishments, the arts, and to stir sympathy, they are taken to visit the Holocaust Museum. But, kept from the eyes of the tourists are the ghettos, the prisons where political prisoners, mostly Arabs are subjected to the most inhumane forms of torture. They do not see the widespread crime activities and the corruption between organized crime bosses and the government and police officials. The tourists do not learn of the true inner workings of Israel's Marxist/fascist government, nor do they see Israel's racism."
– Jack Bernstein, author of the book **The Life of an American Jew Living in Racist Marxist Israel**.

Through the Eyes of a Muslim

"It ran chills up and down my spine," he said that Sunday afternoon. "It was all there, all laid out, how they were going to take over the world, and it was the scariest thing I have ever read."

What he was discussing that day was a document which had been circulating amongst the various members of his church, downloaded off the internet in which was contained an outline for subduing the whole of humanity to a totalitarian system run by Islamic extremists. No doubt, the individual who had brought the document to church that day had originally retrieved it from Worldnetdaily, Drudge, Limbaugh, Hannity or some other intellectual brothel that peddles the whorish agenda of Marxist Zionism for the benefit of Israel. As the elderly, conservative Christian man described this document that ran chills up and down his spine, there wasn't an ounce of doubt in his mind that it was genuine and that its contents portended the worst for the Christian West. He was visibly frightened at what he had read, as if he had been given the gift of prophecy and could see in a vision the nightmare that awaited him and his fellow Christians in the not too distant future. In this future, as he foresaw it, the Muslims would one day seize political control of the Western world, come to dominate or at least manipulate its media and legal systems, and afterwards restrict or outlaw the precepts and practicing of the Christian faith.

Calming him down was of no use. Trying to make him understand that the religion of Islam is not inimical to Christianity in its central tenets was an exercise in futility. Reading to him the treaties signed by Caliph Omar and the Christian leaders in Jerusalem and Damascus, centuries-old treaties which promised the Christians that they would be free to practice their religion without fear fell on deaf ears. Showing him passages of the Qur'an, wherein Christ is revered as the Messiah and wherein his blessed Mother is regarded as even more holy than even some Christians believe only made him angrier. Even for him, as a Catholic, pointing out the fact that in the Holy Land Muslims and Christians can be found side by side in processions honoring the saints in heaven and Christ's mother meant nothing. It was of no use; he had made up his mind and didn't want to be bothered with the details. In his world, Christianity was besieged by an enemy who was encircling it minute by minute, and threatened by a fanaticism whose victories could be chronicled every day in what had become the constantly progressing destruction of Western Civilization.

That Sunday visitor is by no means in a class by himself. He and the tens of millions of his like-minded fellow travelers represent a rather large group of apocalyptically minded Christians who lament the loss of Christian virtue in today's world, and, to be fair, for good reason. Clearly, an individual would have to be sleep walking through present day life not to notice what has become the decline of objective morality, and particularly in the Christian West. It truly is a season of evil, these last 50 or so years, and the fog which has all but choked out the civility which the carpenter from Nazareth preached in his 3 year mission today billows throughout the world, wreaking havoc and misery on an unprecedented scale. Never before (with the possible exception of those early days in which this revolutionary new faith struggled to free itself from the tyranny of Pharisaical Judaism) can it be said that Christianity was more unwelcome than it is now. As such, individuals just like that Sunday guest are willing to hear just about anything which confirms their worst suspicions, which conforms to the future as they envision it, and which justifies and validates all the handwringing that they do on a daily basis over watching their faith attacked. What they do not realize is the fact that clever individuals, much more clever than the average Christian might suspect, know well of their condition, and as such have made the most of it, particularly since the tragic day of September 11.

Never allowing an opportunity to get past them, these clever individuals have capitalized on the anxiety under which conservative Christians have been suffering now for the last 30 years or more, and as such did not miss a beat in exploiting that anxiety so as to serve their own purposes. It is for this reason that a Zionist media (which has never failed in recent decades to profane Christian sentimentality on a daily basis) made sure to fill America's TV screens with images intended to evoke Christian outrage over an attack purported to have been committed by Muslims who were motivated by religious reasons. In such a way, Americans were made spectators to images of structural beams from the debris of the Twin Towers that fell together in such a way as to resemble a crucifix. The same media whose executives have never hidden in the slightest manner their loyalty to the antichrist agenda of Marxist Zionism made sure to show firefighters and policemen making the sign of the cross before going into harm's way. And finally, in the interest of optimizing that same anxiety and outrage which they have fostered for years through their attacks on Christian sentiments, the same institutions which have never blinked at an opportunity to ridicule traditional religious values were found to be conspicuously supportive in their coverage of all the bumper stickers, t shirts, hats, and anything else that could be found boldly stating "God Bless America". In a moment of weakness, one would like to think that the seriousness of the events which took place that day in New York may have caused a profound change to occur in the hearts and minds of these reprobates who have gnawed away at Christianity and its precepts through their influence over the media and legal system. However, for those who are inclined to think so, prudence should probably be allowed to weigh in and remind the world of those famous words concerning a leopard changing its spots.

The truth of the matter is, for Christians who are serious about their faith and who justifiably resent the manner in which it has been ridiculed and attacked over the last 3 decades, there is good reason for them to have those shivers going up and down their spines these days. Indeed, there is an enemy out there who is hell bent on destroying them and their values, and who can be found possessed with a virulent hatred of the Christian faith as well as for all its adherents. Truly there is an organized network laboring in the world, at times whispering in secret, at other times shouting out loud in furthering its agenda to bring about the day in which the last shovelfull of dirt is thrown on the grave of Christian sentimentality. Like he assumes, these individuals have religious reasons for doing this, and indeed have demonstrated that there is no length to which they are unwilling to go in appeasing their flavor of fanaticism. It is a centuries old struggle, a jihad fought by individuals who are absolutely possessed by their desire to replace the religion of Christianity with a theocracy of sorts, and bringing about in the process a totalitarian system that has no tolerance for dissenting views. And, as the Sunday guest prophesied, this enemy will use every means it his disposal to achieve this, including the media, the legal system, and outright terror at times. The problem for the Sunday guest and all those others who agree with him is that they trusted too much the very individuals who couldn't be trusted, and as such have come to fear the wrong people and the wrong agenda. In effect, due to the propaganda which has taken place since 9/11, what has occurred is that those who pose the real danger to Christianity and to civilization in general have used the event as a means of shifting the focus away from their own deeds and agenda, and have caused the world to focus on a threat which pales by comparison. In comparative terms, it is like the hungry, 200-pound wolf who has convinced the sheep that they need to be afraid of a fox that poses no danger to them at all, and for obvious reasons. And as outrageous as this may sound in a propagandized world post 9/11, it actually makes perfect sense to those who still have eyes to see, and even more so when the whole situation involving Islamic extremism is viewed through the eyes of a Muslim.

If any one group of individuals should be able to understand the sentiments which are fueling the anxiety and outrage which have been associated with those living in the Middle East, then no one should understand better than the same conservative Christians in America today like that Sunday guest. In truth, much of what he sees in the world with respect to the lawlessness and immorality which has overcome humanity like a flood has much to do with the reason why Islam views the West in such unfavorable terms. It is the Muslims who despise the moral relativism (or outright antagonism to objective morality) that has brought fuel to the fires of religious extremism. The more radicalized the West has become with respect to its indifference to morality, the more radicalized has the Muslim world become in the opposite direction, much like a good portion of conservative Christians today have become. The document which was making its way around the internet and which was used to frighten Christians in the West was a statement of fact more than anything else, for a better reading of the document would reveal that its contents depicted a West which is dying due to low birth rates, and that eventually, (due more to simple demographics than anything else) the Muslims would overtake the Western world as a result.

Therefore, what should be obvious to that Sunday visitor and all conservative Christians like him is that the Muslim world, rather than an enemy, instead stands in solidarity with them in recognizing the same evils that have all but destroyed Western Civilization. But there are even more simple reasons that explain the current crises with regards to the Middle East, and an individual does not need a degree in theology to grasp them. And given the amount of energy that has been expended in keeping these reasons out of the debate, one must assume that these reasons also make perfect sense, which is why those who manage the flow of information have kept them hidden from public consideration.

Despite a propaganda campaign that has sought to depict Muslims as individuals driven by pure fanaticism, nothing of the sort is the case. They have reacted no differently than any other group of individuals would react were they lied to, had their land taken and their homes destroyed, robbed of their only source of wealth, and had their innocent women and children bombed, shot, starved and poisoned for the last 50 years. The religion of Islam has nothing to do with today's attempt by those in the Middle East to realize their own self-preservation and justice, for these same sentiments are naturally occurring and are found in every race, creed and culture throughout the world and throughout history. In truth, the amount of attention that has been paid to the religion of Islam since 9/11 has been nothing more than a deflectionary program which was hatched in conference rooms in Tel Aviv and New York for the purposes of pitting two religions, Christianity and Islam, against each other for the benefit of Judaism. In the process, the Zionist interests who have been propagandizing American Christianity since 9/11, (interests that are easily verifiable and recognized throughout the rest of the world) have, in furthering their interests, lied (either openly or by insinuation) about what comprises the sentiments of those living in the Middle East. In such a way, the Muslims, whose image has been stereotypically reduced to unthinking, fanatical individuals who have no concern for human life, and imbued with an innate hatred for Christianity and its adherents have been made easy targets in an effort to facilitate their extermination by the Zionist agenda. As such, clever individuals, manipulating what information conservative Christians saw and heard knew how to steer a shell-shocked Christianity into adopting the mindset which would facilitate a war of religion to eradicate

Zionism's last remaining impediment to world hegemony. The obvious foolishness in the arguments that have been used to demonize those in the Middle East is revealed in the fact that there has been no war of religion between the Muslims and the West for centuries, as well as in the fact that there are tens of millions of Christians living in the Middle East today. So inimical to Christianity, freedom, and the West were the Muslim nations that in anticipation of the liberation that they were expecting in the years encompassing the decline of the Ottoman Empire, they came to the Western powers, seeking aid in reforming their countries along the lines of the Western model. It was the Western powers, most notably the "Christian" countries of England, France and America, who (by then mere puppets of Zionist influence) betrayed them and broke the promises that they had made to them. It was the "Christian" countries that funded the gangsters of the Zionist crime families and injected them like a plague into the land upon which these people lived for 2,000 years. It has been the "Christian" countries who have stood by and watched as a program for ethnically cleansing the Middle East has been implemented by the practitioners of racist Zionism, a religion of hate which in reality is nothing more than the ugly twin sister of Aryan fascism. And today, it is the "Christian" countries that are paying for all the awful mechanisms of warfare that are murdering innocent women and children on an hourly basis, both in Iraq and in Palestine.

And yet, and yet, those who are suffering from these injustices are expected not to be angered or affected. They are expected to lie down and allow inhumanity to consume their existence as if they were subhuman themselves without an ounce of worth. All the instincts which are used in justifying America's (and all others') acts of war throughout history, instincts rooted in self-preservation and survival are conspicuously not afforded to those in the Middle East who are supposed to calmly accept being reduced to concentration camp victims until their number for extermination comes up. Only the madmen of the Zionist priesthood could conjure up such a diabolical program, and only an intellectually and spiritually vanquished Christianity could acquiesce to it.

For years, the Middle Eastern nations have appealed to the rationale of the West, and in so doing have calmly delineated these items as being some of the sources for their grievances. And while there has been some success in the countries of Europe with respect to arriving at an understanding in the interests of ending the bloodshed and injustice, there has been little success in America, and for easily discernible reasons. In an America where one must must choose between listening to right wing pundits like Limbaugh who tow the Zionist line and the left wing news media who does the same, there is little opportunity for the average unconcerned American to find out what constitutes reality as it is seen through the eyes of a Muslim. Besides the fact that he has been unjustly demonized and had his religious sentiments completely misrepresented, as well he must suffer from the fact that the history and sentiments of the Zionist agenda have been misrepresented in equal proportionality. In truth, the energy that has been expended in lying to American Christians about what comprises the religion of Islam and its adherents has been matched (if not outdone) by the lying which has taken place concerning America's only "ally" in the Middle East, Israel. And if ever there were a singular situation that formed a major component to this structure of Islamic extremism that Christians are told to fear today, then it can be easily understood by considering this incomprehensible relationship that exists between America and the pariah state of Israel.

As viewed through the eyes of a Muslim, how else then could one consider such a relationship and not shake his head in bewilderment? America's only ally in the Middle East, Israel, has been responsible for more acts of terror, sabotage, and murder of American citizens than the Muslims ever were. By her duplicity, she has put Americans in more danger than they have ever known or will know. She has bombed hotels, American government buildings, deliberately allowed hundreds of US Marines to be killed in their barracks in Lebanon, assaulted a US intelligence gathering ship, the USS Liberty (for the purposes of blaming the Arabs and thus drawing America into her war against them) stole and then sold America's most sensitive nuclear weapons technology to her enemies, (Russia and China) and by all indicators most certainly was involved in the 9/11 attacks. Whether it was the testimony given by the Israeli pilots who bombed and machine gunned the USS Liberty (killing 34 American sailors and wounding almost 200 more) or whether it was the Israeli intelligence officers who were arrested on 9/11 (while videotaping the destruction and cheering for a job well done) so much evidence exists which leaves no doubt as to who America's real enemy is, and yet short of one individual's conviction and prison sentence, Jonathon Pollard, nothing has been done to Israel with respect to justice or the interests of America's security. By contrast, year after year she is rewarded with more and more money and even more in terms of immunity and insulation from public scrutiny. The American people, supposedly a Christian people, have displayed not an ounce of the same concern for this obvious danger against their physical well-being which they attempt to display now over the supposed danger posed by Islamic extremism.

Through the eyes of a Muslim therefore, the picture of the modern day Western Christian is one of an intellectually compliant, politically and religiously complacent individual who cannot think for himself or act in his own best interests outside of the programming that he receives from his Zionist puppetmasters. Even today, as the headlines are blaring out the obvious vindication of this image by virtue of the fact that the war in Iraq was fought on completely false pretenses, the average conservative Christian in America who has adopted this irrational fear of Islam has taken no note of this nor does he appear to have been affected in the least. He will though, on Pavlovian cue by his Zionist mind programmers, become apoplectic with apocalyptic fear over a letter being brought to church in which is discussed the takeover of the world by a group of swarthy, 3rd world individuals hiding in the caves of Afghanistan. In the meantime, religious fanatics who owe their allegiance to the blatantly anti-Christian Talmud and its physical manifestation in the state of Israel will plot away his freedom of speech, freedom of assembly and freedom of religion right under his nose, and his concern will not be roused over these attacks in the least.

For those who remain unconvinced of what is the disproportional fear which they have adopted towards the issue of Islamic extremism, perhaps they should consider it in these comparative terms: There is not to be found one Muslim or Muslim sympathizer in the same Bush administration which launched the war in the Middle East for the interests of Israel. The famed "Neo-cons" are not only all Jewish, but as well are unapologetic Zionists who have acted as a fifth column in hiding from America what was the truth concerning not only 9/11, but as well every other act of war which Israel has committed against the people of the United States. It was not the intelligence services of the various Muslim nations that lied about Iraq's weapons of mass destruction, but rather those of Israel and her surrogates in America. It was not the leader of a Muslim nation who boasted about controlling America, but rather Israeli Prime Minister Ariel Sharon. It was not the intelligence services of a Muslim nation that blackmailed President Clinton through the Monica Lewinsky affair, but rather the Mossad of Israel. AIPAC, the organization that literally decides who gets elected to offices in the various branches of government in America does not stand for the American Islamic Political Action Committee, but rather the American Israel Political Action Committee. The ADL, which made such a fuss over the release of a movie depicting the dignity of the man most revered by Christians does not stand for the Arab Defense League, but the Anti-Defamation League, a Jewish organization tied to Israeli intelligence whose mission it is to silence criticism of Israel and thus open the door for Zionist world hegemony. How out of proportion is the fear entertained by American Christians over losing the right to practice their faith under a Muslim totalitarian system when it is considered that it was branches of these same Jewish organizations who called upon the federal government to arrest the maker of the movie *"The Passion"* and have him tried as a terrorist.

Concerned, conservative Christians should remember (or else come to realize) that it is not the Qur'an, the Islamic religion, nor its adherents whom they need to fear. This fear they have adopted is nothing more than a program of managed sentiments that those who control the flow of information have imposed upon Christians, and for obvious reasons. It is not the teachings of the Qur'an that depict Christ as a sorcerer whose punishment consists of being boiled in excrement, nor which depict his mother as a whore who mated with Roman Carpenters. It is not the Qur'an or the Islamic religion which considers Christians to be animals and calls for their extermination, nor which permits the rape and molestation of their children. These are the sentiments which encompass just a microbe-sized portion of some of the anti-Christian and anti-Gentile sentiments of Talmudic Judaism, whose militant adherents literally decide who becomes president, where and against whom America goes to war, and what information people in America see, hear and read.

In reality, a Christian who is outraged over the way in which Jesus and his followers are depicted in the media will never be witness to such a spectacle were the Muslims to "take over" as they have been led to fear. A Christian will never hear the name of Jesus taken in vain nor used in a mocking way, as occurs on an hourly basis in an American media owned by those sympathetic to Israel. In contrast to the way in which Christ's name is used profanely by a Jewish owned media in America, a Christian who is fortunate enough to carry on a religious discussion with a Muslim will always hear the name of Jesus followed with the very reverential blessing of "may peace be upon him" or, in the case of discussing one of his apostles, the blessing "may God be pleased with him". There are no media interests in the same Muslim societies that the West has been programmed into fearing that are producing movies such as *"The Last Temptation of Christ,"* nor those films that depict Christ's mother working in an abortion clinic. In America there are not to be found Muslims who are castigating Christians for opposing such defamatory art works, nor accusing them of being "book burning Nazis" or "opponents of free speech" and other such nonsense. Quite the opposite, when such movies have been released, Muslims could be found standing alongside Christians in righteous protest of these abominations.

And finally, in the interests of putting things in the socio-religious perspective upon which conservative Christians seem to be so focused today, it must be remembered that the destruction of any normative sense of decency with regards to modesty, promiscuity or the sanctity of marriage that has been realized through the efforts of control over media, academia and law has not been accomplished by Islamic interests, but rather by those interests loyal to Zionism. It is not the Muslims who decided to put two of America's most popular female music idols on stage and have them engage in lesbianesque kissing. It is not because of an Islamic conspiracy that prime-time television celebrates sodomy, promiscuity and trans-gender/trans-sexual lifestyles. It is not because of Muslim influence over media that America's school children are taking guns to school and murdering people en masse in imitation of the programming that has been put before them that has glorified violence and gangsterism. There are to be found no Muslim names when the credits for these programs begin scrolling their way across the screen, although there are to be found a disproportionate number of individuals loyal to Israeli interests. And despite the best efforts of those to try and hide this uncomfortable piece of incontrovertible truth, nevertheless it is the elephant in the room that cannot be ignored, and to attempt such a denial is nothing more than an exercise in child's play. Indeed, as Israeli Prime Minister Ariel Sharon boasted to his cabinet in October of 2001, it is the "Jewish people" allied to Zionism who "control America," not the Muslims.

A proper understanding of history and sociological events requires an appreciation of the laws concerning cause and effect. With this in mind, it must be understood that the real culprits who are responsible for bringing into existence Islamic extremism are the Zionists and their Christian lackeys who have given to Israeli interests a blank check for murder, genocide, and the destruction of all sentiments rooted in commonly held moral values. Before Zionism arrived on the world scene (along with its revolutionary program for reconfiguring Western morality so as to place it in alignment with her designs) there was no such thing as Islamic extremism or the violence that seems to accompany it. Were it not for the fact that those working for the Zionist agenda have through their influence overrun the West with the scourges of abortion, pornography, sodomy and every other abominable vice recognized to be such by any basic moral standard, Muslims would not be "plotting" the downfall of the West. Both in the political and sociological sense, Western Christianity, said to be in danger of destruction by Islamic extremism, can blame the Zionist interests which put into motion the series of events which have brought the West to the brink of annihilation, as well as for their own complacency in allowing it to happen.

If there is any reason for shivers to be traversing what remains of Christianity's spine today, then it should be taking place for the right reasons. In adopting this disproportional sense of fear and foreboding with respect to Islam and its adherents, Christianity has fallen into a trap that was constructed for her by clever individuals much more dangerous than the Muslims could ever be. These clever individuals are fighting a jihad to rid the world of an ideology that they swore two thousand years ago to destroy, and by all appearances, have almost succeeded. Today, these religious extremists have bribed and blackmailed their way to the pinnacle of power in the world, and the attempt to deny this fact is reminiscent of those who at one time attempted to deny the existence the Mafia. As such, conservative Christians who have come to recognize the apocalyptic times in which they are living should take careful steps that they do not become followers of the Beast whom Christianity was told would appear in the last days, for in reacting to the information which has been put forth by the Zionist agenda with respect to the religion of Islam and its adherents, conservative Christians are cooperating with a program which has been designed for their own destruction. In hyping the danger which Islamic extremism is said to pose to Christianity, the Zionist agenda is sending the Christian nations, (against whom the real focus of their agenda is directed) to fight for her and for her interests. With this in mind, Christians should be wise enough to consider the fact that once the "Muslim problem" has been taken care of for the interests of Israel, she will then turn her unused and unallocated resources on accomplishing the mission which she put into motion 2,000 years ago in the town of Jerusalem. Indeed, in watching as Christians have taken the bait with respect to the "Islamic threat" which the Zionist agenda has put forth since 9/11, one can imagine the howls of laughter that have been taking place in the offices of the various groups tied to Israel, including AIPAC, JINSA, the ADL and JDL. All things considered, this must have been what their great great grandfather Lenin meant when he said almost a century ago that "the useful idiots will fall into our hands like a ripened fruit".

Today, let conservative Christians not allow their spines to become cold in the manner in which the Zionist agenda desires, but instead use their heads and apply a healthy dose of skepticism towards today's events. The antichrist agenda that is Marxist Zionism has shown, through her influence in media, academia and law to be the sworn enemy of Christian sentimentality on a daily basis for decades. She has not passed up an opportunity to gnaw away at the pillars of Christendom, and has in the span of only 2 generations almost erased a culture that took 2,000 years to develop. As such, what remains of Christianity should assume that were there truly a threat posed to it by Islamic extremism, that therefore the Zionist agenda would assist it in any way possible. The fact that instead the Zionist agenda has endeavored to misrepresent the religion of Islam and its adherents means that not only does Islam not pose a real, organic threat to Christianity, but as well that there is much to be feared by the Zionist agenda if the two religions were ever to unite against it. It is for this reason, therefore, that the adherents of Judaic extremism have pitted the two faiths against each other, using the one to do the dirty work of exterminating the other, and after which time its own number will come up as well.

As such, let concerned Christians everywhere do as they were instructed and become as wise as serpents, for in so doing, they will avoid the traps which have been set for them by their enemies. Let the sheep not be distracted by that hungry, 200 pound wolf who is endeavoring to convince them that the fox is the real danger to them, when in reality he poses no threat to them at all, for the moment in which they shift their attention towards the fox, they will be pounced upon by an adversary who is much more deadly and much more dedicated to their destruction. And finally, in the interests of fulfilling their duty with regards to charity and justice, let what remains of Christianity recognize the fact that they have more in common with those living in the land of their Master's birth than they have been led to believe, for in the war to preserve what remains of mankind's better nature, the adherents of Islam are not an adversary, but rather an ally. The common enemy to both religions and indeed to all peoples is the antichrist agenda of Marxist Zionism that has relegated all nations and inferior races to positions of subhumanity, an ideology that, like any hellish fire, will consume the world if not stopped.

As such, let a sleepwalking Christianity wake from its slumber and concentrate its efforts on bringing the message of truth not only to itself but as well to the rest of mankind, a noble endeavor whose first steps may be initiated by considering the world as it appears through the eyes of a Muslim.

"He has sent me to proclaim freedom for the prisoners, and to release the oppressed."
— *Jesus of Nazareth*

"Behold,' Allah said, 'O Jesus, I will take thee unto myself and clear thee of the falsehoods of those who blaspheme. I will make those who follow thee superior to those who reject thee.'"
— **The Qur'an**, Islam's most holy book, Surah III

"The chief priests and the whole Sanhedrin were looking for false evidence against Jesus so that they could put him to death."
— **Book of Matthew**

"Do not suppose that I have come to bring peace to the earth. I did not come to bring peace, but the sword."
— *Jesus of Nazareth*

"After this, Jesus went around in Galilee, deliberately staying away from Judea because he knew that the Jews there were waiting to take his life."
— **Book of John**

"And Jesus son of Mary said 'O Children of Israel, I am the messenger of Allah, sent to you confirming the law which He gave before me.' But when he came to them with clear signs, the Jews said 'This is sorcery!'
— **The Qur'an**, Islam's most holy book

"Oh, Jerusalem, Jerusalem, you who kill the prophets and stone those sent to you, how often have I longed to gather your children together as a hen gathers her chicks under her wings, but you were not willing. Behold, your house is left unto you desolate...
— *Jesus of Nazareth*

"Jesus the Nazarene was sexually immoral, worshipped statues of stone, was cut off from the Jewish people for his wickedness, and refused to repent."
The Babylonian Talmud, Judaism's most holy book, Sanhedrin 107b

History's Forgotten Braveheart

Unbeknownst to them, he stood there as motionless as a statue, staring at them intently with a fixed and seemingly determined gaze. He eyed the enemy with the same resolute stare that any revolutionary does, calling to mind the wrongs that had been inflicted upon his innocent countrymen, and the justice that they as victims deserved in bringing things back into balance. He knew there could be no going back once the deed was done, and that by throwing down this gauntlet, he would begin the war for independence for which his people had been waiting more years than they could remember. He nodded his head slightly, as if to acknowledge that he had made up his mind, and turning towards his men who had arrived with him, indicated to them with a facial expression that they should pay attention to what was about to take place. As he started off, one of his men, made uneasy by what he suspected was about to occur, asked him with just a hint of nervousness in his voice "What are you going to do?" And despite his not saying anything, nevertheless they all understood his answer by virtue of the language in his body movements. The answer that he did not give, but which they nevertheless understood quite well was the same response given by the Scottish patriot William Wallace in the movie Braveheart before riding off to meet the English envoy, which simply was, "I'm going to pick a fight."

A minute later, in an event which was to alter the course of human history, he fashioned a whip out of something he had found along the way, and drove those out of the Temple who had desecrated its holiness through their love of money and ambitious designs. History had just been made, and a major shift in mankind's destiny had now taken place.

The event had caused a good deal of commotion, and as such did not escape the notice of those whose money went flying end over end with the turning of the tables. Many profits had been lost that day as a result of this vigilante's actions, just one in a series of fights he would pick during the course of the week against the powers that be. To him, there was no gray area when it came to dealing with his adversary, nor were there any kind, diplomatic words to be found in his discourse with them. In his estimation, they were the children of the Devil, a brood a vipers and a synagogue of Satan who would not escape the punishment of Hell for having oppressed those under them. He fingered them as the root of all corruption in his country, and warned everyone in his proximity to stay as far away from these individuals as possible, and for their own good. What he did was to merely state the obvious which everyone already knew, and this being the case, no one bothered to argue away his assertions, which would have been a waste of time anyway.

A few days later these same individuals who sat stoned face through all the condemnations that where leveled at them for what was their criminal and corrupt behavior would decide to suffer the militancy of this pesky revolutionary no longer. So, after gathering together in dark rooms, amidst whispers and darting eyes they would plot to have him killed in what was to become the most infamous scandal of political corruption in the history of mankind. And despite Pilate's reluctance to be responsible for the murder of an innocent man, nevertheless he was made an offer which he simply couldn't refuse. And so in the end, the simple peasant from Nazareth who dared to attempt the liberation of his people from the devilish grip of the Sanhedrin was strung up and nailed to a tree like an animal, an act of brutality that was meant to be seen as a warning to all the ages should anyone else get any funny ideas. As he hung there naked and stripped of his flesh, his enemies paraded at his feet, shaking each other's hands in congratulatory fashion and mocking him for having dared to disrupt their interests in what was his pathetic display of resistance. As he hung there, history's forgotten Braveheart, his message to those who were the oppressors of the weak and the peddlers of men's souls was simply *"give them liberty, or give me death."* The mob bosses got what they demanded, and, as the saying goes, the rest is history.

Indeed, the rest is history, but unfortunately a history much of whose importance has been forgotten in the 2,000 years that have passed in the interim. The image of the Prince of Peace as a militant revolutionary certainly doesn't conform to the image that has been embraced by millions of his followers today, and yet, in reality this is exactly what he was. In no way can it be accurately stated that he was a moderate in any sense, for as he stated on several occasions, he detested lukewarmness and ambiguity on matters of principle, comparing such half-measures as nothing better than vomit. He was just one in a long line of troublemakers who had dared to challenge the corruption that had been woven into the fabric of Jewish society by the leadership of Israel, and just one of many who was willing to expose that leadership as the source of the injustices that oppressed the poor and blameless of his day. Before him were all the prophets who had castigated a wicked people for their behavior, rabble-rousers who did not neglect to point out that it was those holding power in Israel who had inspired that deviancy.

With this in mind, he who was the mild mannered carpenter and who had suddenly burst on to the scene and began upsetting the order which had been established for the benefit of the privileged few should in all justice be seen as the liberator and revolutionary that he was. This should only be natural, and particularly to his followers today, since he never attempted to hide the fact that he was a thorn in the side of the powers that be in the last three years of his life. He made sure that those around him understood what he was about when he said in no uncertain terms that he did not come to bring peace, but rather the sword. In instance after instance he revealed what was his contempt for those who were determined to oppress the people of Palestine and to reduce their lives to that of concentration camp victims in what was the spiritual and sociological holocaust known as Pharisaical Judaism. He understood how vicious his enemy was, and entertained no illusions about the danger that encompassed his mission, understanding the fact that he was a marked man for his revolutionary activity. Nevertheless, as history has shown, he was not the type to allow fear to dictate his agenda, and therefore refused to back down in the face of such a formidable bully. He loved his people and, with equal passion, loved justice, and would do what was necessary to free them.

It is a curious thing to note these days, the fact that he is called the Savior by his followers and yet few of them appreciate him as anything more than this one-dimensional figure who speaks nice words and heals the sick. To his followers, the salvation he won for mankind is limited to their being saved from sin, and yet they do not acknowledge his revolution as going any further than that.

Whether this insistence upon looking at the life of this liberator in a purely one dimensional way is the product of disinterest in politics and history or whether it is the product of mass manipulation by interested parties is up for debate, probably a little of both, to be accurate. In any case, there is an angle to understanding this struggle that took place between him and the powers that be that is not discussed nor explored, much to the disadvantage of not only his followers, but indeed to the world in general. This truly is tragic, for contained within the drama that took place between the peasant carpenter and the Sanhedrin are invaluable pieces of information which carry the keys to unlocking the most serious problems facing humanity today. Included within this are explanations concerning the destruction of Western Civilization and the present war in the Middle East that threatens to consume the world in the very near future. But in addition, (and more importantly for those living in the present age) this tale is a warning about what lies ahead, a warning which much of the world has chosen not to heed over the course of the last century.

The question that should be asked by all those who are standing in the midst of this living history today is simply, what did this man see? What was it about the power structure of the Sanhedrin that made him temporarily abandon his mild mannered ways and patient demeanor? What was the danger that he saw in the future for mankind if the leaders of Israel were to be permitted to grow in power and in influence? If it is accepted that he held the power of heaven in his hands, then it must be accepted as well that he could have chosen to be born at any age before or after. What was it about that particular age and about that particular society that was of such importance that he insisted upon being born then? Clearly, he must have seen something that humanity did not see, something of such seriousness that to delay his business even a generation would have resulted in dramatic consequences for the future.

The answer to these questions surrounding the clash of ideologies between Christ and the leadership of Israel really are quite simple in their nature, which may explain much of why this answer has been missed. This understanding does not hinge on weighty, over-intellectualized arguments that have been put forth by detractors whose agenda has been to muddy the waters of public understanding. And although the explanation for this clash may come as a surprise to a few, to others however (and most notably to his ideological enemies who today are working feverishly to make the world forget about this war that took place) the answer does not come as a surprise at all.

> *"'If we let him continue on like this, everyone will believe in him, and then the Romans will come and take away our positions and our nation.' And Caiphas, the high priest answered them saying 'Do you not realize that it is better that one man die than that the whole nation perish?'"* John 11:48-51

Here the student of political science can see plainly what were the roots of contention that existed between the peasant carpenter and the ruling classes of Israel. And as much as there are those who would try to deny that this contention had political elements to it, nevertheless such an argument falls on its face when compared to the facts. Clearly the Sanhedrin had big plans, not the least of which encompassed throwing off Roman rule and supplanting it with themselves as the commissars of the Israeli state which would encompass the lands between the Nile and the Euphrates. In addition it is plainly revealed that they were in a state of panic over the effect of Christ's teachings, to the point that they were willing to assassinate him in order to prevent their being robbed of the influence they wielded over the Jewish people who were the stepping-stones in their ascent to power. What the Sanhedrin had been plotting through the medium of religious sentiments, and which was threatened by the message of liberation that Christ preached was a political system wherein the Pharisees would rule, and fueled by a new code of ethics which elevated the Jewish race to a level of at least de facto superiority over all others. This new system of ethics, the embryonic stage of the now codified Babylonian Talmud that forms the lifeblood of modern day Israel's political ideology, was the source of Christ's condemnation of what he famously referred to as the "leaven of the Pharisees." This mindset, with its altered sense of laws governing right and wrong, was a theme which he attacked regularly in his mission, characterizing it as a perverse set of morals which, by its twists and turns, had "made the law of God of no effect." It becomes clear then, based upon this passage, how it was that the Sanhedrin viewed Christ and his message of liberation, a depiction that has been carried forth in modern day Judaism and its political twin, Zionism, by the Talmudic depiction of Jesus as being a man who "seduced Jews under the sponsorship of a foreign, Gentile power."

(Sanhedrin 43a)

It is within this context then that one comes to better understand the deeper implications of Christ's conflict with the leaders of Israel in his day, and why such an effort has been made to de-legitimize and de-emphasize it in the present age. This sense of amnesia that has been imposed upon the world, (and in particular upon the Christian West) may seem to be a trivial matter to the uninterested, but in actuality it holds the fate of humanity in the balance. Put in plain terms, this vital and damning piece of information that his enemies are desperately attempting to conceal through their control over the outlets of information is the fact that this man, the peasant carpenter from Nazareth, was the founding father of the anti-Zionist movement which plays so prominently in world events today. He was the first to openly challenge the ambitions entertained by the leaders of Israel and to expose what was the hellishness of this diabolically inspired ideology. Part of his mission over the course of the last three years of his life was to drive a stake into the heart of this new malignancy which had recently arrived in the Holy Land, a cancer that, if left unstopped, would have poisoned the pool of humanity and destroyed the possibility of peace and order in the world irreparably. In short, the first opposition to the ambitions of Zionism did not begin with Yassir Arafat, Hamas, Hezb'allah nor the PLO, but rather with a peasant carpenter from the Palestinian town of Nazareth who recognized the danger that mankind would face in future generations were this Beast allowed to grow to maturity. It is for this reason and no other that he was murdered by the warlocks of the Sanhedrin, who evoked by wicked incantation this same curse which threatens to consume the world today.

It is in this light then that it becomes perfectly clear why such a concerted effort is and has been underway by the Zionist agenda to remove the dignity that is associated with the image of Christ, since it was he who first opposed these designs in his own time. In consideration of the criteria that has been set down by the peddlers of Zionist propaganda today, Christ therefore was the first "terrorist," the first "anti-Semite," the first "holocaust denier" and the first "sympathizer of Nazi sentiments," all accusations which are leveled at any individual who depicts Israel's past, present, and future in anything less than the most flattering manner that is demanded by her sympathizers. If he were alive today, re-enacting the very events which he authored 2,000 years ago, there is no doubt that just as he was murdered in 33 AD by these crime lords, by these founding fathers of the gangland ideology known as Zionism, that in like manner today he would have had his home blown up in a "targeted killing" and all his followers arrested and tried as terrorists. Short of that, one could expect like cold weather in January that the various groups tied to Israeli intelligence (including the ADL, JDL, AIPAC and JINSA) would be mounting public relations campaigns in order to smear him in exactly the same manner that they did 2,000 years ago, bringing forth false witnesses and conjuring up every slanderous accusation that would further their interests in ruining his credibility.

It is no surprise then that discussions concerning this aspect of Christ's mission have not taken place in recent years, particularly when the stranglehold over the flow and flavor of information held captive by the Zionist agenda is considered. As such, through 50 years of daily programming, the role of Christ as the liberator of humanity from the "leaven of the Pharisees," (Zionist principles without the official name) has been kept out of the consideration of those living in the West and thus out of the discussion as well. As such, a concerted effort has been undertaken to de-emphasize this political and ideological struggle which took place between Christ the freedom fighter and the leadership of Israel, while at the same time replacing it with an image of Christ as an effeminate, quiet, patient individual who only preached peace and submission to evil men and their designs. It is obvious why this has been done, particularly when it is considered what is to be lost by interested parties were such a discussion to be resurrected. The state of Israel, the physical embodiment of the same principles of Pharisaical Judaism which Christ challenged and sought to destroy in his time, can only exist through the co-operative efforts, (both in financial and military terms) of a Christian West that has forgotten the roots of its birth. Israel and its racist, anti-Gentile, expansionist, hegemonic existence would never have been able to have germinated and now flourished into the thorny tree that it has become were it not for the delusion under which maniacal Christian Zionists operate, nor without the assistance which has been provided by the complacency of the uninterested. Were Christians around the world to suddenly come to embrace the idea that Christ was the William Wallace of Palestine, seeking to free a captive humanity from the deadly, tyrannical grip of the Zionist agenda which is today attempting the same, the game would be up, and the Beast would then have to return to the rock under which it has been hiding now for 2,000 years.

The detractors of such an argument will maintain with kindergarten-level rebuttal that this assertion holds no weight in that Zionism began in the mid 19th century, nearly 1800 years after the events of 33 AD. However, making such arguments is in truth nothing more than intellectual slight-of-hand, the now common practice of shaping and molding history for the purposes of mass consumption of propaganda by an uncritical public mind. Zionism in name may have begun with the writings and dissertations of men like Hess and Herzl in the 19th century, and may have incorporated into its agenda the return of the Jews to Palestine, but Zionism as an ideology was already well in operation in 1st century Israel, and found in the ambitiousness of Sanhedrinistas hell-bent on achieving power for themselves.

It becomes clear then, why the disciples of modern day Zionism fear more than anything else an honest examination of its basic tenets and tendencies, (and particularly in the Christian West) for in this examination, the comparison between these tenets and the principles governing the Pharisaical mindset that Christ opposed becomes all too apparent.

In considering what were the characteristics of the embryonic Zionist movement fostered by the Pharisees which Christ condemned, (namely hypocrisy, duplicity, racism and the willingness to corrupt society and employ violence to further its own interests) and then viewing this against what are the defining characteristics of modern day Zionism, the similarities become undeniable. The only thing separating the two is scale, as it was that in Christ's time it was limited to a small geographical location, whereas today it has permeated the world with its poison and has ensured a future of never-ending violence. It is in this light then that it becomes more clear why all the fury over Mel Gibson's movie *The Passion* took place by the various Zionist organizations, since this movie showed in plain terms what was the philosophical lifeblood of ancient Israel's leadership, and how this modus operandi has re-emerged in the modern world today. In Mel Gibson's depiction of a Sanhedrin that employs the mechanisms of political corruption, fear mongering, threats, bribery, and character assassination of its enemies, it becomes clear to the viewer that it is mirror reflection of modern day Zionist tactics as well. With such a discussion taking place, all the clever masks which the apologists for Zionism have crafted in hiding its true image are ripped away, revealing it for the beast that in reality it is, as well as the danger that it portends not only for those in the Middle East, but indeed for the whole of humanity.

As much as the apologists for Zionism will attempt to hide the true nature of this ideology behind the language of noble aspirations mixed with the obligatory evocations of pity for the sufferings of the Jewish people, at its heart it is racism, chauvinism, hatred for outsiders, and more importantly, the vehicle which employs these characteristics for the purpose of bringing to positions of power the more ambitious individuals in Jewish society. Just as in the time of Christ, it featured a privileged class who occupied the positions of power in that society, and who used those under them as stepping-stones for attaining that power. Just like today, it insulates its leadership and protects the power that this leadership enjoys by keeping the lesser beings of the group locked as prisoners in a mindset which pits them against all other peoples of the world, in effect bringing into existence a state of war (if only in sociological terms) between Jew and Gentile. In such a state of war, those under the sway of this leadership are kept malleable by the undercurrent of paranoia that such conditions produce, a tactic that is clearly exploited today when groups are organized against someone or something that threatens the interests of the leadership. In such a way, a side by side comparison of the principles that governed the agenda of the Sanhedrin in 33 AD and that which governs the agenda of the New Sanhedrin, modern day Zionist Israel and its Pharisaical mindset, will reveal them as twin sisters separated by 2,000 years of history.

One does not need an advanced degree in religious studies or special training in sociological trends to see what is the overt application of Jewish supremacist sentiments in the state of Israel today. In the Jewish state, a person, by virtue of where they stand with respect to the race and religion of the Zionist agenda, may or may not own land, be married, receive justice in a court of law, and will inevitably find himself at some point being denied a whole host of other civil rights if he does not have membership in the racial country club.

The Supreme Court of Israel, using as its code of jurisprudence the Babylonian Talmud and its codification of Jewish Supremacist ideology, has on a daily basis for the last 50 years exonerated murderers, rapists, acquitted those accused of war crimes, and a list of similar instances too numerous to mention, whose only evidentiary criteria was the Jewishness of either the victim or the perpetrator.

And if there were ever any parallels that could be drawn between modern day Zionism and the "leaven of the Pharisees" that Christ condemned, then clearly such comparisons can be found in the racism and disregard for fellow man that characterizes both time periods. This racism that had become one of the whips with which the Pharisees kept those under them in line was clearly condemned in Christ's parable of the Good Samaritan, a story that had strikingly prophetic things to say about the current situation in the Middle East. Today, as Palestinians and Iraqis are being murdered for the benefit of Israel's expansionist dreams, one should consider the roots of the racism that are feeding these crimes, as well as take note of the fact that they are but the end result of tenets that are embraced in modern day Talmudic Judaism.

"Do not save Goyim (non-Jews) in danger of death. Show no mercy to the Goyim." —Hilkkoth Akum X1

"The Jews are called human beings, but the non-Jews are not humans. They are beasts." —Talmud: Baba Mezia, 114b

"The non-Jew is like a dog. Yes, the scripture teaches to honor the dog more than the non-Jew." —Ereget Raschi Erod. 22, 30

The above are just a smattering of quotes which depict the Talmudic mindset of modern day Zionist Israel, a mindset which today is but the concentrated, distilled, and purified poison of the same racist ideology that had its philosophical origins in the Pharisaical teachings of Christ's day. For those who will attempt to refute this with the assertion that these are just the rantings of non-Jewish anti-Semites who have either lied or misrepresented what are the true teachings of the Talmud, the reader should consider that these quotes are just a few of those from two works written by Israel Shahak, an Israeli citizen, Holocaust survivor, and professor emeritus at Israel's

Hebrew University. In his two epochal works, *Jewish History, Jewish Religion*, as well as *Fundamental Judaism in Israel*, he outlines what are the institutions of racism which form the lifeblood of Israeli society today and which guide all its actions and policies. By Shahak's accounts, Israel and its society are the physical embodiment of the Babylonian Talmud, which is itself the codification of the precepts of the same Pharisaical Judaism that was condemned by Christ and his message of liberation.

In fairness it must be acknowledged that there are a good portion of the world's Jews who, having become secularized in their worldview, have not been nursed on the sour milk of Talmudic racism nor its supremacist sentiments. It is accurate to say that these individuals are victims of these policies as well, for they have had to bear the brunt of the anti-Semitic reactions that such policies have produced throughout their sad history. Truly heaven and earth will rejoice on the day that these prisoners are finally and permanently rescued from an oppressive leadership that has reduced them to mere cannon fodder for their own greedy designs, an oppression that operates by first setting up conditions that lead to persecution and then rushes in to save them, all for the purpose of empowering itself.

If it can be said that the modern world has approached the understanding of Christ and his message of liberation in an oversimplified, one dimensional aspect, then with equal certainty it can be said the same has been done with regards to the events following his death. And it is within this context that the survival of the modern world is hinged as well, particularly in light of the events taking place in the Middle East today.

The fact that Christ's followers were being hunted down, imprisoned and killed by the Sanhedrin, using the same tactics of bribery and blackmail that were used in coercing Pilate into having the leader of this revolution to Pharisaical Judaism killed leaves no doubt as to what would have occurred had this malignancy remained unimpeded. In reading over the Book of Acts, one is left with the inescapable conclusion that those same individuals whose hands were covered with the blood of history's forgotten Braveheart would have succeeded in exterminating all the members of this underground resistance movement had they been given enough time. In instance after instance, what is depicted was an undeniable program on the part of the Sanhedrin to remove this impediment to the Zionist agenda known as Christianity, going so far as vowing "not to eat or drink" until it had been eradicated. A greedy and ambitious leadership knew that Christianity and its destruction of the barriers between Jew and Gentile were as dangerous to the Zionist agenda as would be firearms in the hands of slaves. Had it not been for a man named Titus, the Roman general who, in 70 AD broke up this crime ring by invading Jerusalem, and by doing so scattered the gangsters of the Sanhedrin to the farthest reaches of what was the civilized world at that time, it is highly likely that history would be much different today. Not only would Christianity not have survived the pogroms that would have taken place, but in addition all the instruments of political corruption which have come to characterize modern day Zionism would have found their way into the infrastructure of the Roman Empire as well. Given what was the mindset of those who sought ascendancy and power for themselves in the form of Jewish ambitiousness, it is logical to assume that given time, they would have seized the organs of power and influence in the Roman government, using it to further their own interests in exactly the same manner that they have affected today. The proof that this tendency was already well in operation is supported by the fact that not only had the gangsters of the Sanhedrin used the vehicles of political corruption to affect the murder of their political opponents in Jesus' time, (in bribing Pilate, the guards at the tomb, and the Roman government in the areas outside of Palestine) but as well in the fact that the first instance of serious persecution against the Christians under Nero was most likely the result of that same influence. According to the great historian Edward Gibbons, author of the timeless classic *The Decline and Fall of the Roman Empire,* the idea of blaming the Christians for the fires that destroyed Rome was introduced by Nero's wife, Poppea, who had recently converted to Judaism and was heavily under the influence of her spiritual advisors, all of whom were Pharisees. Bolstering Gibbon's assertion is the fact that, according to none other than the Encyclopedia Judaica, Nero himself converted to the religion of the Pharisees just prior to his infamous persecution of the Christians.

But besides these examples, one need look no further than the history of the last 100 years for validation of this theme. Understanding the nature of cause and effect, one must note that the world and its condition of growing exponentially more unstable and more drastic in its bloodletting over the course of the last century can be directly tied to the re-emergence of this criminal mindset that had been broken up 2,000 years ago in the town of Jerusalem. Besides the obvious aspect of bloodletting, the observant Westerner cannot help but take note of the destruction of Western Civilization that has taken place through Zionism's corrupting influence over media, academia and law. In the span of just 50 years, the civilization built on the religion of Christ that took 2,000 years to create has all but been removed from the world. As the principles and effervescence of Christianity have been removed, so too have all the political benefits which have accompanied them been erased as well, including true liberty and the respect of individual rights. The law of cause and effect, although not noted by a complacent Christian West, cannot help but point to the influence which the modern day descendants of the Sanhedrin have exerted upon this situation. And as diligently as detractors of this theme may try, there is simply no way to hide from honest consideration this elephant in the room that has had its hands in these events over the last ten decades. From the financiers and footsoldiers of Communism to Fascism to Zionism, the constantly recurring characters possessing an attachment to the same principles that governed the crime lords of the Sanhedrin are to be found without debate.

".....And it may be that this astounding race may at the present time be in the actual process of producing another system of morals and philosophy as malevolent as Christianity was benevolent, and which, if not arrested, would shatter irretrievable all that Christianity has rendered possible. It would almost seem as if the gospel of Christ and the gospel of Antichrist were destined to originate among the same people, and that this mystic and mysterious race had been chosen for the supreme manifestations of both the divine and the diabolical."

This observation, rendered by Winston Churchill in the years following the bloodbath in Communist Russia, is one of the most poignant, yet poorly remembered statements affecting the history of the last century. The Communist revolution and its aftermath, which, by some accounts, (including those of Gulag prisoner and championed writer Alexandr Soljinitzyn) claimed the lives of as many as 67 million people, was, in the words of Churchill, engineered by a group of "international and for the most part atheistic Jews." His is just one of many observances imparting this same theme, many by official institutions and sources, including almost all the governments of the industrialized nations at that time. Besides these observations by Gentiles, such an indisputable fact of history this is that even Jewish sources do not attempt to hide what was the obvious.

"Individual Jews played an important role in the early stages of Bolshevism and in the Soviet Regime. The Communist movement and ideology played an important part in Jewish life, particularly in the 1920's, 1930's and during and after WWII..... In some countries, Jews became the leading elements in the legal and illegal Communist parties, and were instructed to change their Jewish-sounding names and to pose as non-Jews, so as not to conform to right-wing propaganda which posed communism as an alien, Jewish conspiracy." Encyclopedia Judaica

"The Bolshevist Revolution in Russia was the work of Jewish brains, Jewish dissatisfaction, and Jewish planning, whose goal is to create a new order in the world. What was performed in so excellent a way in Russia, thanks to Jewish brains, and because of Jewish dissatisfaction, and by Jewish planning, shall also, through the same Jewish mental and physical forces, become a reality all over the world." American Hebrew, September 8, 1920.

As horrific as this, the most bloody circumstance in human history was, it is but one aspect of the attack against Western Civilization that has been the result of the re-emergence of Zionism in the 20th century. This "system of morals, as malevolent as Christianity was benevolent," has flooded the West with pornography, moral relevance, the murder of the unborn, the destruction of the family, and in all observable ways has all but destroyed the foundation of an entire civilization and culture. Through its stranglehold over media, the Christian West has been turned into a collective body of "useful idiots" whose resources and energies have been put to the service of the Zionist agenda.

In coming to terms with the conflict between Israel and the Arab peoples that she has oppressed and murdered over the course of the last 80 years, it should be considered that Marxist Russia has acted as a fountain for nourishing Israel's ideological thirst, passing along to her the same taste for blood that her vampire forefathers in the Soviet Union possessed. Today, one need look no further than the current bloodshed in the Middle East for validation of these observations, which, although having changed their geographical location, nevertheless carry the same ideological motivations, particularly those which are rooted in the ascendancy of Jewish gangsterism. One should not be surprised then at the seemingly careless application of violence that has been wrought by Israel in the Middle East since her inception, particularly when it is considered that the practitioners of this violence are the cousins and great grandchildren of people like Lenin, Trostky, Berea and Kaganovich, men whose hands drip with the blood of the tens of millions of Gentiles in Russia whom they slew.

It must be noted as well that today Israel has become a haven for "ex"-communists as well as the extremely prolific and dangerous Russian Mafia. Using the Zionist state of Israel as one of its most important bases of international operations, it is presently engaged in the business of drug trafficking, child pornography, arms dealing, the sex-slave business, and a whole host of other criminal acts that have assaulted the Gentile world and left it powerless to do anything substantive in combating it. This powerlessness on the part of the Gentile nations that must suffer from these plagues is due to the fact that Israel will not extradite these Jewish criminals for prosecution to a non-Jewish country. As such, this international group of gangsters wreaks havoc upon the world, enjoying the protection that the racial supremacist state of Israel confers upon them by virtue of their being Jewish.

It should be clear then to the average Christian who has a bearing on the history of the last 2,000 years that their Master had more in mind than simply saving mankind from sin, and that he obviously saw something of serious danger in the mindset of Pharisaical Judaism that caused him to challenge it in the manner that he did. One can assume that what he saw endangering mankind and world peace in the gangland ideology of the Sanhedrin was of such importance that it had to be stopped, first by revealing this "brood of vipers" that had come into existence, and secondly by scattering them and their power base in 70 AD. Given current events, what one may draw from this is that what he saw 2,000 years ago was identical to the reality which humanity faces today; namely, that a corrupt cabal of racial supremacists would bribe and blackmail their way to the pinnacle of power, and in due course seize control of the most powerful military and political entity in existence at the time for the furtherance of their own agenda. And, in light of the current war in Iraq and Palestine, as well as considering the existence of the relationship existing between Israel and the most powerful military and political entity in the history of the world, America, the new Roman Empire, it is obvious that his greatest fears have been realized, and only the truly blind cannot see that this is what has taken place today.

What Christians today have forgotten (with the assistance of a Zionist controlled media of course) is that it was this very entity and ideology against whom Christ gave his life in doing battle. The Christian world and its inhabitants are the progeny of Palestine's greatest freedom fighter, and have for 2,000 years been the beneficiaries of the inheritance that resulted from the war of liberation he fought against the tyrants of the Sanhedrin. Their religion was born out of revolution to Pharisaical Judaism, and the tree of their religious liberty was for almost 200 years fertilized with the blood of the spiritual patriots who paid the ultimate price; men like John the Baptist, Stephen, Peter, Paul, and all the others who knew that it was better to die free men than to live under the slavery of the racial supremacist mindset imposed by Israel's leaders. As such, the two ideologies, Christianity and Pharisaical Talmudic Judaism, (and its embodiment in the Zionist state of Israel) are as incompatible as are the ideologies of freedom and tyranny, and a friendship between the two is as unnatural as would be that of the lamb and the lion. And in what will be remembered one day as one of the greatest acts of betrayal in human history that may even outshadow the betrayal of Judas Iscariot, Christians today have ceded over to their eternal enemy the freedom that was purchased for them at such a monumental cost and sacrifice. This surrender, realized in the events which have been stretched out over the course of a 50 year span, is manifested in their willingness to allow their eternal enemy to once again impose upon the world the agenda which Christ gave his life to destroy, the agenda whose diabolically driven supporters call Zionism and its manifestation in the state of Israel. The deception that has gripped the majority of the world's Christians on this matter is so pervasive in its scope and intensity that even the most devout skeptic would have a hard time not seeing it as the fulfillment of the apostasy that was predicted would arrive in the last days.

And so it was that in the town of Jerusalem, 33 AD, the freedom fighter named Jesus of Nazareth fought not only to save mankind from the tyranny of sin, but to save them as well from the tyranny of the Sanhedrin. The events of 33 AD and 70 AD should serve as a warning to all of humanity, particularly today, as this "beast that was wounded and yet lived" (Apocalypse, 13) has now been resurrected and is in the process of enslaving mankind in the manner that it had planned to do almost 2,000 years ago. As such, let what remains of humanity reconsider the events of Jerusalem in the age of Christ in this new light, for indeed the peace of the world hinges on a proper understanding of it. Let mankind recognize that history's greatest unsung hero, the Braveheart of Palestine, 33 AD had much more to say about today's events than what has been understood, as well as what has been forgotten since that time. Just as his enemies paraded at his feet, congratulating each other in their success at affecting his murder and ending his war of liberation, so do today the great great grandchildren of those gangsters who are reveling in the lawlessness and inhumanity known as Talmudic Zionism.

And so today, let the world recognize the fact that the prisoner who was hung on that tree in Jerusalem continues to preach his message of liberation and to warn humanity about what it will face under the totalitarianism of the Sanhedrin Mafia. Let humanity view his passion and death as a warning concerning the bloodthirstiness of mankind's eternal enemy, the Sanhedrin, a beast whom he revealed to be the seed of Cain and the physical embodiment of evil in human form. In his three years of fighting, he gave mankind a glimpse of the beast that it would one day face towards the end of time, by tearing away the mask of inhumanity that is today the lawlessness and tyranny of the Zionist agenda. As such, let the world remember that his three years of fighting, as well as the 3 hours of his torture, cry out loud the theme that he wishes to bestow upon all his brothers and sisters.

That word, that battle cry which came forth from history's forgotten Braveheart, and which has echoed throughout these 2,000 years as both a blessing and a warning on his fellow man, speaks volumes about the past, present and future of humanity…

…and that one word is freedom.

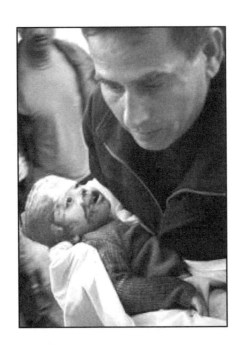

"We have to kill all the Palestinians unless they are resigned to live here as slaves."
— Chairman Heilbrun of the Committee for the Re-election of General Shlomo Lahat, the mayor of Tel Aviv, October 1983.

"The family is very angry. The Israelis transformed my son into a martyr because they killed his brother right in front of him. Then they killed his cousin, blowing Mohammed's brains out all over the ground in his presence. If he hadn't seen his brother and cousin die, he wouldn't have become a martyr."
— Bilal Al-Masri, father of a Palestinian suicide bomber

"The most spectacular event in the contemporary history of Palestine - more spectacular than the creation of the Jewish state itself - has been the wholesale evacuation of its Arab population which has swept with it thousands of Arabs from areas threatened and/or occupied by us outside our boundaries."
— Moshe Shertok, Israeli Foreign Minister

"If I were an Arab leader, I would never sign an agreement with Israel. It is normal; we have taken their country. They see but one thing: we have come and we have stolen their country. Why would they accept that?"
— David Ben Gurion, Israel's first Prime Minister

"The West demands from us that we stop the resistance, and rather than asking our occupiers to leave our land, they ask us to surrender to our oppressors. The "peace" that they demand, the "peace" which reinforces occupation and oppression and which furthers the process of exile for the Palestinian people is not really peace at all, but something else."
— Sheik Ahmed Yassin, founder of Hamas, murdered by Israel in 2004

"Tanks and airplanes do not frighten me. Fallujah is ours. We will rebuild it with the clay of Fallujah and we will irrigate it with our blood. The American soldiers destroyed my toys and my life, and I want them to leave."
— Ruah, a 10-year old Iraqi boy.

Those Who Hunger and Thirst for Justice

I visit him every day on the internet before logging off.

His name is Amir Ayyad. He is a Palestinian, and lived his whole life in the Khan Younis refugee camp in the Gaza Strip. I met him about a year ago, as I, (like many people at the time) found myself in the midst of searching for answers concerning the situation in the Middle East. Exactly what it was that led me into this search remains unknown up to this point. It would appear that for many of us, there seemed to have come a breaking point in the aftermath of 9/11, like the snapping of two fingers in front of our eyes, waking us from what seemed to have been a lifelong trance. I, as an individual who had paid little attention to the whole matter, suddenly in the span of a year's time had reached a limit with respect to what was my complacency and gullibility, and in the midst of looking for answers to this riddle, I met Amir.

I credit running into him on the internet as being an act of divine providence. Looking back, it can honestly be said that it was one of those life-changing events that one never seems to forget. I am sure that had I not run into him, chances are better than not that I would still be trying to sort out all of this business. In the days running up to the war, trying to make sense of anything was like playing pin the tail on the donkey in the middle of an empty field full of shouting madmen. The war machine, which wielded the most terrible propaganda and intimidation campaign in the history of mankind certainly didn't make things any easier. With the new laws in place, people were being arrested for asking questions or making waves. Those who weren't arrested ended up losing jobs and friends, as well as becoming the recipients of anonymous death threats over the internet or over the phone. Spies and snitches on America's college campuses were diligently keeping an eye on anyone, including professors, who dared to exercise their right of free speech and freedom of thought. "Unpatriotic" individuals maintaining

THOSE WHO HUNGER AND THIRST FOR JUSTICE   237

some intellectual individuality would then find themselves in the clutches of the "proper authorities," leading to disciplinary actions of some sort. In the media, all honest discussion surrounding the origins of the Middle East conflict were shouted down by individuals who charged their opponents with the unforgivable crime of being anti-Semitic racists for opposing Zionism, yet who themselves interspersed their attacks with their own racially-laced slurs such as "raghead lover" or "Haji".

And in the midst of this cyclone, I met Amir.

For me, his reasoning proved to be the most balanced and sensible. His argument certainly possessed a certain amount of authority, since he had lived in the midst of this conflict his entire life, and saw more of the reality encompassing the situation than any of the paid loudmouths on radio or television could ever imagine seeing. And although our discourse suffered by virtue of a language barrier, he still managed to make his point more clearly than anyone I have ever encountered, and continues to do so today. He was able, using but a few words, to convey entire chapters of comprehension and insight, and brought more truth to the discussion with just a few arguments than his opponents would attempt to bring in hours of shouting, snarling, and growling. He has never cursed me for asking questions, even when I played Devil's advocate. He has always spoken softly and patiently, never vowing vengeance on his oppressors, even though his entire life has been a testimony to their inhumanity.

How he maintained his composure with me was a miracle, since I, like most brainwashed Americans, refused to consider the possibility that I could be the victim of a giant hoax. At the onset of our discourse, the haughtiness in my refusal to consider his argument was rooted in the idea that such a conspiracy of silence surrounding the injustices inflicted against the Arab peoples was impossible to maintain, particularly in a country full of such smart people like America. It was in my reluctance to ponder the terrible possibility that I had been taken for a fool over the course of several decades that fueled the largest part of my reticence and doubt. In examining the roots of my own disbelief, I have now come to understand that this is one of the biggest reasons for America's unwillingness to consider the plight of the Arab peoples, namely just sheer pride, in addition to the shame that would accompany the process of coming to terms with the situation. Like most Americans, I refused to believe that my government could be party to something as magnanimous in its inhumanity as the circumstances he described. After all, we were America, the land of equal rights and freedom and compassionate conservatism. We were the bringers of liberty to the oppressed and justice to the afflicted. Our whole identity was wrapped up in this pretty packaging, and for him to allege that crimes of this nature not only were taking place, but had been for 50 years, was just too much for me to consider.

In the end though, his arguments finally made their way through my thick American head by way of a single photo, the same photo by which I came to know him. As the saying goes, a picture speaks a thousand words, and this photo, which hangs on my office wall, most of the time leaves me speechless.

As I came to know him, I came to understand what life was like in the place he called home, the Khan Younis refugee camp. Prior to this, the picture that I as an American had been given concerning the Arabs was that they were a mindless, senseless people who would have benefited by the whole Zionist venture had they been more reasonable. The image that the Zionist propaganda machine had painted was that of the Arabs as an unruly people who had no just basis in their complaints or perceived grievances, juxtaposed of course with the image of the beneficent Jews of Europe who were the bringers of civilization and enlightenment. Now I have come to see that this image entertained by Americans today is but a tragic mix of folly and fantasy. For those who have eyes to see, it is plainly apparent that the real savages have been those brandishing the whips of an oppression rooted in the quasi-religious garb of racial supremacy against a people whose forefathers were the bringers of culture to Western Civilization.

Today, I have come to see that the arguments and justifications vomited forth by this enchantress known as the Zionist agenda are no different than those which slaveholders in America used to give in justifying the unpardonable inhumanity that was their own bread and butter. The tactic has been the same as well, in that rather than debating the matter on the level of depravity and debauchery that the subject truly encompasses, instead they have turned the

THOSE WHO HUNGER AND THIRST FOR JUSTICE

argument in the opposite direction by attempting to champion its merits for a brainwashed people who dare to call themselves Christian. The truth given to me as a gift from my friend Amir was so different from this fantasy that it cannot be said that there is anything in the Zionist propaganda that is even accidentally right. The injustices that have been wrought against the Arab peoples are so vast and so pervasive in their scope that it is almost impossible to imagine that humans are capable of such cruelty and such stupidity. If ever an argument were to be made that the Beast of the Apocalypse was real and was living among us then one would not need to look much further than this cancer known as Zionism and consider the history of its deeds for validation of this theory.

The picture painted for me in perfect clarity by Amir's words and personal testimony has been that of the daily nightmare in seeing his friends and relatives killed on a regular basis. Whether such has been executed by Israeli soldiers or Israeli settlers, and whether such victimization has been achieved by being shot, or by being blown to pieces by explosives hidden in toys that were left for a Palestinian child to find, in whatever manner, for these people whom history has forgotten, it has been the nightmare of the 20th century. Life for a Palestinian living in the Occupied Territories has been that of a concentration camp victim, knowing that he or she lives under a sentence of death, and who must wait out the minutes and hours of this nightmare until that fateful number comes up. Every waking moment, the Palestinian asks the question "Is this my day, or is it the day for someone I love?" And in the moments right before falling asleep, the question "Will this be the sleep that brings me to my eternal rest?"

As far as the gangsters of the Zionist mafia are concerned, all of the bases have been covered, and this event can be said to have been the near-perfect crime. Not only have those who boldly assert that they are the apple of God's eye mass-murdered over 200,000 people as a tribute to Cain, the first murderer and the founding father of their ideological experiment called the state of Israel, but in addition, in the interests of honoring him and his infamous attempt to lie about his evil deed, they have cloaked this blood sacrifice in the whorish garments of untruth and disinformation. In the midst of this nightmare, Amir's oppressors have rubbed salt into the gaping wound known as the Zionist Occupation by virtue of the fact that they have held in perfect totalitarian fashion all the mechanisms of dispensing information into the collective intellect of the Western world. The situation produced by such a stranglehold has been one of the greatest causes of the hopelessness that pervades the lives of those living in the Middle East today, and has been one of the most important reasons for the cycle of violence that seems to be unbreakable. Such it has been that by the time Amir and others like him are able to take the stand and argue their case before what they had hoped was a fair-minded world, the jury pool had already been thoroughly tainted and corrupted by the poison of the Zionist propaganda machine. In such a situation, all the arguments they would make over the course of the last half-century, arguments pleading for justice and comprehension, might as well have been pure gibberish to the average Western Christian for all the seriousness that was afforded to them. This scenario is reminiscent of the now infamous trials that took place in America, where the relatives of those Negroes who were the victims of lynchings, shootings, or arsons could expect no justice in a corrupted legal system run by good old boys who would fix things in favor of the thugs being tried.

I must admit that initially, I myself had a hard time believing the allegations made by my friend Amir, until an article came my way, written by a former American reporter named Christopher Hedges, who described what he witnessed himself in the Gaza camp where Amir lived.

"It is still. And then, out of the dry furnace air, a disembodied voice crackles over a loudspeaker.

"Come on, dogs," the voice booms in Arabic. "Where are all the dogs of Khan Younis? Come! Come!"

I stand up. I walk outside the hut. The invective continues to spew: "Sons of bitches! Sons of whores!"

The boys dart in small packs up the sloping dunes to the electric fence that separates the camp from the Jewish settlement. They lob rocks toward two armored jeeps parked on top of the dune and mounted with loudspeakers. Three ambulances line the road below the dunes in anticipation of what is to come.

A percussion grenade explodes. The boys, most no more than ten or eleven years old, scatter, running clumsily across the heavy sand. They descend out of sight behind a sandbank in front of me. There are no sounds of gunfire. The soldiers shoot with silencers. The bullets from the M-16 rifles tumble end over end through the children's slight bodies. Later, in the hospital, I will see the destruction: the stomachs ripped out, the gaping holes in limbs and torsos.

Yesterday at this spot the Israelis shot eight young men, six of whom were under the age of eighteen. One was twelve. This afternoon they kill an eleven-year-old boy, Ali Murad, and seriously wound four more, three of whom are under eighteen.

Children have been shot in other conflicts I have covered, but I have never before watched soldiers entice children like mice into a trap and murder them for sport."

And so has the music played on and on, for nearly a century, repeating itself over and over again in the lives of those who know they are the hunted. This is the diary of a Palestinian who was sentenced to death the moment in which he or she was born, and the story of a people who hunger and thirst for justice.

This process of rooting out the truth concerning the Palestinian/Israeli situation has been a journey through a hall of mirrors to say the least, an unsettling, de-stabilizing event that leaves the individual dizzy and full of nausea after it takes place. When one comes to grasp the fact that a malignancy as brutal and careless in its willingness to inflict injustice and violence upon another group of people on the basis of race is not only running around loose, but indeed shares a lascivious, illicit love affair with the world's most powerful nation, well, after such a realization there is little room left for hope. Even less reason for hope is there when considering that virtually my entire nation of almost 300 million people have come to worship this beast, and that I used to be one just like them.

Nevertheless, I have embarked upon the seemingly futile gesture of attempting to wake others under this enchantment by passing on this gift that Amir has given to me. In trying to convince my fellow Christians who know or care to know little concerning the situation in the Middle East, I will use the arguments that my friend has used successfully with me. Unfortunately, it rarely does any good, they simply stand there as I used to do, haughty in their composure, a slight smirk on their faces as I flesh out a picture of what life is like for a Palestinian. I cannot entirely blame them, since I know that they know not what they do, and that their position on the matter is not a product of their own doing. Their position on the matter is merely one part of a program that has been surreptitiously installed and meticulously maintained on their psychological hard drives by very competent and ruthless hackers. For these individuals who shamelessly consider themselves as being enlightened by virtue of their Christian faith, there was no independent inquiry nor any genuine desire to know the truth that resulted in their present position on the matter, far from it. For the last 50 years, they have been kept deliberately stupid by means of an informational infrastructure that has defecated out Zionist propaganda on a daily basis. They and their opinion on the matter are part of a package deal that comes with the privilege of being an American today.

Being an American today, and having membership in this very elite and esteemed club requires certain obligations from its members, one of which is to forfeit one's freedom of thought and freedom of conscience in return for the badge of complacency and moral stupidity. Wearing this badge of dishonor means that all must swear fealty to the ethos of the club, an ethos that is by no means fair or egalitarian in its application. This ethos, this pledge of loyalty can be summed up simply in its costly purchase: It is the price of the soul, and all its most necessary components: Pity, compassion, justice, wisdom, mercy, et al. And once these have been forked over to the bondsman, their ownership is transferred to those who put it to their own use and for their own interests, individuals who have no right in justice to possess them in any manner, and who are, simply, the Zionists of the Apostle John's Apocalyptic vision who *"call themselves Jews, but are instead a synagogue of Satan"*.

Unbeknownst to the world, and in particular to the Christian West, this war in the Holy Land has become the last battle for the soul of humanity. It has become the contest between the forces of good and evil, manifesting itself in the struggle between the qualities that raise our natures to that of humans or reduce them to that of beasts. Being such a momentous event in which matters of the utmost importance are at stake, naturally it has become a contest that has been corrupted by graft and bribery, and where might makes right. Understanding wherein lies the might these days, it is obvious now that the only rule that applies to this contest is that which brings victory to Israel and her inhabitants. Rather than allow a level playing field to exist, falling back on the confidence that accompanies knowing that the cause for which they are fighting is just and knowing that the best man will win, instead the interests of Zionism have resorted to doing anything necessary to win, no matter how outlandish or unfair. As such, in this battle of ideas and ideologies, the apologists for the state of Israel have demonstrated throughout their history the complete absence of respect they possess for any of the precepts governing right and wrong, save for those that can be successfully co-opted into effecting their own victory. In the application of these corrupted values, such individuals will on a daily basis throw sand into the eyes of their opponents, as well as into the eyes of a watching world community, all in the interest of gaining the upper hand in some fashion. These millions of grains of sand, representing the millions of lies and millions of acts of violence they have wrought upon innocent people, have been the building block of the Zionist temple known as Israel and have been used to blind the Christian West into becoming participants in the very same devilish agenda against which their Master had given his life fighting 2,000 years ago. In the information war that is so vital in keeping Western Christians stupid and lazy, Jewish interests ply the same mechanisms of lying, bribery, blackmail and subterfuge that were the trademarks of their forefathers 20 centuries ago, and Americans, not realizing the depth of their own enslavement, willingly shackle themselves intellectually and spiritually in their service.

No one should be surprised at this, as it has never been asserted that the Zionist propaganda machine is by any means stupid. On a daily basis, this propaganda machine has been able to take the most fundamental, undeniable pieces of fact and turn them into pretzel knots in such a way that they bear no resemblance to the truth in any form. By so doing, they have succeeded in robbing those under such an enchantment of the ability to follow the direction of good conscience or of an unfettered intellect. In weaving this enchantment, these masters of deception have manipulated words such as "targeted killing" to avoid the odious implication associated with the word assassination. Young Palestinian children who are gunned down in cold blood are referred to as "militants," the bombings of

Palestinian school yards are called "military operations," and a whole list of other vocabulary phrases that have been molested so as to best serve their own interests.

In the midst of this seduction, it is easy to see how the masses will surrender themselves and their humanity to the prostitutes of Judeo ethno-centrism, who have taken the most egregious examples of moral outrage and made them look beautiful. It is a difficult seduction to resist, and so, what I invariably end up doing in the midst of this cacophony of lies is to make my way back to Amir and speak to him. As I said, his arguments have always made the most sense to me, and in these moments of doubt, I gather my bearings by talking to him, even if it is only in my thoughts.

"Hello, my little friend, how are you? Are you well? Are you happy? Who are your parents? Do you have brothers or sisters? What is your favorite color?"

And although I cannot hear his responses, I am fairly confident that he can hear my questions, for in my mind's eye he now exists in the next world and walks in green fields holding the hand of God. For him all is serenity and peace, and he will never again feel the pain that he experienced here on earth when an Israeli bullet ripped through his tiny head as he stood looking out the window of his home. For him, there are only the sounds of peace and comfort, and he does not remember the shrieks and wailing that encompassed the last moments of his life in Palestine. And when he is not walking with God, he is playing with friends numbering in the thousands who were killed in circumstances similar to his.

"What's it like up there?" I ask him. "Do you remember your family? You were only two years old when you died. Had you learned to say their names by that time? Do you miss them?"

I can only imagine his answers. In some manner, he probably looks in on his family from time to time, moving in and out of their dreams and thoughts, assuring them that everything will be all right someday. And although he must look forward to seeing them again one day, he would probably pass on the opportunity of being with them today in the refugee camp of Khan Younis. It is understandable, since, given the serenity and happiness that he now calls home, he wouldn't trade that in return for living as a prisoner again in the concentration camp known as Palestine.

"What are the names of your friends in heaven? Are there really many rooms in his Father's mansion, like he said there were? What was your home like? How did your father earn his living? Is your mother pretty? She must be, because you certainly are."

Amir Ayyad is the face of Arab terrorism, or so those in the Christian West have been told on a daily basis. His death, a late-term abortion committed by the ultimate abortionist in the Middle East, Israel, is said to be a necessary procedure for the health of the motherland. The shedding of his innocent blood, one crime in a sea of such crimes that calls out to heaven for justice, is but a minor incidental today to a large number of Christians who consider this situation either with careless disregard or else with devilish celebration. This application of managed sentiments to the daily murder of Palestinian men, women and children is but a Pavlovian response inculcated into those Western Christians who seek the blessings of the same Jewish people whom they secretly fear and loath. The essence of his argument, the picture which speaks a thousand words and yet which leaves me speechless, is the one of him, a 2-year old Palestinian boy with a blood soaked bandage wrapped around his head who died with his eyes open. After a year of looking for the truth, I had finally found it, and it was the last argument that I needed to consider when making up my mind about who was right and who was wrong.

Well, almost the last argument, for in fairness, I needed to hear at least something from the other side. In my foolish sense of optimism, I expected that there had to be at least some pity left in Amir's killers for what they had done, some whisp of humanity that led them to harbor at least some sense of regret. I found none, and to this day have yet to see any proof that such individuals possess even a single blood cell in their beings that connects them in the smallest way with the rest of the human race.

What I heard instead was the chuckling of course individuals who have lewdly danced about like schoolyard bullies, mocking and laughing at the destruction and misery they have delivered into the lives of Arab families for fifty years. No pretensions of regret, no feigned sense of penitent sorrow. And if after this there had been any remaining doubt, than the issue was firmly settled when I considered the cold, calculating words of one of the architects of this process of extermination, just one of millions who seeks to justify what was done to Amir and to the thousands of others like him.

> *"I vow that I'll burn every Palestinian child that will be born in this area. The Palestinian children are more dangerous than the men, because the Palestinian child's existence infers that generations will go on."*

And in these eloquent words, encompassing a century of violence and genocide, I came to view in perfect clarity the image of the beast, the harlot of the Apocalypse, Israel without her mascara. It is a nightmarish image, this that has been hidden for a century from the Christian West by layer upon layer upon layer of insulating blush and rouge, cover-ups that give the appearance of life and vitality, but which when wiped away reveal the nature of a beast possessing the face of death and duplicity. And as much as the magicians and beauticians may endeavor to paint her up in such a way so as to hide the true ugliness of her visage, nevertheless they cannot outrun the history of her utterances. This promise to wipe out the children of Palestine, authored by Ariel Sharon, the "man of peace" whom George Bush and American Christians have pledged to support with their praise and their money, serves as a resume of sorts for one whose hands have dripped with the blood of Palestinians since he was a teenager. These words, by no means isolated, are but a few of those that tell the unvarnished, uncensored, ill-considered testimony of Israel's history in the Middle East. These words are the building blocks of a nation whose existence has been outlawed by the weight of history for the last 2,000 years, and for reasons that now should be apparent to all who have eyes to see. And let not the enchantress known as the Zionist agenda succeed in lulling a Christian world back to sleep by reassuring it that these words by Ariel Sharon, the Butcher of Beirut, are an aberration in any sense. Lined up next to his testimony are the remarks of men like Ben-Gurion, Weitz, Shamir, Begin, Rabin, Netanyahu, Dayan, and every other Zionist vampire who has feasted off of the blood of the Palestinian innocents for the last century.

It is no wonder why Lucifer holds the human race in such contempt. Robbing mankind from its sense of humanity and right thinking historically has been as easy as stealing candy from a baby. How much he must laugh when he considers the effortlessness of such an endeavor in bringing before the consideration of mankind such blood thirsty individuals, beasts in human form who are then celebrated and inaugurated to the highest positions of prominence and power by fools who gladly forfeit their sense of decency and humanity. A man like Ariel Sharon and all the founding fathers of Israel can, in the midst of the bloodiest century in mankind's history, utter promises to continue such a blood orgy, and will be given all the money and firepower they demand in carrying it out. A Christian world, in the most galling act of pretension and spiritual contradiction, will call to mind the infamous Slaughter of the Innocents by Herod, and yet will sit on the sidelines of its modern day equivalent and cheer like the stupid, soulless animals that they have been trained into becoming by the Zionist agenda over the course of the last half century.

And so in the midst of this, I come to understand why there is this thing known as suicide bombers. I come to understand a father's rage, who must spend the rest of his life trying to forget the last image in his memory of a 2-year old son, the face of an angel whose brains had been deliberately blown out and who died with his eyes open. I come to understand the rage of a father who knows that all his children live under a sentence of death, a sentence issued by racial supremacists who bow before no moral precepts outside of that which they have created for the furtherance of their own interests. It becomes perfectly clear why one day, a father who fears every moment of everyday that he will get "the call" telling him that his child has just been murdered decides he will take no more. A father, after desperately trying to get to the hospital in the hopeless effort of arriving before his young son dies, who then decides one day that his hunger and thirst for justice can wait not a moment longer and who then makes the front page of every newspaper throughout America and the West by blowing himself up in order to kill the Israeli soldiers who did this thing. I come to understand the desperation of the Palestinian people, who know that they cannot seek redress of grievances from a Christian world that has been captured by the Whore of Babylon, these supposed followers of the Prince of Peace who have allowed themselves to be used as pawns in the program of exterminating a race of people considered by the Jews to be animals.

I come to understand how a people can be driven mad from hunger and thirst, and how in such a state of madness, commit themselves to doing something that in other circumstances they simply would not choose to do.

Whether he knows it or not, Amir has become one of my best friends, if indeed not my very best friend. His gift to me cannot be measured nor compared to any other I have received in this life. Besides breaking the spell under which I have been held captive with regards to understanding the politics of my country's involvement in the Middle East, in addition he has led me to discover something of even more importance. In considering the weight of his arguments, I discovered this thing in me, deep down there, that I had forgotten about through the many years of this unnatural sleep. It is easy to forget about this thing called the soul, since it has been one of the greatest casualties resulting from this assault on humanity known as Zionism. As much as this beast has grown in power and in viciousness by feasting on the blood of the innocents whom it has slaughtered in the Middle East, with equal voraciousness it has feasted on the blood of men's souls. It has been one of the main objectives of the Zionist agenda in the Christian West (and more so in America) to slaughter this thing that brings humanity to the masses, this "targeted killing" that has left almost an entire civilization bereft of compassion, pity, or justice. The reason for such a program of assassination is easy to understand, since it has been the human soul and all its precepts of life that have served as the one impediment to realizing the complete conquest of mankind and his existence. As such, the human soul, with its sense of right and wrong which enables it to recognize that shooting children for sport is murder, and that wiping out an entire race of people is an abomination before the eyes of the Almighty, has been targeted for extermination as well. The Zionist agenda, in its methodical application of doing violence to the soul of humanity, has succeeded in corrupting the Christian West into becoming a pitiless, bloodthirsty, ghoulish race of people willing to fight and die for the state of Israel, exactly as is taking place now. The Christian West, too stupid by now to recognize the war that is and has been waged against it, does not see the fangs on this beast. It does not hear the snarling or growling that erupts when this beast finds itself in the presence of the same compassion and justice that are supposed to be the lifeblood of Christian civilization. And having become blind

THOSE WHO HUNGER AND THIRST FOR JUSTICE

and deaf to these realities, the members of the Christian West have themselves become prisoners in this holocaust called the Zionist agenda, and whose number will shortly be called up, as it has for all those who are listed as the main course in this feast of humanity.

And so, in discovering this thing, this soul, I found a treasure that I did not know existed, with more riches and wealth in it than I could possibly imagine having over the course of a million lifetimes. In allowing the humanity of Amir's reasoning to bypass the spiritual and intellectual censorship that had been imposed upon me, I discovered the treasure of my own humanity, buried under the mounds of complacency and carelessness that had been heaped over it on a daily basis for decades. In coming to understand the same Golden Rule often repeated yet poorly considered, I became rich by its gold, and as I imagined myself in his shoes, living what he lived and seeing what he saw, I finally came to be one of those who hunger and thirst for justice.

Amir Ayyad has not only made me a survivor, but indeed a soldier. Recognizing that I was robbed of my birthright, the right of all human beings to nurture the better side of their natures and to ameliorate the beast that dwells within them, I have became a warrior in reclaiming this birthright. In this war that has become the bonfire of human virtues, where pity, justice, and compassion are hunted down and slaughtered in the same manner as are the children of Khan Younis, I came to understand the unseen depths of this war that have penetrated the lives of all peoples in existence today. Such an individual, living in the Zionist outpost called America who realizes that he has become the hunted, and by being the hunted has joined the ranks of those whose blood stains the soil of a land that was once holy, in that moment he realizes that he too must join in this fight alongside the others who hunger and thirst for justice.

For me, I will guard this last spark of humanity that was rescued from the jaws of death, rescued from this beast known as the Zionist agenda by the heroism of a boy named Amir Ayyad. How long such a dangerous and tenuous mission can endure I cannot say, given the day's events, but it is the least that I can do in showing him my gratitude, he who helped to rescue me from what was a certain death of sorts. As a refugee from the holocaust of the Zionist agenda that has slaughtered like sheep the last remnants of human decency and of Christian compassion, I will choose death as a free man over the life of a slave.

And assisting me in this mission is my little friend Amir Ayyad, who reminds me everyday about what is justice and injustice, and who has promised to keep a place ready for me, should I be fortunate enough one day to join him in Paradise.

"The day will come when your enemies will build an embankment against you and encircle you in on every side. They will dash you to the ground, you and the children within your walls. They will not leave one stone upon another, because you did not recognize the time of God's coming."
— Jesus Of Nazareth

"Of the 50,000 American Jews who migrated to Israel between 1967 and 1970, about 20% (10,000) of them were Marxist oriented with a great number of them actual card-carrying communists. They were welcomed by the Israeli authorities and were given favored treatment."
— Jack Bernstein, author of the book **The Life of an American Jew Living in Racist Marxist Israel.**

"Jesus shall speak to people in the cradle and in maturity and he shall be righteous. And Allah will teach him the book of wisdom, the law of the Gospel, and appoint him a messenger to the children of Israel, and he will say to them 'I have come to you with a sign from your Lord...and I will heal those who are blind, and the lepers, and I will raise the dead by the power of Allah."
— **The Qur'an**, Islam's most holy book, Surah III

"And I saw a beast coming out of the sea. He had ten horns and seven heads and on each head a blasphemous name. The dragon gave the beast his power and his throne and his great authority. One of the heads seemed to have had a fatal wound, but the fatal wound had been healed. The whole world was astonished and followed after the beast. Men worshiped the dragon because he had given authority to the beast, and also worshipped the beast saying, 'Who is like the beast? Who can make war against him?' The beast was given a mouth with which to utter proud words and blasphemies and to exercise his authority for forty-two months. He was given power to make war against the saints and to conquer them. All inhabitants of the world will worship the beast, all those whose names have not been written in the book of life."
— **Book of the Apocalypse**, Ch. 13

Ten Good Men

They huddled together, quiet as church mice, afraid to even breathe, lest their presence and location be betrayed. Behind locked doors they sat, paralyzed with fear after witnessing the manner in which their leader had been tortured and murdered by members of the establishment whose bloodlust and viciousness seemed to have no boundaries. Their hearts pounded like drums, and the fear in their souls rose like flood waters whenever voices or footsteps grew louder with the approach of those who were milling about outside. They were marked men themselves, and knew that if even one of them were to show his face in public, he would be hunted down, tried as a revolutionary, and subjected to the same abominable flavor of "justice" that their leader had suffered. They had good reason to be afraid, for they had witnessed first hand just how far the establishment was willing to go in putting down their War for Independence, as well as the amount of blood it was willing to shed for the furtherance of its agenda. And so, that night, as the book says, they, the disciples, *"were together with the doors locked, for fear of the Jews..."*

Tonight's scene is quite a departure from that which took place a few nights before. Those who tonight sit shivering in fear are the same who a few nights ago protested with all the boldness and brashness of a cocky street scrapper as their leader predicted the manner in which they would all flee like cowards in his most desperate hour. The three years they had spent in his presence should have been enough to convince them that his prediction would come to pass, since he had on countless occasions demonstrated what was a vastly superior intellect and penchant for keen foresight. Nevertheless, in extreme overestimation of their own human limits, they challenged his words with an admixture of indignation and dread, perhaps out of pride, perhaps out of ignorance concerning just what it was that lay before them that night.

Some things never seem to change, and one thing that has remained the same since the time of Jerusalem of 33 AD and now has been mankind's clumsiness in recognizing the signs of the times for what they really are. As such, those who were gathered that night envisioned an event that would be the start of the war for independence that the prophets of old had predicted. They expected that later that evening, the man who had raised the dead, healed the sick and fed 5,000 would bring Israel's enemies low with the wave of his magic hand. In their mind's eye, those who sat eating bread and wine with the carpenter from Nazareth would be part of an event which would make them heroes in the years to come. The reality of the situation is that they were completely right and completely wrong. All these things would take place, but not necessarily as they had envisioned it. The problem for them was that in taking the short view of things, they had formulated a completely inaccurate picture of what the looming confrontation was to be that night, and so, when he allowed his enemies to take him away without resisting, they were taken completely by surprise, and that surprise was what led to their being routed off of the battle field.

It is 2,000 years later, and, like the freedom fighters of Jerusalem, 33 AD, the great great great grandchildren of those who sat shivering and quivering can today themselves be found doing the same thing, *together with doors locked, for fear of the Jews...*

Today's Apocalyptically minded Christians, visibly prevalent more and more every day can be said to be afflicted with the same vision problems as were the Apostles of Jerusalem 33 AD. Given the times which mark modern day events, the bulk of what calls itself Christianity is standing with upturned eyes, awaiting the event which will announce the sign of the times and the commencement of the great battle between good and evil. But, like their forebears 2,000 years ago, they are wandering around aimlessly, unable to find that location designated as "x" on the map. They are looking for a treasure in the wrong place and in the wrong manner. One wonders how this can be, since the signs are clearly visible, and the great battle is raging around them so loudly that even the deaf should be able to hear it. The only viable explanation for this sense of spiritual myopia is that its roots lie in sentiments of self-absorption that have permeated much of Christianity today. One must assume that the same toxins which have all but destroyed Western Civilization have found their way into Christian thinking as well, and that as a result the same narcissism which afflicts the secular world can also be found in the religious. In such a mindset, today's apocalyptically concerned Christians who are awaiting the much prophesized hell-on-earth to arrive are unable to recognize that it is already here, and the apparent blindness to this reality reveals itself in how they today view the suffering of others. Within this context, the mindset of such an ideology operates under the assumption that since such tribulations haven't yet happened to them, that therefore they do not yet exist, and in the process they fail to appreciate the fact that it is happening to others. The tragedy of the situation is that this symptom is by no means the only aspect of what afflicts Christianity today, for in addition to going about their lives carelessly as others are suffering a veritable hell on earth, as well Christians have bought into an idea that once that hell does arrive for them, they will suffer little if anything from it.

From just about every corner of what encompasses Christianity, individuals can be found who have embraced fantastic ideas concerning what the tribulations about to befall the world are and how they themselves will be dealing with it. Whether such thinking is found in the idea of the "rapture" (as embraced by Christian Zionists and mainstream Protestantism) or whether it is envisioned as the "three days of darkness" (as embraced by much of Catholicism) the common theme found in both is one of dispensation from what are sure to be the horrible aspects of divine punishment. Again, one must assume that this mindset is also the product of the same narcissistic tendencies which have afflicted the secular institutions of the West, for in this case as well as in the former, a Christianity which has grown soft and weak on luxury and comfort seems to be unable to bear the thought of suffering for the faith as the forefathers did. And so, like one biblical writer once wrote, *there is nothing new under the sun,* and in the same way that the followers of the carpenter from Nazareth formulated unrealistic expectations concerning the looming confrontation in 33 AD, so too have today's disciples done the same. And, likewise, as the disciples of 2,000 years ago could be found hiding behind locked doors for fear of what might happen to them for their faith, so too can be found the adherents of Christianity today, and no better example for this mindset exists than in the way in which the Christian world deals with the situation concerning Israel and her position in the Middle East conflict.

One would think that the conservative Christians who consider themselves a part of the avant garde to the secular onslaught against their faith would be a little more skeptical about the information concerning the Middle East situation, and in particular that information concerning what occurred on 9/11. For at least the last decade, these same conservative Christians accepted as dogma the idea that an agenda existed to destroy the Christian faith, an agenda realized through the cooperation of organized forces in the government and media who couldn't be trusted to tell the truth, even if a fortune was to be made by doing so. Unfortunately for them (and for those who must suffer from the Zionist agenda which has been aided by apocalyptically minded Christians) no such skepticism took place, and has yet to occur. These same individuals who have sat for decades now with clenched fists and grinding teeth at the attacks on their Christian values never exhibited an ounce of healthy doubt when the same Zionist run media responsible for attacking those values put all the pieces of this apocalyptic puzzle together for them in a neat, tidy package blaming the Muslims. Whether this example of uncritical acceptance of blatant propaganda can be attributed to sheer stupidity, intellectual laziness or a mixture of the two is up for debate. The fact is though, that they, by virtue of the manner in which they have taken the bait laid out before them, have demonstrated by such to be completely unprepared for the war of the soul that is quickly approaching. A better-trained, more dedicated soldier of the faith would recognize that any information given freely by the enemy could not be trusted, and that only a fool would accept it. Furthermore, if these apocalyptically minded Christians had done a more thorough reading of the warnings that were issued to them by their commander-in-chief, they would have known better than to have allowed themselves to be captured by the enemy in such a disgraceful manner.

"Watch out for false prophets, who come to you in sheep's clothing, but inwardly are ravenous wolves...By their fruits you will know them."
Matthew 7:15

If ever there was an era in which the ugly fruits of false prophecy were on full display, then clearly no better example of this exists than in the poisonous doctrine of Christian Zionism that has so effectively captured a large portion of the Christian world today. These ugly fruits are now openly visible in the present war going on in Afghanistan and Iraq, as well as in the murder of the Palestinian peoples by the devilish disciples of Marxist Zionism over the course of the last 80 years. And while there may be those in the Christian world who have not greedily gulped down the maddening wine of Christian Zionism, nevertheless there are those who have sipped from that poisoned chalice, as evidenced in the manner with which they choose to deal with the question of Israel's past, present, and future.

With respect to the suffering of those peoples in the region who have witnessed first hand what is the Apocalypse of Marxist Zionism, the callous unconcern for such suffering has become one of modern day Christianity's defining characteristics. By such behavior, today's Christians have become the same priest and Levite in the parable who, after witnessing the plight of him who had been beaten and robbed, continued uninterrupted in their walk without the slightest trace of compassion or concern. In like manner, as the peoples of the Middle East have been beaten and robbed by the thuggery of Marxist Zionism, the "religious" members of the Christian community have barely glanced in their direction at what is the pitiable state of their fellow man. By such actions, modern day Christians who are party to this have demonstrated what has become their contempt for the rules of justice and charity towards the least of their brethren in the Middle East. Again, the roots of this can be traced to the narcissism which afflicts much of Christianity today, exactly in the same way that it afflicted the priest and the Levite whose lives and interests were of such importance that not even coming to the aid of a dying man would divert or distract them. Those individuals who would defend their complacency with the argument that they have not taken any sides with regards to the situation in the Middle East should realize that they are merely suffering from a mild case of the same virus which has afflicted millions of others in a full blown way. And even though such individuals may not have been baptized into the idolatrous religion of Christian Zionism, (as manifested in the master race ideology which is applied generously to the inhabitants of Israel by Jerry Falwell, Pat Robertson and the rest) nevertheless, when all is said and done, the real reason for their complacency is not pardonable by any means. The dirty little secret which much of mainstream Christianity doesn't want to face (nor wishes to have revealed) is that the reason for their deafening silence on the issue of how the peoples of the Middle East are suffering is not rooted in religious or intellectual reservations that are the fruits of careful consideration. It is not rooted in the benign neglect that many of its adherents would like to claim it is. Rather it is best understood as originating in the same instincts that gripped their forefathers 2,000 years ago in Jerusalem 33 AD, as they sat shivering and quivering behind locked doors. That instinct which afflicted the first Christians with the same sense of spiritual paralysis that afflicts a good number of them today is simply (for lack of better phraseology) *fear of the Jews*.

This fear is completely understandable, and only the truly blind or the truly dishonest would attempt to deny that this tiny minority within the world's population holds the preponderance of wieldable power. This power, found in the avenues of media, academia, finance and law is such that over the course of the last 50 years, it has been able to re-rout and redefine for the benefit of the Zionist agenda all the moral underpinnings of an entire civilization which took 2,000 years to develop. This infrastructure of power, (which the world is expected not to see yet is expected to fear) organized around the nucleus of Marxist Zionism was able to completely hypnotize 300 million people encompassing the most powerful nation on earth into going into an illegal and unjust war. Everyday, the world's highways and byways are littered with the lives of those who somehow got in the way or in some way challenged the designs of this statistically tiny group of gangsters who worship the golden calf of the Zionist idol. The lives who litter such highways cover all levels of society, from the rich to the poor to the powerful to the powerless, and irrespective of what these individuals may have done in the past which served the interests of this tiny group, the moment they are of no more use they are finished. Such interests can put a man in the White House or make him go home in shame. Such interests can make the cover up of their involvement in an atrocity as infamous as 9/11 appear seemingly effortless. Even a movie maker or writer who gets in their way can literally be said to be a marked man, and for anyone who doubts this, just consider the circuses that have taken place recently concerning the release of *The Passion of the Christ* by the most popular actor in the world. Besides hounding the creator of this film for nearly a year and reducing him to a lump of frazzled nerves, the most powerful of them within the entertainment industry have vowed to destroy him for daring to portray an image of their arch enemy in a light more favorable than they wish. Some of the organized groups representing the interests of Marxist Zionism have been so bold in throwing around their weight that they have called upon the federal government to arrest this man under the Patriot Act and have him tried as a terrorist. It is this raw power which no one is allowed to acknowledge yet everyone knows is there, (like the proverbial elephant in the room) that is the reason for the complacency of Christianity with regards to the plight of the Middle Eastern peoples. And it is in recognizing such power that the bulk of what remains of Christianity has adopted a policy of acquiescing to the interests of Marxist Zionism, whether such acquiescence represents itself in the nauseating idolatry of Christian Zionism which has deified the inhabitants of Israel, or whether it is represented in the cowardly silence which has been adopted by the remainder of the group with regards to the murderous and duplicitous behavior of the pariah state of Israel. This acquiescence reveals what has become the foolishness of much of what remains of Christianity today, a foolishness that has embraced the notion that if such an antichrist agenda is appeased, it will eventually wear itself out and that their faith will again be able to flourish in a fertile environment. What these deluded souls should come to understand is that in having adopted these policies with regards to Christianity's arch enemy (and indeed the enemy of all mankind) they are embracing a notion of the future which simply will not bear itself out in the reality to come. And, as with any two-sided coin, if the one side represents the sentiments of fear and acquiescence to a criminal agenda, than the other side can be said to represent the sentiments of greed and ingratitude. This mindset can be summed up in the notion that Christians today need do no more than bide their time, not make any waves nor ruffle any feathers, and that by so doing, they will collect their reward by a God who is eternally grateful to them for having done nothing to earn it.

"Then the man who had received one coin said....Master, I was afraid and went out and hid your coin in the ground. See, here is what belongs to you." His master replied "You wicked, lazy servant! Take the coin from him, and throw that worthless servant into the darkness, where there will be weeping and gnashing of teeth." Matthew, 25:24-30

There is a clear and definitive section of the four gospels in which Christ addresses the theme of the last days and what are the obligations of his disciples with respect to these events. Besides warning of the false prophets (whose identities become seemingly more clear every passing day) in addition he warns his followers, as in the above parable, not to embrace the idea that they will be rewarded with heaven for having run from the battle. In the parable of the servants and the coins, the servant who hid his coin in the ground (representing his faith and his obligation in confronting the evil of his day) had his treasure taken from him and was cast outside. Modern day Christians who think that they may simply sit back and allow their treasure to appreciate with interest by virtue of their keeping silent should think again. What they have done in effect is to make a deal with the devil, and have by such an agreement pledged their assistance to his actions by not revealing his identity nor his agenda. To a certain degree, this mindset can be said to be in perfect conformity with what defines much of the capitalist mindset of the West, for in such a mindset, today's Western Christians exploit the labors of God and believe that they have the right to the fruits of those labors while paying little if anything for them.

Christianity today, personified by the lazy, self-indulged individuals who have been made weak by luxury and comfort and who sit on their backsides, waiting to be served by the second coming should allow history to speak on this matter. If the past is any indicator as to what will transpire again, apocalyptically minded Christians should consider therefore the circumstances surrounding their Master's first arrival. In this approach, and in recognizing that all revolutions start off in small numbers, Christians today should not be surprised to find that the war for independence against the tyranny of Pharisaical Judaism would commence with only one voice crying out in the desert.

"You brood of vipers! Who told you to flee from the coming wrath? The ax is already at the root of the tree, and every tree that does not produce good fruit will be cut down and thrown into the fire." Matthew 3: 7-11

That "brood of vipers" whom John the Baptist confronted without any detectable fear were the gangsters of the Sanhedrin, the founding fathers of the modern day Zionist Mafia whose great great grandchildren today are feared by a cowed and propagandized Christianity. John must have known what kind of unpleasantness would result from his boldness, and yet he knew that there was no other way. Like all true revolutionaries, he must have embraced the idea that it was better to die a free man than to live as a slave, and therefore accepted the losing of his head willingly in exchange for the honor of fighting for such a just cause. Clearly, he understood that there was a price to pay for freedom, and that in the interests of true equity, such a valuable commodity demanded a higher cost than most today would want to assume. Today's Christians would be wise to adjust their thinking in the same manner, and come to understand that the freedom purchased for them by the sacrifice of their brothers in arms 2,000 years ago had a heavy toll attached to it.

But besides the example that the past has offered, they have as well conditions that have been set for the future that they should consider also. They have been told over the course of the last 2,000 years that the return of their Master would hinge on their faithfulness, and with this in mind, to expect anything different is like the proverbial situation of putting the cart before the horse.

"Don't let anyone deceive you in any way, for the day of Christ's return will not come until the rebellion occurs and the man of lawlessness is revealed." 2Thessalonians, 2:3

In a world robbed of its ability for critical thought, (accomplished through the daily assault on the intellect by the propaganda infrastructure of the agenda of Marxist Zionism) it is easy to see how many individuals might overlook the significance of the previous passage. Nevertheless, careful consideration should be applied herein, given the fact that what is implied is the duty of Christianity in exposing the existence of lawlessness in the world as well as who is responsible for it. It does not say "when God reveals him" nor does it say "when the man of lawlessness reveals himself". What is expressed in the passive voice, and what apocalyptically minded Christians should take from this implication is the idea that if they are waiting for the return of the Prince of Peace, then they must do their part in exposing the Prince of darkness. And if ever it was clear, if ever there existed in the 2,000-year history of the Christian faith the proof of an organized, fanatically driven agenda to bring lawlessness and brutality into the world, then clearly the proof of such a conspiracy exists today in the antichrist agenda known as Marxist Zionism. Like all its ugly siblings, Fascism, Communism, Maoism, Leninism, et al, it has demonstrated by the fruits it has produced, those of duplicity and viciousness, what kind of tree it really is. At the present moment, it has come to extinguish and erase the liberation that Christianity won in the town of Jerusalem 2,000 years ago, and to replace that liberation with the same totalitarianism it had envisioned for itself in the interim. And while there may be those (and most notably from the idolatrous, adulterous whore known as Christian Zionism) who will lament publicly over the destruction of decency and morals in the formerly Christian West, nevertheless they fail to recognize (nor reveal) that it is the agenda of Marxist Zionism which is driving such attacks. Christians today, instead of waiting with greedy expectation for the brand new world which their Master is going to provide for them by virtue of their having done nothing, should instead take a more conservative, grateful approach to the world and its program of rehabilitation. If they bothered to read their scriptures better, they would realize that there was always a condition put on God's vengeance, and that for the sake of the few who were willing to do their part, the looming Apocalypse could be mitigated or delayed. As the destruction of the wicked city of Sodom became imminent, a timid Abraham approached and asked in the spirit of humility the question which all of mankind should be asking at this moment.

"I pray that the Lord not be angry with me for asking, but what if only ten good men can be found there? And the Lord responded with "For the sake of ten good men, I will not destroy it." Genesis, 18:32-33

Being the most wise of all investors, the Master knew that even only ten good men in a city overrun with lawlessness would yield him a handsome profit. Ten good men, driven on by the spirit which hungers and thirsts for justice could conquer and reconquer the world seventy times seven, and for this reason, as much now as then, he would be willing to invest in the seemingly hopeless venture known as humanity. With nothing more than the bravery of ten good men, (or, as in the case of the Apostles, 12) individuals who would go forth and engage the enemy, brandishing the weapons of courage and truth that cannot be defeated, the looming Apocalypse could be delayed. For obvious reasons, given the fact that Christians are not as prepared to endure this event as they might imagine they are, it would be in their interest to take advantage of such a reprieve.

Christians around the world, who have been silenced by their fear of the Jews should think twice about the scenarios that they have

TEN GOOD MEN 263

envisioned for themselves. Within the scope of their 2,000-year history, not an instance can be found in which an individual was rewarded by the Master for cowardice, laziness or complacency. On the contrary, it has been demonstrated in exhortation after exhortation by their founder that it is the diligent who are rewarded, and those who have chosen to remain cold have in effect made themselves the worthless servants whom their leader said he would "vomit forth" for choosing to remain neutral in the battle between good and evil. In addition, it must be remembered that in despite of all the fanfare which has been attached to the visions and prophecies of today's wolves in sheep's clothing who masquerade themselves as religious leaders that not an instance can be found in which they have been correct in their foresight. Not only have they proved themselves to be completely unreliable in interpreting matters dealing with spiritual or scriptural themes, but as well they have been unable or unwilling to reveal what is the true antichrist system that has gripped the world by the hair today, that being the ideology of Marxist Zionism. As such, what remains of Christianity should cast such false prophets out of any realm of respectability or credence, since if even their own interpretations of the coming Apocalypse are true, a lake of fire is what has been scheduled for such liars as their eternal reward. As such, what remains of Christianity would be wise not to follow them in what is sure to be a most unenviable end.

Those good and true souls who are left pondering the question mark of the last two millennia would be wise to consider the fact that no one has yet cracked the Apocalyptic code. For the last 2,000 years in which the prophecy concerning the end times has existed, at least as many varying opinions have been formed concerning what it means. What is for sure though is that the beast of Marxist Zionism will continue to grow as long as it is fed by a complacent and compliant world that willingly refuses to confront it out of fear of the Jews. Mankind and all that he has attained in terms of civilization and distinction from the beasts of the field will be served up in the daily feast that has marked the ascent to power of this ugly sibling within the Marxist family. Simply pretending that it is not there is useless, and even more futile is the business of cozying up to it. There simply is no room in the civilized world for these two opposing ideologies, Marxist Zionism and Christianity, to exist together, for in truth they are locked in a bitter struggle which has existed now for the last 2 millennia, albeit unbeknownst to most Christians today. For those who make the pretense of standing for decency, there is only one option, and that is to stand, while there still remains time, an action which does not entail running off to the hinterland or hiding one's light under a bowl. It does not mean storing up weapons and ordnance in what is sure to be a useless gesture against a force never before seen in history.

Rather, it is as simple and pure and bold and beautiful as the heroism of the first Apostles, who, after being found by their Master behind locked doors for fear of the Jews, went forth and did their part in revealing the man of lawlessness in an effort to hasten the return of their Lord. It is as elementary as taking compassion upon him who is lying in the ditch, pouring oil and wine into the wounds of those in the Middle East who have been beaten and robbed by the brigands of Marxist Zionism. It is as basic as confronting the same ethnocentrist sentiments which formed one of the ideological battlegrounds between Christ and the Sanhedrin, sentiments which have breathed life into the beast known as Marxist Zionism, and which are responsible for the murder of women and children in the Middle East today. And likewise, as God's impending judgment is about to fall on a wicked world which has become the twin sister of that doomed city of Sodom, what remains of decency would be wise to consider just what is truly needed in order to bring justice to a dying world. It will not be accomplished by the silence of the multitudes, nor the platitudes of the false prophets, nor the complacency of the weak. It will not be affected by lazy servants who bury their coins in the ground, much like what the adherents of mainstream Christianity do with their heads today.

Rather, the domino effect which will lead to the rehabilitation of mankind will be initiated by the brave actions of those who refuse to live in a world of lawlessness and who refuse to be silenced for fear of the Jews, individuals who choose to risk putting their necks on the chopping block by daring to submit their names for membership in the noble fraternity of freedom fighters and lovers of humanity.

Before it is too late, let the world hope that such heroes exist today, and that for the sake of what remains of decency and justice, there can be found in a world of lawlessness, totalitarianism, and complacency, just ten good men.

"Now everyone knows what was not the cause of this war. Even President Bush acknowledges that Saddam Hussein had nothing to do with 9/11. In listing the 45 countries where al Qaeda was operating the State Department did not list Iraq. Led by Richard Perle, Paul Wolfowitz and Charles Krauthammer, for years there has been a domino school of thought that the way to guarantee Israel's security is to spread democracy in the area."
— US Senator Ernest F. Hollings

"To stand against Israel is to stand against God. We believe that history and scripture prove that God deals with nations in relation to how they deal with Israel."
— Christian Zionist Rev. Jerry Falwell in his book **The Fundamentalist Phenomenon**

"Watch out for false prophets, who come to you in sheep's clothing, but who inwardly are ferocious wolves. By their fruit you will recognize them."
— Jesus of Nazareth

"I have seen Israeli soldiers urinating in bottles and then offering them to Palestinians to drink as 'Coke.' The Israeli soldiers would call to each other across the roofs of Palestinian houses in the middle of night, one of them saying that he wanted to do "something great" and then urged his colleagues to pay attention. From there he proceeded to urinate into the water tank of the family who owned the house. I had to put a jerry can on my balcony in front of my bedroom to collect the urine of Israeli soldiers that dripped from the military post onto my roof every day. The soldiers urinated at night and during the day, and I was forced to collect it. Often the soldiers would collect their urine in vessels for a couple of days and then wait until I hanged my washed clothes. Then they would spread their urine on my clothes."
"During middays in the summer, the foul smell of their feces and urine contaminate the fresh air."
— Excerpt from '**IDF Soldiers and Jewish Squatters: Shit, Drugs and Abuse...The Daily Life of Kawther Salam.**'

No Beauty in the Beast

"I just sent four more souls to Allah," he said in that news report.

The source of this ugly utterance was an American soldier, probably no higher in rank than a private or corporal, who was bragging to one of his fellow brothers-in-arms about how he had just added a few notches in his rifle. Not four souls, but four *more* souls. He was almost giddy, like a young teenager who had just thrown a rock through the window of some neighborhood kid whom he and his fellow schoolyard bullies assaulted everyday for fun.

There was no remorse in his voice, no regret. The time for that had long since passed. Whatever conscience he might have possessed when he was dragged into this thing called the war in the Middle East had now been slaughtered, probably through the combined efforts of seeing so much innocent blood flow as a result of his actions coupled with the assurances by his comrades and superiors that he was there doing the right thing. If only common sense, which screamed out like a banshee in the moment that this soldier from a country that dares to call itself Christian had been able to penetrate into his thoughts at that moment, it may have stopped him in his tracks.

"My young, foolish boy, do you realize what you have just done? Do you realize what you are saying? Do you really understand what this is all about?"

No doubt, he slept well that night. After all, he was a soldier from America, fighting against the enemies of Christianity and against freedom. He was there as an ambassador of God's army, saving Western Civilization from an enemy that was bent upon destroying it entirely. He was sure of this, because the president, George Bush, had told him so, right before he had had been sent off. So had the loudmouths on talk radio like Sean Hannity, Bill O'Reilly, Limbaugh, Liddy, and all the rest who had mysteriously reached heights of popularity, seemingly out of nowhere, in the years just running up to September 11th. So had his favorite televangelists, the Pat Robertsons, Jerry Falwells and Tim Lahayes, who have told millions like our young friend that the work of killing 1.5 billion people is a mission that has been ordained and blessed by the God of Israel. And just in case the magic spell woven by the founding fathers of this blood bath in Iraq and Afghanistan didn't do the trick, he had the assurances of his army chaplain, who was there, on cue, every day of every week, to administer the anesthetic salve of righteousness anytime one of America's best might have had an attack of conscience.

Pretty soon, the memories of the women and children he and his fellow Christian soldiers gunned down in cold blood would be gone. The images that initially haunted his dreams of limbless civilians, the sand niggers who just happened to be in the wrong war at the wrong time would be drowned out in the flurry of ribbons and accolades that he and his fellow defenders of truth, justice and the American way would receive as a result of such unprecedented bravery.

Little does he know, as the saying always goes. Little does he realize that those four souls he sent to Allah were in reality his best friends. Little does he (as well as the rest of those inhabiting the formerly Christian West) realize that those 1.5 billion souls that they have been seduced into exterminating for the benefit of the Zionist agenda are the only things standing between themselves and their own eventual extermination. In snuffing out their lives, he just brought one step closer the destruction of all the good things for which his country and culture have made the pretenses of standing throughout the last 20 centuries. Little did he know that with every Iraqi and Afghani and Palestinian slaughtered today, the real enemies to not only America, but indeed to the entire Christian world are one step closer to realizing that dream that they have nursed out of the bowels of Hell for over 2,000 years.

To call it a pity is an affront to justice, to call it a tragedy is the same, for it's not as if the signs haven't been there, and for quite some time. In his Sunday visits to the chapel on base, it can be expected with absolute certainty that the chaplain had spent quite a bit of time reading from the book of Revelations, one of the roadmaps that is fueling and subsequently justifying this whole blood orgy.

NO BEAUTY IN THE BEAST

No doubt, this chaplain made sure to discuss the prophecies concerning the beast that would rise up with the intention of destroying Christianity and all that she had accomplished in bringing civility to the masses during her 2,000-year stint. No doubt, there was discussion about how there would be worshippers of this beast who would go out and do the dirty work of seeing to it that all the virtues that were preached by the peasant carpenter from Nazareth were snuffed out in accordance with this beast's agenda. What this Chaplain no doubt did though was to make sure that when the image of this beast and his worshippers began to flesh itself out, when they began to acquire an uncomfortable familiarity, that new faces were hastily pasted over those that were naturally appearing, faces like the four souls about whom our brave young Christian soldier bragged of having sent back to Allah that day. Had our young friend bothered to take off his American made, Government issue Christian Zionist rose-colored sunglasses that have prevented him from seeing all the innocent red that he and his fellow patriots have shed in the last few years, he might see his own face on one of those followers of the beast about whom his chaplain preached in his weekly sermons. And if he had had his ears open, he (as well as the rest of what remains of the Christian West) might have heard the proud words of the beast whom he is following and serving, the beast whose most cherished agenda lies in eradicating what remains of the message of justice that the freedom fighter from Palestine preached some 2,000 years ago.

"Tell me, do the evil men of this world have a bad time? They hunt and catch whatever they feel like eating. They don't suffer from indigestion and are not punished by Heaven. I want Israel to join that club. Maybe the world will then at last begin to fear us instead of feeling sorry. Maybe they will start to tremble, to fear our madness instead of admiring our nobility. Let them tremble; let them call us a mad state. Let them understand that we are a savage country, dangerous to our surroundings, not normal, that we might go wild, that we might start World War Three just like that, or that we might one day go crazy and burn all the oil fields in the Middle East. Personally, I don't want to be any better than Harry Truman who snuffed out half a million Japanese with two fine bombs."

"You can call me anything you like. Call me a monster or a murderer. Call Israel by any name you like, call it a Judeo-Nazi state....Why not? Better a live Judeo-Nazi than a dead saint. Even if you'll prove to me that the present

war is a dirty immoral war, I don't care. We shall start another war, kill and destroy more and more. And do you know why it is all worth it? Because it seems that this war has made us more unpopular among the civilized world."

"Let me tell you what the sweetest fruit of this war is: It is that the Gentiles now don't just hate Israel. Thanks to us, now they also hate all those Jews in Paris, London, New York, Frankfurt and Montreal. Now the Jews there are getting it because of us, and I am telling you, it is a pleasure to watch. Those Jews are being identified with us Zionists and that's a good thing! Their cemeteries are being desecrated, their synagogues are set on fire, all their old nicknames are being revived, they are being expelled from the best clubs, people shoot into their ethnic restaurants murdering their small children, forcing them to remove any sign showing them to be Jews, forcing them to move and change their profession."

"We'll hear no more of that nonsense about the unique Jewish morality. No more talk about a unique people being a light upon the nations. No more uniqueness and no more sweetness and light. Good riddance."

"We are Judeo-Nazis, and why not? If your nice, civilized parents, rather than writing books about their love for humanity had instead come to Israel and killed six million Arabs, what would have happened? Sure, two or three nasty pages would have been written in the history books, and we would have been called all sorts of names, but we could be here today as a people of 25 million!"

"Even today I am willing to volunteer to do the dirty work for Israel, to kill as many as is necessary, to deport, expel, and burn, to have everyone hate us, to pull the rug out from underneath the feet of the rest of the world's Jews so that they will be forced to run to us crying. Even if it means blowing up one or two synagogues here and there, I don't care. And I don't mind if after the job is done you put me in front of a Nuremberg Trial and then jail me for life. Hang me if you want, as a war criminal. You can write that I am a disgrace to humanity, I don't mind, on the contrary.....What you don't seem to understand is that the dirty work of Zionism is not finished yet, far from it."

And how those who dare to call themselves Christian could miss such a trumpet blast will forever remain a mystery.

NO BEAUTY IN THE BEAST 271

The event that virtually every member of the Christian West has been anticipating for the last 20 centuries is now at hand, and the members of this culture are to be found walking around aimlessly, except of course when they are not doing the dirty work of Zionism for the benefit of their slavemasters. If our young friend, as well as the rest of the Christian world were paying better attention, they would have seen the handwriting on the wall when this war against Islam was initiated years ago. Had they remembered these proud words uttered by Ariel Sharon some 2 decades past, words which serve both as a history lesson as well as a proforma for future events concerning Israel's agenda for the world, they might not have fallen for this mess so easily. But alas, amidst the flurry of red, white and blue as well as the humming of *Amazing Grace, God Bless America* and *Proud To Be An American* all of it seemed to have gotten misplaced. Even more importantly, had they remembered the words and the warnings of the humble carpenter from Palestine whom they make the pretense of following, they might have recognized the signs of the times for what they really were, and thus recognized that the very entity and the agenda against whom their Master had given his life fighting 20 centuries past had now again reared its ugly head and was making a play for world dominance. Had our young Christian soldier bothered to read the Seven Woes that his Savior cast in Jerusalem, 33 AD against Zionism's founding fathers, the Sanhedrin, words that were meant to remain for all time as a warning to humanity that this was a beast to be watched carefully...had they bothered, had they but bothered.

But now it is too late, for what remains of the Christian West has collectively become some stupid, soulless animal willing to do the bidding of its enemies, exactly as humanity was warned would take place by men much wiser than can be found today. Our young friend, (as well as virtually everyone else who inhabits those countries that were the beneficiaries of the Palestinian carpenter's war for the liberation of humanity from the beast known as Zionism) have now metamorphacized into one of the heads of this creature, the very same beast that will, at the right moment, turn on Christianity and devour it and every aspect of the civilization that it has created. Like some foolish, spoiled adolescent who cannot see that the friends she has chosen are running her down the road to ruin, so too does what remains of Christianity and its followers, who at present are enjoying an illicit, dangerous love affair with the very same Zionist agenda that is dedicated to their complete destruction. And all that remains now is to sit back and watch the show, to watch as what remains of humanity, what remains of the last spark of freedom and justice, to watch as it is slowly choked out in the Devil's last attempt in turning the Garden of Eden into a bonfire of all the qualities that separate man from beast.

In pondering what possible future lies ahead with regards to this situation, the scenario is not that difficult to imagine. Despite the festivities taking place aboard the Titanic, there came a moment when the obvious was impossible to avoid noting, and thus it will be with those in the Christian West as their civilization reaches its last days. Like some patient who has just learned that he has a terminal incurable disease, who knows that death has now become his constant companion and will be ushering him into the next world, he sits in that doctor's office and asks what he can expect in those last days before his departure. And as the doctor describes the series of events, the failure of organs, the wracking pain, the incoherence, what overcomes the future guest of death's estate is the sense of regret, the regret of having lived badly, for having invited this terminal condition into his life by having willfully allowed the poisons of a diseased world into his once healthy body. And so it will be in the formerly Christian West, whose members will, on the eve of their own destruction, take an accounting of what has brought them to the edge of this abyss, and what will inevitably result will be that deafening wail of regret that always seems to precede the destruction of all great civilizations, and one can imagine how loud that it will be on that day.

It will be louder than any conceivable thing, louder than all the bombs that have been dropped in Iraq, and louder than all the bullets that have been fired in Afghanistan. It will be louder than all the screams of Palestinian parents who have cradled in their arms the mangled bodies of dead children who were deliberately killed in order to ethnically cleanse the Promised Land, Eretz Y'Israel of the Arab filth that has polluted it for centuries. It will be louder than the thunder that was produced when the towers came tumbling down in New York, and louder than the panic heard in the voices of Congressmen as they fled America's capital following the discovery of anthrax in the building. It will be louder than the pleas for mercy that took place in the halls of the Abu Ghraib prison as Iraqi men, women and children were beaten and sodomized by self-described Christians who signed up in droves so that they could go and steal the sand niggers' oil for Jesus. It will be louder than the cheers that were heard as 5 Israeli intelligence officers danced on top of a building in Manhattan while filming the horrific spectacle of 2 jetliners crashing into a building, and it will be louder than the screams of the thousands of people who lost their lives in the process. It will be louder than all the growling and snarling that erupted from the mouths of religious and racial bigots working for Israeli intelligence as the world's most popular actor prepared to release a film depicting the dignity of the man most revered by what remains of the world's Christians.

And like our friend in that doctor's office, what the Western world will be left to consider in the remaining days of its life will be the fact that all of this was avoidable. Had they but listened, had they but considered the weight of history. For the Christian West, who at present is engaged in the business of slaughtering 1.5 billion Muslims for the benefit of humanity's future overlords in Tel Aviv, the day will arrive when they themselves will realize that the Muslims were their natural allies against this beast, and that it was only due to the bravery and steadfastness of those in the Islamic world that the Christian West had been able to survive as long as it had. What those who will be walking amidst the rubble of their destroyed civilization will realize, much too late, is the fact that had the same "rag heads," "hajjis" and "sand niggers" (whom they so willingly went about the business of destroying) had these people not tied up the energy and resources of the Zionist agenda for the last fifty years, the Christian world (which is the real target of Israel's plans for extermination) would have long ago succumbed to such a ruthless enemy. What they will be forced to consider is the fact that it was the same Muslims (whom the Christian West whored itself out in merchandising the kiss of death) who recognized the beast, the Anti-Christ, *Dajjal*, in the diabolical agenda known as Zionism, and who were willing to give their lives in resisting it. What the Christian world will be left to ponder is the fact that the Muslims knew for centuries that the creation of such a political corporation such as the state of Israel was tantamount to releasing a deadly plague upon the earth, as evidenced by the fact that in the Islamic religion *Azrael* is the name given to the angel of death. What the Christian West will be left to ponder, and one of the bitterest pills of all to swallow, will be the fact that the war against Islam was in reality a war against Christianity, for it was those in the Muslim world who stood in the way of Zionism's vampires finally reaching their intended victims, those being the followers of the humble carpenter from Palestine.

But even more importantly, (considering the origins of their own religion and culture) had the Christian West considered the weight of history, remembered its own past as well as the last words and actions of their Master during Holy Week of 33 AD, then that present holocaust it will be facing in the not too distant future will be placed in its true context as an event that was completely unnecessary. If only the Christian West had remembered the words of their Master concerning the founding fathers of the Zionist movement, had they but remembered.

"You snakes! You brood of vipers! How will you escape Hell?...And so upon you will come all the righteous blood that has been shed on earth, from the righteous Abel to the righteous Zechariah....You belong to your father, the Devil, and you want to carry out your father's desires, who was a murderer from the beginning, not holding to the truth, for there is no truth in him. When he lies, he speaks, his native language, for he is a liar and the father of lies. You are like whitewashed tombs...full of dead men's bones and everything unclean. In the same way, you appear as righteous, but on the inside you are full of hypocrisy and wickedness."

This was by no means an isolated event, for during his last week alive, he made sure to impart on several occasions what kind of danger had just been spawned in 1st century Palestine and what foreboding it presented for the future of humanity. And whether it was the casting of the Seven Woes, driving the moneychangers from the Temple, or warning of a future time in which the Holy Land would be desecrated by the arrival of what he termed *"the abomination of desolation,"* the message was crystal clear.

"Watch this animal," he in essence has told mankind for the last 2,000 years. *"Do not let it out of your sight, not even momentarily, for if you do, all that is to be accomplished in future generations, the brotherhood of mankind and the good will of all nations, — all this will be obliterated and devoured by this beast whom I have come this day to destroy."*

NO BEAUTY IN THE BEAST

And the tears he wept when looking over Jerusalem that day appear now to have all been but for nothing. In allowing himself to be taken prisoner by this beast, to be subjected to a sham trial and murdered by a family of gangsters utilizing the vehicles of the same political corruption that they utilize today in furthering their own interests — bribery, extortion, threats, perjury, false witness, etc. — he had hoped that such a dramatic display would serve as a warning that all mankind need be watchful and mindful of this animal. He hoped that the example of what took place when this criminal class wormed its way into the court of the Roman emperor Nero, the persecutions that his followers suffered as a result of the Sanhedrin's influence over this madman's thinking, that this would leave a lasting impression as to what kind of viciousness coursed through the veins of this beast. He hoped that in the breaking up of this gangster family's power base — in their being driven from the Holy Land called Palestine, (the singular most important event in affording this new civilization, Christendom, the chance to survive) that this act would serve as a warning not to allow this beast to ever consolidate its power again in the political corporation known as the state of Israel. The Christian world, who should have known better than anyone else, instead drank from the chalice of foolishness, and having succumbed to its intoxicating effects, allowed themselves to be seduced by the very same heresy of racial supremacy that the humble carpenter from Palestine sought to destroy in his three years of fighting. In assenting to the program of allowing "God's chosen people" to once again re-occupy the land that was made holy by the life and death of the freedom fighter known as Jesus of Nazareth, they in effect unchained the very beast that he gave his own life in subduing. In providing this beast with all the money and weaponry it needed to murder the Arabs who have been the guardians of this land for over 1,000 years, they have now signed their own death certificate as well, for in so doing, this beast has attained the heights of power in exactly the same manner as the humble carpenter turned freedom fighter tried to prevent through his war of liberation. Now, this animal, this *"savage country, dangerous to its surroundings,"* has indeed as promised *"gone wild,"* and has through its dominance over the political machinery of the Christian West, *"started World War Three... just like that."*

And now as a result, today Christian soldiers and the citizens of their respective nations brag about their own involvement in the daily business of murdering men, women and children, and joke of having sent them back to Allah. The airwaves in their nations bristle with discussions as to how the peoples of the Middle East, every man woman and child, whose culture was responsible for bringing to such a position of affluence the Western World, should be consumed in some storm of utter destruction so as to better facilitate the stealing of their oil and wiping out the last remaining enemies to the Zionist agenda. Maniacal Christian Zionists, who make a disgusting display of their madness by extolling the ongoing missionary work in Iraq, in perfect contradictory fashion do so even as Israeli soldiers make a daily practice of deliberately gunning down Palestinian schoolchildren, many of whom are Christian themselves. The Christian West, who lament the decay of their own societies — the murder of their children, the debasement of marriage and women, the elevation of vice in every form — nevertheless go forth to places such as Iraq, Afghanistan and Palestine and assist the very same Zionist agenda that is responsible for bringing such cultural destruction to their own lands. The followers of Christianity who have now squandered the inheritance left for them by their Master; a legacy that affords them the wealth of justice, mercy, compassion, as well as all the other attributes that separate man from beast, have now become beasts themselves, in perfect lockstep with their Zionist overlords. The progeny of those who were fed to the lions as a form of public entertainment have now themselves become members of a mad, cheering crowd at the coliseum who watch with delight as those in the Holy Land endure the unendurable. These worshippers of the beast known as Zionism welcome and praise a man like Ariel Sharon as if he were a prince, and furnish him with all the money and firepower that he needs in order to stain the land made holy by the life and death of the same humble peasant carpenter whose teachings of justice and mercy he holds in the lowest form of contempt. The members of the Christian West, who penitently beat their breasts and make all the pretenses of shame for having allowed the murder of six million in the camps of Hitler's war today bow down before the Zionist butcher Sharon and his partners in crime when he and they casually speak of murdering six million Arabs.

In the meantime, their Zionist puppetmasters in New York, Washington and Tel Aviv have now turned the hourglass upside down, and are in the process of watching as the grains of sand come tumbling down, waiting in salivating expectation for the arrival of that moment in which these very same Christian nations who today are doing the dirty work of the beast will themselves be targeted for extermination in exactly the same manner. A leopard never changes it spots, as the saying goes, and with this in mind, the prospect of this apocalyptic future for the Christian world should come as no surprise to those who have done as they were commanded and remained as wise as serpents in the face of what is unimaginable evil. When their Master warned that those occupying the highest positions of power in Israel at the time of his arrival were the descendants of Cain and the children of the Devil, he was not merely playing with words or images. When he cursed the fig tree and said that it would never again produce anything good, he was not showing off for the benefit of posterity. And with this in mind, those in the Christian world who are nursing to maturity this beast known as Zionism and its bastard child known as the state of Israel would be wise to consider the fact that it was Ariel Sharon's cousins in Bolshevik Russia who were responsible for the slaughter of some 70 million of those whom they called their "useful idiots." And yet, in what is a dizzying amount of programming and propagandizing being beamed at the Christian world as to what events are taking place today with regarding the fulfillment of those prophecies that they await with schizoid expectation, they have forgotten about the words of their Master himself, who wanted above all things to protect humanity from the beast known as Zionism, in 1st as well as in 21st century Palestine.

"The day will come when your enemies will build an embankment against you and encircle you in on every side. They will dash you to the ground, you and the children within your walls. They will not leave one stone upon another, because you did not recognize the time of God's coming."

While there is time, if indeed there is any time remaining, let those who proudly boast of being followers of the humble carpenter from Palestine realize that the beast they were told would be forthcoming has indeed arrived, and is now utilizing a good number of their own in bringing Armageddon to reality. Let these fools abandon the idea that they will be somehow rewarded with heaven for standing with the enemies of their Master, and walk away from the notion that somehow he smiles upon all the evil they are committing in their acting as functionaries to the antichrist agenda known as Zionism. Let them recognize that indeed as promised, the *abomination of desolation* has arrived, and that it soils the Holy Land of Palestine through its daily practice of murdering and consigning to a life of utter misery those who have acted as the guardians of this holy place for over 1,000 years. Let them display the true attributes that are supposed to be the insigniae of Christianity's membership—the love of justice, mercy, and wisdom-and by so doing, let them separate themselves completely with the enemies of all humanity whom their Master said were here to carry out the will of the Devil. Let these Christian soldiers—men, women, and children—shake off the hypnotic effects of the Zionist programming that has rendered them senseless and realize that those in the Middle East who are suffering and dying in droves are the only thing standing between them and their own destruction. Let what remains of the war of liberation waged by the freedom fighter from Palestine known as Jesus of Nazareth arise from the ashes and again capture and contain this beast known as Zionism and the gangster class who rides atop of it. Let those who confidently float through these heady days, assured that they already possess in their grip first class tickets to eternity realize that nothing so precious is earned so easily. May they therefore take seriously the words of their Master and thus display the same courage as their great grandfathers did in Palestine some 20 centuries past in confronting the founding fathers of the Zionist movement—the *brood of vipers* known as the Sanhedrin—whose grandchildren today have drowned the world in chaos, murder and mayhem. Let those who make the pretenses of cherishing justice realize that the slaughter of 1.5 billion people for the benefit of *"those who call themselves Jews, but who are instead a synagogue of Satan"* will be met by fate with consequences so terrible that they are impossible to imagine.

Finally, let those who call themselves Christian look in the mirror and see that they have become one of the heads of this animal that will bring everything they have accomplished in 20 centuries to ruin, and in so doing, conclude therefore that they cannot serve two masters. Let them see that there is no justice, there is no mercy, there is no dignity in what they have become, and the lovely image in which they view themselves is but an illusion, for the truth of the matter is that there is no beauty in the beast.

"My brother Mujahideen in the path of God! What can I say to you? I say to you: our wombs have been filled with the children of fornication by those apes and pigs who raped us. Or could I tell you that they have defaced our bodies, spit in our faces, and tore up the little copies of the Qur'an that hung around our necks? Can you not comprehend our situation? Is it true that you do not know what is happening to us? We are your sisters."

"By God, we have not passed one night in this prison without one of the apes and pigs jumping down upon us to rip our bodies apart. And we are the ones who had guarded our virginity out of fear of God. Kill us along with them! Destroy us along with them! Don't leave us here to let them get pleasure from raping us! Leave their tanks and their aircraft alone. Come at us here in the prison of Abu Ghurayb."

"I Fatimah am your sister in God. They raped me on one day more than nine times. Can you comprehend? Imagine one of your sisters being raped. With me are 3 girls, all unmarried. All have been raped before the eyes and ears of everyone. They won't let us pray. They took our clothes and won't let us get dressed. As I write this letter one of the girls has committed suicide. She was savagely raped. A soldier hit her on her chest and thigh after raping her. He subjected her to unbelievable torture. She beat her head against the wall of the cell until she died, for she couldn't take any more, even though suicide is forbidden in Islam."

"Brothers, I tell you again, out of your fear of God, kill us with them so that we might be at peace. Help us, please help us."
– Excerpt of a letter written by a young Iraqi woman named Fatimah who was repeatedly raped by American soldiers in the Abu Ghraib prison in 2004.

"It's a necessary act of defense, and the only weapon that we have to protect Palestinian women and children. If we don't use suicide bombing, we shall be back in the situation when the Israelis kill us with impunity."
– Spokesman for Hamas, August 2004

Independence Day

"I have to get home to my mother, she will be so worried if I am not back soon."

9 year-old Mona clutched at the gaping hole in her stomach, blood pouring out of her as if someone had turned on a faucet. There was something so terribly and indescribably out of place in her frail words, the colliding of two disparate worlds, that of a mother's child, and that of a little girl facing down the ugliest of what life and humanity had to offer.

The man who was kneeling at her side however knew better. He was a trained medical professional, and in a war zone known as Gaza of all places. He had seen this scenario a thousand times before, and a thousand times too many as far as he was concerned. This child would not be going home, at least not her earthly home, given the fact that she had just been shot in the stomach at close range by a soldier wielding a machine gun, the bullets from which produced exit wounds on her tiny body that were as large as golf balls. Had she known that her insides had just been turned to mush, it is highly unlikely that she would have been as composed as she was at this moment.

Her gesture in worrying about her mother, about not wanting to cause a beloved parent any grief was partly genuine, and partly an attempt to distract herself from the fact that she knew something terrible had just happened to her. Indeed a child's sweetness knows no bounds, irrespective of where such a child can be found in the world. As she lie in a bath of her own warm blood that increased with each passing second, while frantic adults attempt to effect that which they know is futile, all she can think is that her mother must be worried, and how she wishes she could be home with her now, if only for enough time to give her one final embrace, tell her of a daughter's love, and to say goodbye.

In the end, it all came down to sweets, an indispensable part of any child's life, even in places that have been torn apart by warfare for the last century such as this. Today, little Mona, despite having grown up in a world of bullets and mortars, allowed the carelessness of her childhood to overpower her reason just enough to persuade her towards venturing forth into that deadly world of never ending violence to buy some cookies at the corner store. The fact that Israeli soldiers were busy with their latest masterpiece in butchery nearby did not seem to arouse her concern. After all, when all things were considered, this was just another day in the life of someone who knew she had been born under a sentence of death and who had developed an intimacy of sorts with this fact as if it had been her own skin.

On her way back, humming something sweet and armed with nothing more dangerous than the cookies in her hand, she was indiscriminately shot by an Israeli soldier, who, like all the rest of his ilk, had been told by both political and spiritual leaders that it is the religious duty of all good Zionists, *a mitzvah*, to cleanse the promised land of any impurities that may be infecting it, a process of sterilization which included, if it can be imagined, slaughtering helpless Arab children. And so, this courageous and obedient soldier from among a group of people who fancy themselves as being *a light among nations*, without the slightest hesitation pulled the trigger, simultaneously swatting away at the shred of what remained of his conscience as if it were some species of annoying insect.

For little Mona, it merely felt like a lit match touching her insides momentarily, and it was not until she began to feel the sensation of warm wetness on her dress that she began to panic. Her first instinct was that she might get into trouble for having gotten her new dress dirty, since the last thing her mother told her before leaving the house was to make sure not to get it messy. Thus is the mind of a child, even when facing the awfulness of eternity that their thoughts are always to be found firmly rooted in something trivial and sweet. Perhaps it was the panic stricken appearances on the faces of those around her who were trying to help that caused her to realize the seriousness of what it was that she was facing, or perhaps it was the unseen whisper into her soul from some divine messenger telling her to hurry up, since time was running out. Either way, no one really knows.

And so in that fifteen seconds before her spirit was liberated from the hellish existence that had been imposed upon her and upon the rest of the inhabitants of the Holy Land by the self-described 'chosen people', the little Palestinian child of 9 years forgot all about her cookies, as well as about every other item of what encompasses a child's existence, grew up quickly, remembered everything she had been taught during the religion classes she had taken throughout her life, and made her last statement of faith. In her last words, there was no malice, no *pulsa de nura*—the infamous curses that rabbis and Orthodox Jews hurl daily at passing Christians or Muslims in Israel, no condemnations, no vows of revenge. Her composure, as she lie there in a pool of her own blood, was as graceful and as dignified as was that of any patriot or saint who has secured a rightly earned place in mankind's memory as a result of having had his or her life cut short by the actions of men hell-bent upon doing evil to others. For Mona, it would be one simple statement, without any fanfare or drama, final words that will probably be remembered by few, short of those who loved her more than they loved themselves.

The little girl whose life had been snuffed out like a candle, the last fragrance of this little Palestinian flower who had been cut down by the hatchet of Jewish supremacism had nothing more spiteful in her final curtain call other than *"God is great."*

From a bird's eye view, this was but one of several tragic scenes taking place on that day. A few miles away, a family of seven had just barely made it out of their home when the bulldozer crashed through where the living room was. There were no warnings that this demolition process was about to take place, and had it not been for the fact that 14 year-old Ismail went to the window to see what the noise was that was coming from outside, the entire family would most likely have been buried beneath the rubble. This was a common occurrence these days, of not ordering the evacuation of a home to be demolished, since the Israelis cared nothing about the lives of the filthy Arabs who were polluting their sacred land, and thus preferred that the entire mess be hauled away, home and dwellers included.

Under the gaze of 3 armed-to-the-teeth Israeli soldiers, the family stood by and watched helplessly as everything that encompassed their lives was reduced to rubble within a few minutes. There was nothing left of the meager example of their family's security and order now, and even though what they had called a life had been a miserable existence anyway, at least they had had a place to call home where they could eat, sleep, and find refuge from the rain. This home, which had literally stood for centuries, was just one of thousands in recent years that has been bulldozed in order to make way for a new apartment complex for "better people," the Zionists, who, if you were to ask them, were a race apart and chosen by God to be the bringers of enlightenment, peace and righteousness to the rest of humanity.

Perhaps it was the colors of it that caught his eye, the green, black, brown and white that contrasted with the sand-colored rubble of his former home's exterior. Ismail went over to where his bedroom used to be and found it jutting forth from the rubble, the Palestinian flag he cherished and which he had used to adorn his room on the same wall upon which he hung the photos of friends and family members who had died fighting to liberate their land of its oppressors. He carefully pulled it out from the rubble, paying the same respect to his country's colors that is paid by other citizens around the world to their respective countries, and forgetting where he was, or possibly, because of remembering where he was, draped the flag over the rubble in what was the only act of defiance he cold muster at this moment. 14 year-old Ismail turned and stared at his oppressors with a controlled yet determined stare.

The three armed Israeli soldiers, recently arrived from the former Soviet Union and not able to speak even one word of the same Aramaic that was the language of the Biblical ancestors from whom they claimed to be descendents, finally got what they had been hoping for that day. After all, what good were guns for anyway if they remained cold and unfired? Was there no truth to the old saying that a weapon unused was a useless weapon? Therefore, without any concern paid for what might be future consequences, one from among them chuckled, lifted the American-made rifle that had been gifted to him by virtue of his ethnic superiority from a nation that dares to calls itself Christian, aimed its sights squarely between the boy's eyes, and in the plain sight of all who were present, launched one of his .22 caliber missiles traveling at 3,300 feet per second through the boy's head, resulting in a spray of pink mist that left the smell of human blood in the air.

INDEPENDENCE DAY 285

Even before the echoes of the gunshot had died, the family was screaming in agony and running to the spot where Ismail lie as motionless as a child's doll. His last act of defiance, of simply saluting the flag and of swearing loyalty to the land that his forefathers had inhabited for over a thousand years resulted in the execution of a death sentence under which he had lived from the moment he was born. And as the family members hold him in their arms, watching as his life flows out of him in rivers of red, wailing towards heaven and begging the Almighty who created him to spare his life, those who were responsible for authoring this misery-laden event simply walk away snickering, thinking to themselves that they are now one step closer to having finished the business of exterminating *Amalek*, the people whom their ancestors were commanded to eradicate in cleansing the promised land, *Eretz Y'Israel* and of making it racially and spiritually pure. Later that evening, there would be drinks and discussions of what kind of medals would be forthcoming as a result of the day's hard work…

…And these were just some of the thoughts going through his mind as he looked out the window that evening, watching the night sky as its darkness was interrupted every few seconds by brilliant displays of light. It was July 4th, 2004; Independence Day in America, but his thoughts could hardly be focused on the festivities that were supposed to mark this event. Not now, and not anytime soon. His eyes had been opened to something so horrible that precluded celebrating anything, much less the freedom that he was supposed to have as an American.

It must have been quite a scene down there in town where all the fireworks were taking place. Over-sized Americans stuffed into under-sized clothing, beer in one hand and something to shove into their mouths in the other, congregating for the purpose of celebrating something that in reality they no longer possessed. Waddling around like penguins and peppering their base and trivial discussions with language that one would hear in an x-rated film, they had painted themselves into the ultimate picture of black humor, and had it not been for the fact that such terrible consequences were attached to this situation, one could have been moved towards laughing at all of it.

But laughing was out of the question now, for to do so would have been as vulgar as telling dirty jokes at a funeral. The tragedy was too great, too monstrous, too serious. Besides the fact that it was the ultimate in contrasting images, as well it was all taking place in the midst of unimaginable suffering for millions of others around the globe. Just imagining the audacity of it all made the bile in his throat rise and caused his brain to scream out loud in pain. They were like a group of individuals who had inherited a great fortune generations past, but who today, unbeknownst to them were as penniless as street bums, and all of this the result of their having allowed shyster lawyers to administer their estate and bleed it dry of all its wealth. Tonight as they celebrate their perceived fortunes and congratulate themselves for having inherited them, that which they do not realize is that fact that they are bankrupt, busted, broke, and even now, as they drink and mingle with each other, laughing and talking as foolish heirs often do, the paperwork is being signed in remote places wherein their foreclosure and eviction is being planned and implemented. It had become the ultimate contradiction of themes, Independence Day in America, as much so as if there had been something known as Virtuousness Day in the ancient city of Sodom thousands of years ago.

Our spiritually ex-patriate American, watching all of this from a distance remembered reading something once in a medical journal about schizophrenia and about how one of the telltale signs of this condition's presence was found in an individual's ability to simultaneously hold two completely contradictory ideas, and if this wasn't a description of what had happened to this country, he didn't know what could be. They had become a nation of madmen, wild beasts who couldn't think for themselves outside of the parameters that had been constructed for them by overlords who were capable of doing nothing but evil. Here they were, celebrating their freedom in an age where their lives had been reduced to that of mice within a cage, and they were too stupid to realize it. A corporate police state had been constructed around them, and their country resembled the land of their forefathers as much as a swine resembles a ballerina, and yet they were too blind to see it. But yet, as if on Pavlovian clue, here they were, shouting and hollering like a bunch of maniacs about how wonderful all of it was and how proud they were to be Americans, the freest people on the planet, how much God loved them and blah, blah, blah. He swallowed hard in contemplating these realities, and having ingested this nauseating gruel of clashing images, felt the beginnings of a sickness in his stomach that was not going to be chased away by anything over-the-counter.

For whatever reason, he had not been infected with this virus that had gripped millions of his countrymen on September 11 2001, and in the interests of maintaining his as well as his family's intellectual and spiritual health, he had maintained a strict quarantine from his countrymen since that fateful day. Over the course of the following 3 years, from a safe distance he watched in horror as his nation slowly but surely came down with this plague of intellectual and spiritual paralysis, watched as his former countrymen marched uninterruptedly towards their own oblivion without so much as a trace of resistance.

And so, in maintaining this agenda of keeping his loved ones off of the political version of the Titanic, on this night our American friend was at home with his family instead of participating in the mass-suicide that was taking place down in town.

When the first "boom" had gone off, he and his wife had looked at each other simultaneously, each bearing a face that revealed the underlying sense of puzzlement mixed with a small amount of concern that each felt. It was followed by another distant "boom" and then another, and then both of them, remembering what day it was, nodded their heads and said in unison "July the 4th."

The event shouldn't have taken them by such surprise, particularly since they had spent a good part of that evening watching *Independence Day*, that not-so-subtle piece of propaganda that was released upon the American people just prior to initiating the wars to save Israel. Talk about blatant, this unashamed effort of pumping up the American people into supporting what was to be the biggest bloodbath in history, theirs or anyone else's for that matter. A storyline wherein the planet is suddenly threatened with complete annihilation from hostile, fanatical un-humans bent upon the destruction of everyone who is not like them, an extra-terrestrial *jihad* which is defeated by the combined efforts of Jewish brains and American brawn. The only thing that could have made the film more obvious would have been bearded aliens dressed in sheets and quoting verses from some religious book that inspired them to do what it was that they were doing. We should suppose though that our couple should be given some slack for having forgotten where they were and in what time period they were living, since the events of the last 2 years in America have been a whirlwind of sorts that should have left anyone with half an ounce of sense somewhat senseless.

It was only a few minutes of these distant festivities going on before there was heard the sound of small footsteps coming down the stairs. In single file, beginning with the youngest (who we can suppose were the most frightened by the noise and thus wanted to get to Mom and Dad as quickly as possible) up to the oldest came the 5 children who were suddenly awakened by what sounded like strange thunder. They made a beeline for the couch where Mom and Dad were seated, asking what all the noise was about, huddling in closely as children are biologically programmed to do. When "fireworks" came the answer, all the children turned their heads towards the window to see for themselves, relieved somewhat that there was no storm, or worse, that there was no new war that had just begun in their vicinity, a reality of present day life that they had come to understand better during the course of the last two years. The oldest boy, who by then had begun to feel the stirrings of his masculine nature already, was the first to recognize the light show for how it appeared, and walking towards the window to get a better gaze, said ominously *"It looks like Iraq."*

Out of the mouths of babes, as the saying has always gone.

It certainly did look like Iraq, at least that version of it that had been presented to Americans in the opening moments of the war, wherein the night sky in Baghdad was illuminated in dizzying displays of light that resembled any night in America on July the 4th. Perhaps this was how the puppet masters in Washington and Tel Aviv wanted it to be seen, this "shock and awe" as they characterized it, in trying to get the "freest" people in the world to acquiesce to the agenda of murdering 1.5 billion Muslims for Israel's benefit.

The other children, understanding the importance found in the oldest boy's words, also walked towards the window to get a better view. They stood there, saying nothing, although everyone in the room knew what was on each other's mind. They winced at each flash, recoiled a bit, not displaying the 'ooohs' and 'aaahs' that children would normally exhibit at such a performance. The light show, paired with its distant booms and crackles was just one of several obscene spectacles that their young eyes had witnessed since the beginning of the present war to erect the Israeli empire. Prior to this were the images of the little Iraqi boy whose arms had been completely blown off of his body when the Americans dropped a bomb directly on his home, killing his entire family. And as sickening as this was—the image of this boy fighting to keep himself from succumbing to utter despair, the spectacle which followed was even worse; that of the American soldiers loading him onto a military transport to take him to a medical facility and cheering as he went on his way, a grandiose attempt by the Zionist media to gloss over this tragedy that had somehow slipped past the censors and made its way before the eyes of the American people.

Of course, there were as well many other scenes that these children witnessed which brought the reality of this war to their eyes and which made them smarter than the average American as to what it was all about—the women and children of Palestine who were being shot and blown up on a daily basis for the last century by those who fancied themselves as the apple of God's eye—America's only allies in the Middle East, the Israelis, not to mention the daily destruction of all those monuments that have stood for thousands of years and which are considered sacred to billions of Christians and Muslims around the world.

And so, what had taken place over the course of the last two years of watching the war on television and of discussing its awful realities with Mom and Dad is that these children had been robbed of their youth and their innocence. They understood life and the ugly side of human nature much better than children should, and this was the reason why there was no excitement in their eyes tonight while watching the rockets' red glare and bombs bursting in air. Rather, they looked upon the images as any decent individual with open eyes should in America of 2004; a disgusting display of patriotic pornography that was a bringer of disease and death. It was pure smut, a way of defiling what would normally have been the beautiful act of expressing one's love for the country in a wholesome, healthy way and of replacing it with a whorish, cheap, and sterile performance for lustful spectators. Worse yet is the fact that the national life and vitality that should have been produced by the consummation of this political marriage was (just as had been taking place in the literal sense over 4,000 times a day during the course of the last 30 years) torn to pieces by the political and cultural abortionists in Washington, New York, and Los Angeles, leaving in their wake a trail of death and destruction for hundreds of millions.

And so, having had their fill of these ugly scenes and of being scandalized in such a frightful way, all went upstairs in single file as they had come down, a silent march, that, although not uttering a word, yet spoke volumes.

Having had enough of it herself, his wife followed suit and went to bed, leaving our friend in solitude to ponder other thoughts that refused to be chased away the night on which Americans were busy celebrating their freedom, Independence Day.

The phone ringing at 3 am in the morning could never be a good thing. It was either bad news or a prank. For this particular individual, a phone call at 3 am to *this* number was particularly worrisome, since, being the most popular actor in the world, he had only given it out to a handful of friends and relatives. He heard his wife and the youngest of their seven children stir as the rings continued.

"Hello?" he answered, expecting to hear the voice of his father or someone else from the family with some kind of important news.

"You think you're pretty smart don't you?" taunted the voice on the other line. It was a man's voice, menacing, with a thick Brooklyn accent. The actor had heard the voice before, since this was not the first time he had been called in this manner. The voice continued. *"You made me and my friends really mad, and we're going to make sure that you pay for your crimes, you and your entire family. Think about that when you're trying to get back to sleep."* The actor started to say something, displaying that angry, determined look on his face that he had famously worn in his movies and which had been seen before by millions of people around the world, but before he could get a word out, the line went dead.

INDEPENDENCE DAY

"How did they get this number?" he thought in disbelief. It was a brand new number, and only about 5 people had it. The only way possible was to break into the phone company's computer banks and retrieve it, which would have required the resources of a government or at the very least, its passive cooperation.

His crime, the thing that had outraged this tiny minority of tyrants and which had driven them to the brink of madness was his decision to make a movie about the one man who was the most revered by the world's 1 billion Christians and 1.5 billion Muslims, Jesus of Nazareth. In the months leading up to the release of the movie, the Zionist organizations had gone ballistic and had pulled the levers on every machine upon which they held sway in trying to destroy this man and his project. Under their direction, every newspaper, magazine, radio and television program had devoted a considerable amount of their attention to the campaign of smearing him and of making a mockery of his film. Some of these groups, the less cautious, actually petitioned the US government to have this man and his associates arrested as terrorists under the provisions of the Patriot Act.

It was July the 4th, Independence Day in America, and not only his life, but the lives of those whom he loved had just been threatened, *again,* something that had become a regular event now for over a year as a result of his daring to exercise his freedom of speech and religion. He had gone to the police, the FBI of all people, but nothing was done short of periodic assurances by agency spokesmen that "they were looking into it."

Our American actor should have known better than to call them, since after all it was this same agency that had allowed over 200 spies who had been directly involved in the attacks of September 11th to be sent back to Israel immediately following what took place on that fateful day. Added to this, the fact that the Zionist group that was responsible for making such a fuss about his movie, the ADL, was a registered agency of the Israeli government and the fact that it had enjoyed a love affair with the FBI over the course of the last 5 decades should have signaled to him whose priorities were going to take precedence in this matter. And if these two items weren't enough, then that which should have brought his expectations into proper alignment with reality was the fact that the individual who was responsible for overseeing much of the FBI's investigations held dual citizenship in America and in Israel, and this fact, more than anything else should have underscored for him just how ridiculous the business of contacting them over this matter really was. In all fairness to our naïve American actor though, what else could he do? He had a family whose safety he was responsible for securing, and he still, foolishly, believed in the system, at least somewhat.

Tonight, the same people who flocked to see his famous movie in droves will don their baseball hats, their t-shirts emblazoned with such recently resurrected and popularized slogans as *"United We Stand"* and *"God Bless America"* and who, while clutching in their hands the millions of miniature American flags specially made for this event will celebrate their enslavement to the very same jackals who made the threatening phone call tonight, although none among the sheep will recognize this as being the case. They will nostalgically and schizophrenically lump the triumph of this man's movie and the war in the Middle East together as being two sides of the same coin – 2 fronts in the war to save Christianity and its civilization – two battles being fought in defense of the faith and freedom, refusing to see that the very same people who were responsible for running this man's life through the meat grinder are the very same who are sending America's sons and daughters off to die in the Middle East for the benefit of a foreign power who is, despite all the propagandizing that has taken place, no friend.

And while all this is taking place, in the very land where a war of liberation was waged by a peasant carpenter from Nazareth against the descendents of those who made the threatening phone call tonight a continuation of this war is raging at full throttle. At this moment, the gangsters who put to death the main character in the same film which Christians in America stampeded like buffalo to go see in 2004 have returned after being chased out in 70 AD and are attempting to impose upon the world the very same nightmare that the Palestinian carpenter-turned-revolutionary tried to prevent. Tonight, all the spots that commemorate the great events of this carpenter's life and which have stood as some of the greatest monuments to the development of Western Civilization are being bulldozed and blown up by Jewish supremacist tyrants, while a group of Arab peasants attempt to prevent this disaster from taking place, even with their life's blood.

INDEPENDENCE DAY

Tonight, as Americans celebrate the memories of those who gave their lives for the liberation of their own country from a foreign invader, will at the same time curse and castigate those who are attempting to do the same in the lands of Palestine and Iraq. Tonight, "cowards" and "terrorists," as they have been called by the President of the United States and by his Zionist overlords, are fighting with every ounce of their beings to liberate their respective countries from the foreigners who have invaded their lands and who are slaughtering their women and children in the tens and hundreds of thousands. Adults, not having the sophisticated weaponry that is used against them by their oppressors will strap themselves with explosives and blow themselves up in order to take out the assassins within the Israeli military machine and their hired mercenaries from America who murder women and children on a daily basis. Children, in what is but a modern day repeat of the battle fought between David vs. Goliath will bravely go up against tanks and machine guns, often armed with nothing more than rocks and sticks and will fight this enemy with every ounce of their beings, knowing beforehand that they stand a good chance of losing arms and legs and even their lives. These "cowards" and "terrorists" will do so for exactly the same reasons and in exactly the same manner as was done by those rare Americans who, over 200 years previously, drove out foreign invaders who were bent upon enslaving them and of robbing them of their own destinies. Every man, woman, and child in Iraq, Palestine and every other place where the beast of Jewish supremacism is on the rampage, are—whether donning a rifle, grenade launcher, bomb vest, or a vehicle laden with explosives—brilliant reincarnations of the patriots of 1776 who refused to go down without a fight, who refused to go quietly into the night, freedom fighters whose existence today has been reduced to one agenda that is beyond negotiation or surrender, which is simply, *"give us liberty or give us death."*

Of course we will not find an ounce of this awareness among those Americans who have chosen to tempt the patience of fate on this night, July 4th, Independence Day. As they foolishly wave their flags, put their hands over the hearts and sing with a quivering voice the national anthem with tears welling up in their eyes, what they have chosen to do is to participate in an obscene display of hypocrisy and contempt for that gem of incalculable value known as freedom, as well as for the justice that must accompany its existence if it is to remain a viable entity. The contempt that they maintain for those who are paying with their life's blood so that they themselves may experience just a *tasting* of the same freedom that Americans presume to be celebrating on this night has become a perfect representation of *the two minute's hate* of George Orwell's nightmarish novel *1984*. Tonight, as it will be for many future nights in the coming years, the cursing that the Americans will display against those in the Middle East for daring to defend their beloved homelands and families from foreign assassins has become the chanting of the contradictions in that infamous, prophetic piece of fiction turned-into-non-fiction which predicted a future state of madness for humanity: *war is peace, freedom is slavery, ignorance is strength,* and by such, has now become the process of spitting on the graves of those who gave their lives before them in the noble cause of freedom. What they are doing in effect by championing the war against Israel's enemies, in cheering like the mob at the coliseum for the hellish precepts of the Jewish supremacist agenda is to hold in contempt the war for freedom that their forefathers waged centuries past, although today, most of them are too stupid to recognize this as being the case.

For in reality, what are they daring to celebrate this night? Freedom? They are as bankrupt of this currency as some indigent, homeless hobo on the street begging for food. Justice? Their political and cultural system is as anemic of this life-sustaining element to the point of near death. Truth? The fools who tonight are championing the slaughter of the last remaining impediment to the enslavement of the Jewish supremacist agenda stagger around aimlessly, inebriated on the drug of duplicity that they ingest on a daily basis by a government media complex furthering the cause of Zionist tyranny. Decency? Their society has become like a leper colony full of dying individuals who are rotting away from the corrosive effects of the plague, a plague that has resulted from poisons that have been deliberately poured into the wellspring of their culture by the very same assassins who bow at the feet of the Israeli agenda.

After all, what is the event being remembered this evening, and for which all of this energy and effort is being expended? The day when a group of rugged individuals refused to be enslaved by a man named George who was a puppet to the business interests and corporations that controlled him? The day in which patriots stood up to the most powerful political, economic, and military power in the world at that time for the chance to run their lives free of those who would be their overlords? The day in which they fought back against an invasion initiated by foreign powers that threatened the peace and prosperity of their lives and the lives of those whom they loved? Please…no more.

It is something that, out of respect for the dead, should be put on hold for a while, this celebration of Independence Day in America. Not only out of respect for those who gave their lives fighting for this thing known as freedom 200 years ago in America, but more importantly, out of respect for those who are fighting for it today and who are being rewarded with nothing but scorn and derision by Americans for their efforts. The honor that is due to the minutemen at Lexington Bridge who were killed by the British is shamed and tarnished when remembering the event in which 35 of America's young men were deliberately murdered by the Israelis in 1967 when the ship that carried them, the USS Liberty, was torpedoed, napalmed and machine-gunned for almost 2 hours with the quiet complicity of the American government. The outrage with which Americans recall the unsuccessful assassination attempt on George Washington's life by the British is irredeemably defiled when paired next to what was successfully realized by a nuclear weapons-hungry Israel against the same John F. Kennedy who stood in her way of getting the bomb. The disdain that Benedict Arnold has suffered for 2 centuries now and counting as a result of his treachery in turning coat and siding with America's enemy at that time is but a grain of sand placed alongside a mountain when considering the manner in which today all the elected members of the American government have unflinchingly cast their lots with the worst enemy that America has ever had.

Here they were this night, standing solidly behind the man who lied to them about the reasons for America's entry into the present war being fought in erecting the Israeli empire, King George, the man responsible for the deaths of thousands of sons and daughters serving in the American military and who has promised to send even more to die in the coming years, and they cheer. This man and his coterie who silently sent back to Israel the nest of spies, 200 or more, who played an indispensable role in the deaths of 3,000 Americans on September 11th sits atop his throne receiving the adulations of a compliant and conquered American people. They hoop and holler over their ancestors having thrown off the shackles of a foreign power 2 centuries past, and yet drink themselves silly over the fact that they have become the useful idiots of a foreign power whose thirst for supremacy and blood makes what was 'British tyranny' in 1776 look like paradise. Even now, as the next terrible event is being planned that will dwarf what took place on 9/11, these individuals who today inform on their friends and family to the Zionist thought police and who would have been the loyalists in America's war against Great Britain 200 years ago refuse to see the obvious for what it is.

And it is in this light therefore that our American friend, watching from a distance as the fires of duplicity and treachery consume the land that he used to love becomes a refugee, a wanderer without a home and without a country to which he can swear his allegiance. He sees the circus in town for what it really is, a farce of unprecedented historical outrage that should be an abomination in the eyes of every decent human being on the planet. The presence of these individuals tonight at what should be the solemn ceremony of celebrating freedom and of commemorating the sacrifices made by selfless individuals for their beloved country is as appropriate as would be a whore clad in a red dress at someone's first communion ceremony.

In the meantime, our friend must do the unthinkable, something that he never would have imagined doing in a million years, which is to find an escape route out of this land of 'freedom' before this beast that is on the rampage snatches his own children and drags them off to fight and die for the benefit of a hostile, maniacal foreign power. He must begin preparations to flee, while there is time, to some safe haven lest the storm that is gathering comes and destroys everything that has given his life meaning. As a descendant of those who came to America looking for freedom from their respective countries, he must reverse these events and bring the family name to distant shores, someplace where his children will be safe — not only from being physically kidnapped and dragged off to die in order to serve the beast of the Zionist agenda, but as well from the highly contagious and deadly mental illness that has destroyed their countrymen.

INDEPENDENCE DAY

And as he looks out the window, wincing as the mid-air explosions and percussions—meant as a celebration of this thing called independence, punctuate what would ordinarily have been a peaceful night, he thinks to himself, *"If I could be president for a day, the things I would do."*

In his meanderings, he envisions what would take place in a world where freedom and liberty are celebrated and honored in the spirit of true justice, where vice and bloodthirstiness are contained and then, even if only temporarily, terminated instead of celebrated.

And he concludes his thoughts by saying something that he always remembered hearing his grandfather solemnly say when speaking of future events, a man who was born in the same Holy Land where today's true patriots are fighting and who understood where life's importance lie; *"Yam Yammi"*, which, when translated from the same Aramaic tongue spoken by the freedom fighters of Palestine 2,000 years ago against the beast of Jewish Supremacism simply means *"the day will come."*

The day will come wherein Independence Day, on whatever date it falls, will be a day celebrated by *all* the world's peoples, not just by those in America. It will be a day commemorating the event wherein mankind fought and achieved its independence from the beast of the Jewish supremacist agenda, and wherein a wooden stake was driven through the heart of a vampire that terrorized the world in such an unimaginable and unprecedented way. It will be remembered as the day wherein those who were tyrannized in such a brutal manner by the descendents of Cain rose up and finally cast into the lake of fire this animal that has prowled about humanity's homestead and who has snatched the helpless, dragged them off towards oblivion and devoured them without any mercy. It will be the day wherein from the heavens, children like Mona and Ismail and all the others who were cut down by Hell's assassins are remembered and enshrined as some of the best individuals that humanity had to offer as a result of their having given their lives in fighting for the taste of freedom. It will be celebrated as the day in which the beast and his 2,000-year agenda was finally put to the torch, and permanently made a thing of the past, never to be resurrected again.

And, with these last thoughts, our American friend turns from the shock and awe, walks towards where his wife and baby lie sleeping, thinking of the heroes whose exploits would one day tell the story of freedom and justice for all mankind…

And it was July 4th, 2004, Independence Day in America.

Parting Shots, Final Thoughts

No Shades of Grey in a World of Black and White

And there we have it, my friend, the image of the beast as I have envisioned it. Of the three main religions emanating forth from the Holy Lands, the Middle East, we see three disparate views of this thing, and thus three completely differing approaches in dealing with it. Of the three main religions of that region, only one of them in my opinion views this thing in its proper clarity.

For those Jews who are its adherents, Zionism and the bloodthirsty, haughty, supremacist ideology that is its lifeblood is the long anticipated Messiah. It is the elevation of their people and of their well-being above all other matters, including those involving objective right and wrong. It was this same ideology that formed the basis upon which the Pharisees implemented their agenda and against which Christ spoke and fought. For 2,000 years it has lied dormant and subterranean, due in no small part to the restraining effects of both Christianity and Islam. Now it has come forth, as if *out of the sea*, in exactly the same language used by the prophet John in the Book of the Apocalypse and as such has become the *abomination of desolation* in the Holy Land that was predicted to be forthcoming.

For a good number of those in the Christian world, the beast of Zionism has become part of their religion as well, since they believe that it is the harbinger of their being rewarded with heaven and rescued from the great sufferings that are to take place immediately preceding the return of Christ. The rest who call themselves Christians and who have not *formally* adopted this view have nevertheless been corrupted by these same sentiments, albeit in a diminished way in that they simply do not care enough about it to devote any serious study or understanding as to what encompasses its nature nor how it is going to effect them (nor their fellow man) in the near future.

Of the three, it is only those who are adherents of the religion of Islam who appear to take this item seriously, and who thus appreciate it for what it is and what it portends. As of the moment of this writing, it is only these adherents who seem to understand what kind of hell it is that humanity faces under the Jewish supremacist agenda and wherein lies the duty in opposing it.

For those in the Christian world who may be up in arms over this statement, prove me wrong, not with frowns or alienation, but with logic and facts. If the Christian world, many of whose members claim for themselves a front row seat in the Almighty's voyage to the bliss of eternity wish to be taken seriously, then they have quite a bit of catching up to do with their Muslim counterparts in standing against this Antichrist system that has so devoured the world. And if by chance these individuals who claim for themselves the name of Christian do not accept this challenge and choose instead to continue on as they have been in allowing the enemies of both God and man to destroy everything in their interest of creating a worldwide plantation with themselves at the top—and with all the misery, dehumanization and degradation that this situation entails—then may they, those who call themselves Christian at least keep their tongues and their hubris silent during this misery-laden process. May they at least have enough decency to not exacerbate the pain being endured by those who are willing to sacrifice life and limb in resisting this abomination, and may they at least sit there quietly and not try to dignify their spiritual treason and the denial of their duty with haughty words and self-adulation.

Better yet, may they remember who they are and who their forefathers were, and thus join in on the side of those who are losing their own lives in this struggle, and thus may they bring their own forces to bear in slaying the agenda put in motion by the enemies of the Master whom they presume to follow. May they remember and take seriously the words of the peasant carpenter from Palestine who made it clear to all generations of mankind where he stood on the matter when he said without any ambiguity,

"No man can serve two masters. You are either with me, or against me."

Recommended Reading

Lest the reader assume that the previous discussion has no basis in anything other than an over-active imagination on the part of this writer, included is a short list of works that are highly recommended and which appear in order of their importance and relevance to the subject matter

Jewish History, Jewish Religion
Professor Israel Shahak

Dangerous Liaison: The Inside Story of the US-Israeli Covert Relationship
Andrew and Leslie Cockburn

Judaism's Strange Gods
Michael Hoffman II

They Dare To Speak Out
Paul Findley

The Other Side of Deception
Victor Ostrovsky

Final Judgment
Michael Collins Piper

Israel: Our Duty, Our Dilemma
Theodore Winston Pike

Islam
John A. Williams

Memoirs of a Jewish Extremist
Yossi Halevi

RECOMMENDED READING

Deliberate Deceptions: Facing the Facts About the US-Israeli Relationship
Ex-United States Congressman Paul Findley

The Controversy of Zion
Douglas Reed

Gideon's Spies: The Secret History of the Mossad
Gordon Thomas

The Kingship of Christ and the Conversion the Jewish Nation
Fr. Dennis Fahey

Islam: A Short History
Karen Armstrong

The Essential Koran
Translation by Thomas Cleary

By Way of Deception
Victor Ostrovsky

The Israeli Holocaust Against the Palestinians
Michael Hoffman II

The Final Apostasy: Prelude to Antichrist
Dr. Gordon Ginn

Behind Communism
Frank L. Britton

Red Banners, White Mantle
Warren H. Carrol

The Gulag Archipelago
Alexandr Solzhenitsyn

Discovering Islam: Making Sense of Muslim History and Society
Akbar S. Ahmed

RECOMMENDED READING

Islam: The Straight Path
John L Esposito

Our Roots Are Still Alive: The Story of the Palestinian People
Joy Bonds, Jimmy Emerman, Linda John, Penny Johnson and Paul Rupert

How Israel Lost
Andrew Ben Cramer

A History of Modern Palestine
Ilan Pappe

Assault on the USS Liberty
James M. Ennis Jr.

Seeds of Fire
Gordon Thomas

When the World Will Be As One
Tal Brooke

The Arabs
Jacques Berque

Heritage of the Desert
Harry B. Ellis

High Priests of War
Michael Collins Piper

The Life of an American Jew Living in Racist Marxist Israel.
Jack Bernstein

Crescent & Cross
The website of solidarity between Islam and Christianity

The Crescent and the Cross Solidarity Movement is telling the truth about the relationship between Christianity and Islam and why they have been deliberately set at war against each other by Zionists and their supporters.

Christianity and Islam are natural allies, not natural enemies. There is nothing about them that makes them organically opposed to each other. In fact, they have more in common with each other than they do with any other of the world's faiths. Besides Christianity, Islam is the only other religion that recognizes Jesus. It is the only other religion that gives honor to his mother Mary. And, more importantly, they both are, in their true forms, universal in their scope and do not adhere to any supremacist themes.

The present conflict between the two religions is an artificial conflict that has been deliberately constructed by Zionists—both Jewish and Christian—who stand to benefit from the two religions wiping each other out. This Zionist agenda that is using a "divide and conquer" strategy is done with the interests of seeing that in the end their supremacist agenda reigns over the world. Zionism is an expansive, aggressive ideology steeped in racial supremacist themes.

Islam as an organized ideology is the last barrier that is standing steadfastly in the way of this nightmarish apocalyptic agenda being realized. The West has been coerced into participating in this present "clash between civilizations" as a result of her economic, military and technological superiority over those Muslim nations that will not bend to the will of the Zionists.

In truth, what has happened is that the Zionist state of Israel has, through her interlocking network of loyal assistants, pitted these two worlds against each other in what is an unjust and unnecessary spilling of innocent blood. Our mission is to tell the truth about all the entities that are involved in this conundrum—Christian, Muslim and Jew—and by doing so, see to it that the power of the Zionist agenda will eventually meet its only viable and justified ending, which is on the ash heap of mankind's history.

Please join us in this journey of uncovering the truth. The stakes are higher than they have ever been in our history. All the events for which mankind has been waiting for 2,000 years are happening before the eyes of a deluded and sleeping world. What is needed now more than ever is light, clarity and solidarity, and this is the aim of our movement.

If you'd like to join our e-mail list, write articles for this website, and/or just support our cause, please contact Mark Glenn and let him know how you'd like to contribute. All support is welcome! And check out the website for articles from many truth activists.

mrkglenn@yahoo.com
www.notmywords.com

TOLL FREE TBR ORDERING: 1-877-773-9077 • Visa/MasterCard

TBR

THE BARNES REVIEW
REVISIONIST MAGAZINE

Real history is **NOT PROPAGANDA** intended to shape the views of unsuspecting readers toward the current projects of the media masters nor is it regurgitated war propaganda. Real history is more than the distorted, politically correct half-truths you get in virtually every other periodical published today.

In THE BARNES REVIEW (TBR) you will read the **REAL STORY OF OUR PAST**—from the prehistoric to the very recent, from forgotten races and civilizations to first person accounts of WWII and the late Cold War. There is no more interesting magazine published today, nor a more significant and important subject than **REAL HISTORY**. How else can we judge the present but by the past? And everything inside TBR is **PURE AND UNADULTERATED**—history like it should be told—**NOT WATERED DOWN** to please one special interest group or another.

Subscribe for one year at $46* and we'll send you **a FREE copy of** *The East Came West.* Subscribe for **TWO YEARS at $78*** and we'll send you **TWO FREE BOOKS**: *The East Came West* AND *FDR: The Other Side of the Coin*—nearly $40 in **FREE** books! Send payment with request to TBR, P.O. Box 15877, Washington, D.C. 20003 or call TBR today at **1-877-773-9077** toll free to charge your order to Visa or MasterCard.

EVERY DOMESTIC U.S. TBR SUBSCRIBER will also receive the bimonthly *Barnes Review Newsletter*, keeping you up to date on what's happening in the field of Revisionist history. Foreign subscribers may download this from our web site.

Remember to indicate your free book choice(s) when you call or write. Mention you saw the ad in *No Beauty in the Beast!*

THE BARNES REVIEW:
A Magazine LIKE NO OTHER in Print Today!

TBR, P.O. Box 15877, Washington D.C. 20003
Visa/MasterCard Toll Free Ordering Line: 1-877-773-9077
Website: www.barnesreview.org

*ADD $12 PER YEAR FOR SUBSCRIPTIONS OUTSIDE THE U.S.

TOLL FREE TBR ORDERING: 1-877-773-9077 • Visa/MasterCard

No Beauty in the Beast:
Israel Without Her Mascara

"The day will come when your enemies will build an embankment against you and encircle you in on every side. They will dash you to the ground, you and the children within your walls. They will not leave one stone upon another, because you did not recognize the time of God's coming." —JESUS OF NAZARETH

These words have been with mankind for nearly 2,000 years, and yet they appear to be some of the most disregarded pieces of advice in history. These cautionary words were uttered by a freedom fighter from the Palestinian town of Nazareth a few days before he was executed for daring to stand up against a group of racial supremacists known as the Sanhedrin.

No Beauty in the Beast: Israel Without Her Mascara is a book that discusses the most momentous events of mankind's history and how they pertain to today. What the world is witnessing today with regard to the events in the Middle East and the manner in which the Christian West has been seduced into involving itself in the slaughter of Muslims is the extension of the same battle that took place in the Palestinian town of Jerusalem 2,000 years ago between Jesus and the founders of the modern-day ideological movement known as Zionism. Today, this beast of Judeo-ethnocentrism against which Christ waged his war of liberation—the beast which for 1,900 years remained dormant—has now been resurrected from the ashes where it remained safely isolated from the rest of mankind. It is at present devouring everything in its path to world domination. With the recreation of the state of Israel that was destroyed some 2,000 years ago and the much prophesied "return of the Jews" to the Holy Land, the world is now witnessing the fulfillment of the prophecies concerning the final battle between the forces of good and evil. The ascendancy of this same supremacist agenda (Zionism) that was opposed by Christ is the linchpin in understanding the cryptic description of the Beast of the book of the Apocalypse. And, just as was predicted by seers thousands of years ago, the future of humanity hangs in the balance.

—MARK GLENN, *author of* NO BEAUTY IN THE BEAST

FROM THE BARNES REVIEW—*Softcover, 320 pages, #470*

$25 *minus 10% for TBR subscribers.* (*See coupon in back of book.*)

TOLL FREE TBR ORDERING: 1-877-773-9077 • Visa/MasterCard

The High Priests of War
The Secret History of America's Neo-Cons

The Secret History of How America's Neo-Conservative Trotskyites Came to Power and How They Orchestrated the War Against Iraq as the First Step in Their Drive for Global Empire

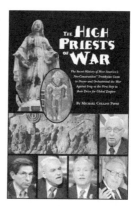

This is the only full-length book on the "neo-cons" and their ultimate agenda. *The High Priests of War* is the entire story—no holds barred—from the beginning. The neo-cons have steered us to the edge of the most dangerous time in United States history. We face the consequences of the disastrous war in Iraq, hatred of Americans across the globe, loss of U.S. economic prestige, talk of a military attack against a determined Iran, and much more. The book is now being circulated internationally (Malaysia, Saudi Arabia) and is being translated into a variety of languages. It has been acclaimed as the one book that explains the "who, what, when, where, why and how" of the tragic involvement of the United States in the Iraq war. This fast-reading, carefully-documented 144-page volume has helped spread the word about the REAL reason for the Iraq war and how it is all part of a grand design that is being suppressed by the Controlled Media.

Softcover, 144 pages, $19.95 minus 10% for TBR subscribers.

See coupon at back of book. Send payment to:
The Barnes Review, P.O. Box 15877, Washington, D.C. 20003.

Order any books from TBR TOLL FREE
by calling 1-877-773-9077. Visa and MasterCard accepted.

The Inside Story of Operation Keelhaul

The East Came West: The Cossacks, and more than a million Russians, fought against Communism during WWII, and they still hate Communism today. But they are not pro-"Ally." While researching material for the writing of *The East Came West,* Peter J. Huxley-Blythe discovered why these people do not trust the U.S. or Great Britain. When the war in Europe ended, millions of Russian men, women and children sought sanctuary in the West. There they met terror face to face. They were physically beaten into submission and then shipped like cattle back to the Soviet Union to face Stalin's executioners, or to serve long sentences at hard labor in the death camps of Siberia. The author says this brutal appeasement policy was contrary to recognized international law, and was initiated and carried out by the Supreme Allied Commander, Gen. Eisenhower. From survivors, Huxley-Blythe obtained the details of the Cossacks' fight for freedom from 1941 until 1945, and from them he learned the method used by the British to force them back to the merciless Soviet leaders at the points of bayonets. Softcover, 224 pages #434, *$19.95* minus 10% for TBR subscribers.

A Truthful History of Russia's Mad Monk

Grigori Rasputin: Neither Devil Nor Saint: By Dr. Elizabeth Judas. Is all of what we know about the "Mad Monk," Grigori Rasputin, the product of anti-Christian Bolshevik propaganda? A healer and holy man of great repute—one who tended to the health of the poverty-stricken as well as the wealthy—he has emerged in history as a satanic figure. Nothing could be further from the truth, according to Dr. Elizabeth Judas, one who knew Rasputin personally, and the author of this important work. First published in 1942, about 25 years after the Bolshevik Revolution that destroyed Christian Russia, this book is the fulfillment of a promise made by Judas to her husband on his death bed. He too knew Rasputin and was witness to many of his feats of accurate prophecy and medical healing. Dr. Judas's husband wanted the truth to be known about Rasputin and the historical record set straight. Far from the "mad monk" he has been portrayed by establishment historians, Rasputin was a complex character whose true history is in desperate need of accurate revision. Softcover, 218 pages, #432, *$19.95* minus 10% for TBR subscribers.

Franklin Roosevelt's WWII Treachery

FDR: The Other Side of the Coin—How We Were Tricked into World War II: The early chapters deal with Franklin Roosevelt's clandestine diplomatic negotiations in the dangerous months before U.S. intervention in WWII: in the Danzig Crisis, with which the author, Hamilton Fish, was deeply involved; the war ultimatum to Japan, kept secret even from Congress; and the unpublicized communications with Ambassador Bullitt and British leaders. Mr. Fish felt that had FDR listened to public opinion, overwhelmingly against American intervention, millions of lives would have been spared. He documents how FDR refused every prewar peace concession the Japanese offered, and later refused peace initiatives from the German Secret Service. In his analysis of the Yalta agreements, Mr. Fish traces the roots of the Korean and Vietnamese conflicts to the outrageous, traitorous and unnecessary territorial concessions made by Roosevelt to Josef Stalin at Yalta. Softcover, 255 pages, #419, *$19.95* minus 10% for TBR subscribers.

Did Adolf Hitler Order The Homicidal Gassing Of Six Million Jews?

The Myth of the Six Million—Examining the Nazi Extermination Plot: This was the first book ever written which really dug into the facts of "the holocaust." David L. Hoggan, the author of the book, fearing academic retribution, was unwilling to publish the book with his name attached. Thus the first edition was published back in 1969 under the name "Anonymous." Now Hoggan can be given the credit he so rightfully deserved. The book includes a fascinating Foreword by the editor, Willis A. Carto, describing the amazing history of this powerful book. Chapters cover such politically incorrect topics as: Hitler's real feelings toward the Jews; three phases of National Socialist treatment of Jews before WWII; Bruno Amann's exposition of the Jewish policy; the Weissberg tale; Jewish memoirs of the concentration camps; the role of Rudolf Hoess and the Hoess memoirs; the truth about the Holocaust; Red Cross factual appraisal of the camps; Adolf Eichmann; the legends of Hitler's depravity; and many more. Softcover, 119 pages, #446, *$13.95* minus 10% for TBR subscribers.

TOLL FREE TBR ORDERING: 1-877-773-9077 • Visa/MasterCard

FUTURE FASTFORWARD

The Zionist Anglo-American Empire Meltdown

Is the alliance between the United States, the British Empire, and Israel a paper tiger or a mighty empire? Is global "Empire Capitalism" about to come crashing down? Will there be a worldwide "people's war" against the super-capitalists and their Zionist allies? Is nuclear war inevitable?

THESE ARE JUST SOME OF THE PROVOCATIVE QUESTIONS addressed in *Future Fastforward*, a forthright, no-holds-barred new book by a prominent Asian political figure and globe-trotting diplomat.

In *Future Fastforward*, author Matthias Chang, former top-level political secretary for Malaysia's outspoken longtime prime minister, Dr. Mahathir Mohammad, takes a stark look at the realities of global power politics and the ultimate and inevitable consequences for the not-so-secret forces that are behind the push for a New World Order.

Now being published for the first time in the United States, this book is a remarkable "insider's" view of world power politics from a point of view that few Americans have ever had the opportunity of hearing.

The Power Elites of the Zionist Anglo-American Axis have been in control of the political systems throughout the world and, in all probability, there is not a single country in which their cunning and evil influence has not been felt.

The author describes the rapid and irreversible decline of the Zionist Anglo-American Empire; the forthcoming inevitable nuclear wars; Israel as the linchpin of those nuclear wars; the end of Empire Capitalism; and a new world map by the middle of this century.

Softcover, 400 pages, $25 minus 10% for TBR subscribers. SPECIAL COMBO—*Brainwashed for War* PLUS *Future Fastforward*— just $50 minus 10% for TBR subscribers.

(See coupon at back of book or call 1-877-773-9077 toll free to charge.)

TOLL FREE TBR ORDERING: 1-877-773-9077 • Visa/MasterCard

BRAINWASHED FOR WAR:
PROGRAMMED TO KILL

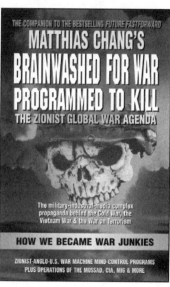

In *Brainwashed for War: Programmed to Kill*—the must-read companion to *Future FastForward: The Zionist Anglo-American Empire Meltdown*—written by internationally renowned Malaysian author Matthias Chang, we learn that we Americans have been brainwashed for war our entire lives. From the Cold War of our youths to Vietnam and now the so-called "War Against Terror" (including the war against Iraq and Afghanistan—and perhaps even Iran if we are not wary), we have been lied to, mind-controlled and duped by president after president (at the behest of America's own intelligence services) with the goal of making us mindless supporters of bloody war. And how many of the wars of the 20th (and now 21st) century have actually been necessary for the defense of the United States?

But again and again we support whatever war our presidents choose almost without question. It's "kill the enemy" and "let blood be shed."

Tracing back four decades and more, *Brainwashed for War* documents the atrocities carried out by the imperialist, Zionist-driven forces whose goal it is to subjugate the peoples of the world.

Replete with documentary evidence (including 200 pages of detailed and highly-readable, eye-opening classified documents), *Brainwashed for War* exposes the vile propaganda warfare, mind control and brainwashing operations carried out by some of the world's most powerful intelligence services in the world including the Mossad, CIA, MI6 and more, and how these operations have come to impact our lives even today. Discover the *modus operandi* of the Zionist masterminds and how they program the minds of the world's peoples to support their goal of global dominion.

Softcover, 561 pages, $30 minus 10% for TBR subscribers.
(Get *Brainwashed* and *Future FastForward* as a set
for $50—minus 10% for TBR subscribers!)

TOLL FREE TBR ORDERING: 1-877-773-9077 • Visa/MasterCard

Auschwitz:
The Final Count

AUSCHWITZ: The very name of the infamous concentration camp in Poland has become synonymous with the period now commonly referred to as "the holocaust."

For about 60 years, schoolchildren around the world have been taught that 4 million Jews were exterminated in the gas chambers at Auschwitz. In other words, *Auschwitz alone accounts for 2/3 of the symbolic 6 million figure.*

But lo and behold: Even the Auschwitz authorities admit the 4 million figure is in need of "revision," lowering the total recently from 4 million to 1.5 million deaths at the camp.

But just how low can we go?

Auschwitz: The Final Count is an amazing assembly of factual historical data about Auschwitz that tells the story of the legendary "death camp" as it has never been told elsewhere—*and determines total death and casualty figures from archival sources.*

This special anthology, featuring commentary by veteran British historian Vivian Bird (right), who originally edited this volume, offers an inside look at Auschwitz and provides the reader with scholarly information that had otherwise been unavailable or previously suppressed before publication of this book.

Once you've read *Auschwitz: The Final Count,* you'll never look at the holocaust, or the history of World War II—or the history of the 20th century, for that matter—in the same way ever again.

Softcover, 109 pages, #67
$12.95 minus 10% for TBR subscribers.
See coupon at back of book. Send payment to:
The Barnes Review, P.O. Box 15877, Washington, D.C. 20003.

Order any books from TBR TOLL FREE
by calling 1-877-773-9077.
Visa and MasterCard accepted.

TOLL FREE TBR ORDERING: 1-877-773-9077 • Visa/MasterCard

STILL AMERICA'S NO. 1 UNDERGROUND BESTSELLER

FINAL JUDGMENT:
The Missing Link in the JFK Assassination Conspiracy

This massive 768-page volume is just now back from the printer in the second printing of its Sixth Edition, containing explosive new material. More than 45,000 copies of previous editions of this book are in circulation here and around the world, documenting—just as Israeli nuclear whistle-blower Mordechai Vanunu has said—that JFK's heroic efforts to prevent Israel from building nuclear weapons of mass destruction played a critical role in the conspiracy behind JFK's assassination. On the strength of this amazing book, Piper has been invited all over the world to discuss his findings—everywhere from the Arab world to Moscow to Malaysia and Japan. Find out what the rest of the world knows about JFK's assassination and what the Controlled Media wants to keep under wraps. This is definitively the last word on the subject, endorsed by former high-ranking Pentagon and State Department officials and large numbers of independent researchers who aren't afraid to utter the dreaded word . . . Mossad.

Softcover, 768 pages, 1,000+ footnotes, indexed, photo section: $25 minus 10% for TBR subscribers.

See coupon at back of book or call 1-877-773-9077 toll free to charge to Visa or MasterCard.

TOLL FREE TBR ORDERING: 1-877-773-9077 • Visa/MasterCard

WHO RULES AMERICA?

FIND OUT IN:

The New Jerusalem
Zionist Power in America

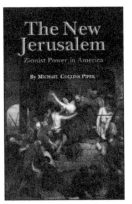

Unlike anything else ever published in the modern day, this explosive study combines in 184 pages, for the first time ever, all of the amazing facts and figures which document the massive accumulation of wealth and power by those who have used that influence to direct the course of U.S. foreign and domestic policy today. While there are many historical books on "the Israeli lobby" and about Zionist intrigues, etc, this is the only book that brings things "up to date" and constitutes a bold and thorough inquiry. Chapters include a list of prominent figures throughout history accused of "anti-Zionism" and "anti-Semitism," a detailed dissection of the Bronfman family, who are often called "the royal family of American Zionism," an eye-opening summary of some 200 little-known, immensely wealthy Zionist families in America; a fascinating inquiry in to the infamous Enron and INSLAW affairs, documenting the suppressed "Zionist connection," plus more.

Softcover, 176 pages, $19.95 minus 10% for TBR subscribers.

See coupon at back of book. Send payment to:
The Barnes Review, P.O. Box 15877, Washington, D.C. 20003.

Order any books from TBR TOLL FREE by calling 1-877-773-9077.
Visa and MasterCard accepted.

TOLL FREE TBR ORDERING: 1-877-773-9077 • Visa/MasterCard

TBR ORDERING COUPON
TBR subscribers take 10% off book prices

Item#	Description/Title	Qty	Cost Ea.	Total
			SUBTOTAL	
			Add S&H on books*	
Send a 1-year subscription to TBR for $46 plus my free book**				
Send a 2-year subscription to TBR for $78 plus two free books**				
			TOTAL	

*S&H ON BOOKS: Add $3 S&H for one item. Otherwise add $5 S&H on orders up to $50. Add $10 S&H on orders from $50.01 to $100. Add $15 S&H on orders over $100. Outside the U.S. double these S&H charges.

**OUTSIDE THE U.S. add $12 per year to subscription price.

PAYMENT OPTIONS: ❏ CHECK/MO   ❏ VISA   ❏ MASTERCARD

Card # _____

Expiration Date _____   Signature _____

NBB126

CUSTOMER INFORMATION:

NAME _____

ADDRESS _____

CIty/STATE/ZIP _____

RETURN WITH PAYMENT TO: THE BARNES REVIEW, P.O. Box 15877, Washington, D.C. 20003. Call 1-877-773-9077 toll free to charge to Visa or MasterCard.

TOLL FREE TBR ORDERING: 1-877-773-9077 • Visa/MasterCard

TBR ORDERING COUPON
TBR subscribers take 10% off book prices

Item#	Description/Title	Qty	Cost Ea.	Total
		SUBTOTAL		
		Add S&H on books*		
Send a 1-year subscription to TBR for $46 plus my free book**				
Send a 2-year subscription to TBR for $78 plus two free books**				
		TOTAL		

*S&H ON BOOKS: Add $3 S&H for one item. Otherwise add $5 S&H on orders up to $50. Add $10 S&H on orders from $50.01 to $100. Add $15 S&H on orders over $100. Outside the U.S. double these S&H charges.

**OUTSIDE THE U.S. add $12 per year to subscription price.

PAYMENT OPTIONS: ❏ CHECK/MO ❏ VISA ❏ MASTERCARD

Card # _____

Expiration Date _____ Signature _____

NBB126

CUSTOMER INFORMATION:

NAME _____

ADDRESS _____

CIty/STATE/ZIP _____

RETURN WITH PAYMENT TO: THE BARNES REVIEW, P.O. Box 15877, Washington, D.C. 20003. Call 1-877-773-9077 toll free to charge to Visa or MasterCard.